Kashmir's Untold Story

Kashmir's Untold Story
Declassified

Iqbal Chand Malhotra
Maroof Raza

BLOOMSBURY
NEW DELHI · LONDON · OXFORD · NEW YORK · SYDNEY

BLOOMSBURY INDIA
Bloomsbury Publishing India Pvt. Ltd
Second Floor, LSC Building No. 4, DDA Complex, Pocket C – 6 & 7,
Vasant Kunj, New Delhi 110070

BLOOMSBURY, BLOOMSBURY INDIA and the Diana logo are trademarks of
Bloomsbury Publishing Plc

First published in India 2019
This export edition published in 2019

Copyright © Iqbal Chand Malhotra and Maroof Raza 2019
Illustrations © Iqbal Chand Malhotra and Maroof Raza 2019

Iqbal Chand Malhotra and Maroof Raza have asserted their right under the Indian Copyright Act
to be identified as the Authors of this work

All rights reserved. No part of this publication may be reproduced or transmitted in any form or by
any means, electronic or mechanical, including photocopying, recording or any information storage
or retrieval system, without the prior permission in writing from the publishers

Bloomsbury Publishing Plc does not have any control over, or responsibility for, any third-party
websites referred to or in this book. All internet addresses given in this book were correct at the time
of going to press. The author and publisher regret any inconvenience caused if addresses have
changed or sites have ceased to exist, but can accept no responsibility for any such changes

ISBN: HB: 978-93-88912-84-6; eBook: 978-93-88912-85-3

2 4 6 8 10 9 7 5 3 1

Printed and bound in India by Replika Press Pvt. Ltd.

Bloomsbury Publishing Plc makes every effort to ensure that the papers used in the manufacture of
our books are natural, recyclable products made from wood grown in well-managed forests. Our
manufacturing processes conform to the environmental regulations of the country of origin

To find out more about our authors and books visit www.bloomsbury.com and
sign up for our newsletters

Contents

Images vii

Abbreviations ix

Preface xi

Introduction xiii

Chapter 1: Unfathomable Depths — 01

Chapter 2: Cloudy Waters — 18

Chapter 3: Emerging Ripples — 35

Chapter 4: Swelling Crests — 43

Chapter 5: Lashing Waves — 58

Chapter 6: Temperamental Tides — 75

Chapter 7: Stormy Seas — 89

Chapter 8: Emerging Abyss — 111

Chapter 9: Deeper Waters — 132

Chapter 10: Rising Tsunami — 151

Postscript 171

Endnotes 175

Index 189

Images

Image 1.1: Map of the Silk Route
Image 1.2: Map of Maharaja Ranjit Singh's Sikh Empire
Image 1.3: Map of the boundary of Jammu and Kashmir as depicted by the Treaty of Chushul, 1842
Image 1.4: Maharaja Gulab Singh, the first ruler of the Dogra Dynasty (1846–57)
Image 1.5: Map of the Dogra Empire with a picture of its coat of arms (1846–47)

Image 2.1: Maharaja Hari Singh, the last Dogra ruler (1925–49)
Image 2.2: Map of Sinkiang's boundary with Jammu and Kashmir
Image 2.3: Map of Gilgit Agency sharing its boundary with Jammu and Kashmir
Image 2.4: Captain William Brown, Acting Commandant of the Gilgit Scouts
Image 2.5: Map of all the vassal states of the Maharaja of Kashmir

Image 3.1: Ram Chandra Kak, Prime Minister of Jammu and Kashmir (1945–47)
Image 3.2: Sir George Cunningham, Governor of NWFP
Image 3.3: Lord Hastings Ismay, Chief Military Advisor to Churchill

Image 4.1: Clement Attlee, Prime Minister of UK (1945–51)
Image 4.2: Map of Chinese presence in Sinkiang and Tibet
Image 4.3: Map of Gurdaspur's location

Image 5.1: Bannu district in erstwhile NWFP

Image 6.1: Pakistan Occupied Jammu and Kashmir

Image 7.1:   Pandit Nehru with Yuvaraja Karan Singh, 1949

Image 8.1:   Roads through Aksai Chin Area in 1953
Image 8.2:   Pakistan ceded Shaksgam Valley to China

Image 9.1:   West and East Pakistan, which later became the independent country of Bangladesh
Image 9.2:   Line of Control/Ceasefire Line

Image 10.1: Map of all the rivers of Indus Basin
Image 10.2: Location of Siachen Glacier
Image 10.3: Location of Daulat Beg Oldie
Image 10.4: Map showing connectivity from Gwadar Port to Kashgar

Abbreviations

AFSPA	Armed Forces (Special Powers) Act
BSF	Border Security Force
CENTO	Central Treaty Organization
CFL	Ceasefire Line
CIA	Central Intelligence Agency
CPEC	China-Pakistan Economic Corridor
CRPF	Central Reserve Police Force
EMP	Electromagnetic Pulse
IB	Intelligence Bureau
INA	Indian National Army
ISI	Inter-Services Intelligence
JKLF	Jammu Kashmir Liberation Front
JKPF	Jammu and Kashmir Peace Foundation
LoC	Line of Control
MUF	Muslim United Front
NEFA	North-East Frontier Agency
NHPC	National Hydroelectric Power Corporation
NWFP	North-West Frontier Province
PIB	Pakistan Intelligence Bureau
PLA	People's Liberation Army
POK	Pakistan Occupied Kashmir
PPF	People's Political Front
RAF	Royal Air Force
SEATO	Southeast Asia Treaty Organization
SF	Students' Federation
SOG	Special Operations Group
UN	United Nations
UPA	United Progressive Alliance
USSR	Union of Soviet Socialist Republic
YML	Young Men's League

Preface

Kashmir has been in the news, for various reasons, for the past three decades or more. Much has been written about its various dimensions, and how it was the cause of wars between India and Pakistan since 1947. However, there are fewer studies on the events that led to Kashmir becoming such a contentious issue between India and Pakistan, especially over the century preceding the Partition (from 1846 to 1947). There is, thus, the need for a much deeper understanding of the subject. It was with this intent in mind that I suggested to my co-author Iqbal Malhotra and our publishers, especially Nitin Valecha of Bloomsbury, that a book like this one needs to be published. And this led us to this book that you now hold in your hands.

My own understanding of Kashmir began during my postgraduate studies in the UK, when I chose to write my MPhil dissertation at Cambridge University on low-intensity conflicts in India. On leaving the army prematurely, I was awarded a fellowship from *The Times of India* and wrote my earlier work titled *Wars and No Peace Over Kashmir*. For both these projects, I did a fair amount of research and travelled to Jammu and the Kashmir Valley, in the mid-1990s, and met people from all sections of the society. The current insurgency was in its nascent stages and there were many seminars debating the Kashmir issue. But, there was no single narrative that would be acceptable across India. Unlike Indians, who are at the helm of these debates, the Pakistanis always asserted that Kashmir should be theirs and that India had outmanoeuvred them at the Partition.

Obviously, it wasn't that simple as my research and reading over the past 25 years have led me to believe. Besides, I have participated in hundreds of prime-time television debates where I have been pitted against Pakistanis, who have a selective understanding of the post-independence history of the region. Many of their perspectives are coloured by their loyalty to their deep state and they are often unaware of actual facts. Among the Kashmiris I have engaged with, there is now an obsession for 'independence', although neither India nor Pakistan is willing to accept the state's autonomy. For Indians who've had enough of the bad news that continues to come from Kashmir, the big question is, 'Why don't we settle the issue once and for all, through a war if necessary?' But as I've always emphasised, it is not that simple. The subject has multiple dimensions with a long history of intrigues, and unless leaders from India, Pakistan and Kashmir are all able to make serious compromises and prepare for the resulting political fallout, this matter will continue to fester.

It is thus important for us to understand the story of Kashmir, and how the problem has come to take its current shape. This book has been put together with considerable research, citing sources from the public domain as much as possible to keep things transparent. Whatever the optimists might say, I do not think that the Kashmir issue will be resolved in my lifetime. Though I hope, I am proved wrong!

Maroof Raza

Introduction

Once, on a Saturday afternoon, during the monsoon months of 1961, we were having our ritual family lunch at my grandparents' home in Carmichael House, on Carmichael Road, in what was then Bombay.[1] Suddenly, the doorbell rang. Hearing a minor commotion, I ran from the dining room to the hall, where I saw several *hamaals*, or bearers, unloading bundles of linen and carpets. I overheard my grandmother telling my aunt that my grandfather[2] had bought an entire store's unused stock of specially monogrammed 'HM'[3] linen. He had also bought three large, customised Kashmiri 'Maharaja' Carpets; they were exquisite. These carpets, along with some pieces of royal furniture and artefacts belonging to the late Maharaja Hari Singh of Jammu and Kashmir, were sold in a public auction following the Maharaja's death in April 1961. He had passed away in Bombay while in exile.

My grandfather was born in Muzaffarabad, which was then a part of the princely state of Jammu and Kashmir.[4] My great-grandfather, Faqir Chand Malhotra, was a barrister; a friend and advisor to the then monarch, Maharaja Pratap Singh. My grandfather and Maharaja Hari Singh were acquaintances who would meet every Sunday afternoon at Bombay's Royal Western India Turf Club; they had the two best adjoining boxes at the Turf Club and shared a common passion for fillies.

Two summers later, in May 1963, my grandparents drove up our Cadillac Eldorado from Delhi to Gulmarg, with our whole

---

1   In 1995, Bombay's name was officially changed to Mumbai.
2   My grandmother, Vidya Malhotra, my aunt Raj Thapar and my grandfather, Puran Chand Malhotra.
3   HM linen was customised Egyptian cotton linen, embroidered with 'HM' or 'His Majesty' motif.
4   Muzaffarabad, following the Partition, is now a part of Azad Kashmir, POK.

family on board. We rented a hut[5] in Gulmarg and I remember going for daily horse rides, accompanied by the hostlers who would provide horses to my grandfather every time he drove down to Gulmarg from Lahore to spend his summers in the pre-Partition years. I remember my grandfather telling me about the Partition; how we lost our ancestral home in Muzaffarabad and, with it, our collective history and how the Kabaili[6] tribesmen raided, burnt and looted Gulmarg and other parts of the Kashmir Valley.

During the summer of 1966, I met Dr Karan Singh and his now-deceased wife Yasho Rajya Lakshmi for the first time when they attended a dinner at our house in Delhi's Aurangzeb Road. Dr Singh is Maharaja Hari Singh's son and the former Governor of Jammu and Kashmir. They are, of course, Uncle Tiger and Aunty Asha for me. They were an elegant and sophisticated couple and I vividly remember being moved on hearing Dr Singh sing some Punjabi and Dogri songs, while the dinner guests sipped coffee from the family's Rosenthal china.

In February 1970, when my grandfather passed away, Uncle Tiger was one of the first mourners to visit our house. Over the next 50 years, as the next generation of the Kashmir royal family came of age, my wife Anu and I have enjoyed a warm friendship with each of the members.

As a documentary film producer, I once met Dr Karan Singh for a project in 2013 at his then office at the Nehru Memorial Trust in Teen Murti Bhavan, New Delhi. When I started talking about producing a documentary on what he believed had gone wrong in Jammu and Kashmir, he grew cautious. He started speaking in chaste Punjabi since no one else present would be able to fathom the nuance and idiom of the language. It was a language that was spoken by very few people on the Indian side of the border. He felt that if he revealed the truth, it would

---

5   Partially furnished cottages on rent in Gulmarg were called a 'Hut'.
6   The *Kabailis* were the Pathan tribesmen from the NWFP who invaded the Kashmir Valley on 22 October 1947.

cause significant tremors in Raisina Hill[7]. He wanted to carry his secrets to the grave.

In 2014, Discovery Channel commissioned two hour-long feature documentaries from my company, AIM Television Pvt. Ltd. These were called *Revealed: Line of Control* and *1965: Heroes and Battles*. Maroof Raza, my co-author, was the consultant on both these films. The popularity of these two films encouraged Discovery to commission another documentary called *Revealed: Siachen* from us. This film provided insight into the real reason behind the sustained pressure from the Sino-Pakistan forces on the Indian state. This was the war for water and the important military advantage that the Siachen Glacier and the Shaksgam Valley enjoy.

Two years later, in the spring of 2017, Maroof asked me to write a proposal for a documentary on Kashmir that he would pitch to M. K. Anand, CEO of the Times Network. He felt that the earlier three films, we made for Discovery, skirted the subject. I was sceptical of such a project. Surprisingly, in June 2017, Maroof asked me to fly down to Mumbai to meet M. K., as M. K. Anand was called by his acquaintances. M. K. stated that because Kashmir-related news generated over 45 per cent of the Gross Rating Points of the news channel Times Now, he wanted us to produce an hour-long documentary on the actual story of the state. He assured us that there would be no editorial interference. I convinced him that an hour would be insufficient to tell such a complex story and requested him to commission two one-hour-long documentaries. That way, we would be able to bring together the entire story in a cohesive manner. He was convinced. Soon thereafter, our contract was signed, and we set out on our recce in September 2017. The show we produced was called *The Story of Jammu & Kashmir*.

Another of my very close friends, Rakesh Mathur, had an extensive network of contacts in Kashmir, as he had served as

---

7   Raisina Hill is often used as a metonym for the seat of the Government of India. It is an area in New Delhi that houses most of India's government buildings.

the General Manager of the then Oberoi Palace Hotel in Srinagar, in the 1980s. The hotel is now called The Lalit Grand Palace. He introduced me to two former police officers, A. M. Watali and Javed Makhdoomi, who would play key roles in my documentary. Meanwhile, Dr Karan Singh and Yuvaraja Vikramaditya Singh agreed to participate in the project and allowed us to film in their homes in Srinagar, Jammu and New Delhi. My lawyer in Srinagar, Javed Iqbal Wani, introduced me to his father-in-law Mian Qayoom, who is very close to the Hurriyat. Speaking to him enabled me to explore their point of view.

We commenced filming in October 2017 and completed in January 2018. At a meeting in Mumbai in December 2017, when we screened some sequences from our film, M. K. was convinced that the story could not be told in less than six one-hour-long episodes. So, we went from one 60-minute episode to two, and then finally to six 60-minute episodes! We handed in the six episodes by mid-April and received our final payment by the end of the month.

Things had been smooth so far but there was an unexpected twist in the tale. The Times Network had apparently signed a contract with Facebook which required them to scale down the duration of each episode and have them uploaded on the network's Facebook page. When we passed on this requirement, the network assigned another firm the responsibility of scaling down the content. In the process, they also scaled down the six 60-minute episodes to six 30-minute TV episodes. This was a departure from the original, puritan version and left out much more than it retained. As the writer and producer, I was deeply saddened.

But every cloud has a silver lining; towards the end of November 2018, Maroof appeared in my office one afternoon with an offer that was too tempting to refuse. Bloomsbury had decided to commission us to jointly write a book on Kashmir. Since I had already done all the research and had written the scripts for several documentaries on the subject, it would not be difficult to restructure them all into a book. Also, the limitations of documentary filmmaking in India, with the measly budgets, prevents the filmmaker from exploring the depths of the subject matter. Writing the book would not only prove to be a healing experience from the Times Now fiasco, but also enable me to do full justice to a story that had never been comprehensively reported on in the public media. Co-authoring this book has been a very enjoyable and fulfilling experience. Our research brought to light the hard reality of Pakistan's deep dissatisfaction over inheriting a 'moth-eaten' country from the British. They had to play out their hateful agenda by making India bleed with a thousand cuts. Today, with their new overlords—the Chinese—the Pakistanis are continuing with this strategy and because of the reasons argued in this book, no amount of candlelight marches are ever going to make them change their policy. Militancy in Kashmir is here to stay; it will only be controlled by the joint forces of Pakistan and China. Both Pakistan and China fear India's soft power and need to tie India down with their military power. Only time will tell if my assessment is accurate.

I would like to thank my assistant Sania Syed who has tirelessly worked as a liaison between Bloomsbury and me. I would also like to thank my colleague, Sudhesh Unniraman, who worked with me, with great dedication, on the Discovery Channel films and the Kashmir film series. He has been an excellent sounding board. I am confident that this book, in the near future, will be transformed into a great film series.

Iqbal Chand Malhotra

Chapter 1

Unfathomable Depths

Legends reveal that the Kashmir Valley was once submerged under water. Ancient texts have referred to the existence of a mountainous land, known by several names through history—Kashyapamir, Kashyapa Meru, Kashyapapur, Kasperia, Kaspapyros, Kaspatyros. Archaeologists have also traced the earliest signs of human life in the Indian subcontinent to Kashmir.

In 535 BC, the Persian Achaemenid Empire, under Cyrus the Great, extended its boundaries eastwards—almost to the Pir Panjal Mountain Range that divides Kashmir from the plains of the Indian subcontinent.

Alexander and Christ in Kashmir

Over 200 years later, in 326 BC, Alexander the Great, after conquering the Achaemenid Empire, turned his attention to India, which he believed was the end of the world. North-western India already formed the eastern part of the Achaemenid Empire, at this time.[1] He divided his invading army into two contingents: one entered the plains of India through the Khyber Pass and the other, led by him, crossed into India via the Hindu Kush mountain ranges, which the Greeks called Caucasus Indicus. After capturing the mountain fort of Aornos, which lay near present-day Swat, Alexander's contingent descended into the foothills of Jammu and Kashmir, where the river Jhelum flows into the plains of Punjab. On the east bank of Jhelum, in a place known to the Greeks as Hydaspes, Alexander the Great killed the son of King Porus in a battle. However, before succumbing to Alexander's sword, the brave warrior managed to kill Alexander's horse, Bucephalus.[2]

The town of Bafliaz on the Old Mughal Road between Jammu and Srinagar probably derives its name from Alexander's much-beloved horse. Common folklore claims that this is the place where Bucephalus was buried. They claim that a shrine was erected here in his memory, but there exists no trace of it. Thereafter, from 206 BC, Kashmir was part of the ancient Silk Route that connected China with southern Europe. Contemporary revisionist scholars of Christianity like Holger Kersten, Fida Hassnain and Suzanne Olson argue that Jesus Christ took this route to Kashmir when he escaped from the cross.[3] According to them, the famous Rozabal shrine in the Khanyar suburb of Srinagar is the tomb of Jesus Christ, who was known in Kashmir as 'Yuz Asaf'. The shrine consists of a wooden structure built over a gravestone. Access to the inner sanctum, which is believed to contain a sarcophagus laid east to west in Hebrew tradition, has now been shut off to the public. Near the gravestone lies a rock carving of a wounded pair of feet. Though the shrine has a Sunni Muslim caretaker, he was unable to convince the authors of why there was a stone engraving in this shrine, given that mainstream aniconism in Islam proscribes the creation of images of sentient beings.

Image 1.1: Map of the Silk Route
Source: Archives of AIM Television Pvt. Ltd.

Kashmir's famous epic, *Rajatarangini*, written in 1148 AD by Kalhana, records that Rozabal is the grave of a king. The epic also reveals that Ashoka brought Buddhism to Kashmir in the mid-3rd century BC,[4] where it took root and spread to Tibet, China and Central Asia.

It was only during the reign of the Sultan dynasty from 1339 that Islam overpowered Hinduism and Buddhism in the region. Sikandar Butshikan, the iconoclastic sixth sultan of the Shah Miri dynasty, who ruled from 1389 to 1413, had attempted to 'sanitise' the valley of all its non-Muslim inhabitants and their culture. This was the period when Kashmir's patron saint Nund Rishi, realising that there was no other option, converted to Islam and came to be called Sheikh Nur-ud-Din Wali or the 'Light of the Faith'. Nund Rishi preached and practised a faith of tolerance and inclusivity called 'Kashmiriyat'.[5] This involved respecting all religious traditions and celebrating each other's festivals. At this time, both beef and pork were dropped from the Kashmiri diet.

In 1752, five years before the victory of the British East India Company in Plassey, the Durranis from Afghanistan seized Jammu and Kashmir from a weakened Mughal Empire. The Mughals had annexed the state from the Sultan dynasty in 1586 and politically incorporated it into their empire and ruled it for 166 years.

The minority Hindu community of Kashmiri Pandits or Brahmins were highly educated in the Persian language, and this knowledge helped them serve the state's Muslim rulers for centuries and emerge as the cornerstone of the ruling dynasties. The Muslims in the state were mainly artisans and peasants. There was a clear trade-off—the Pandits accepted the dominant Islamic culture, but they controlled the state's economy by virtue of their superior education and mobility.

The entire state of Jammu and Kashmir, as it stood in 1947 on the eve of Partition, was a constituent part of Maharaja Ranjit Singh's kingdom of Punjab till as late as 1846. Maharaja Ranjit Singh had wrested Jammu and Kashmir from the declining

Durrani Empire in 1819. This brought the state under a non-Muslim ruler for the first time in 455 years.

Emergence of Gulab Singh

When Maharaja Ranjit Singh conquered the state in 1819, he recognised the talents of one of his soldiers called Gulab Singh, a Dogra from Jammu. The Maharaja installed him as the ruler of Jammu in 1822 and personally anointed him as his vassal ruler.

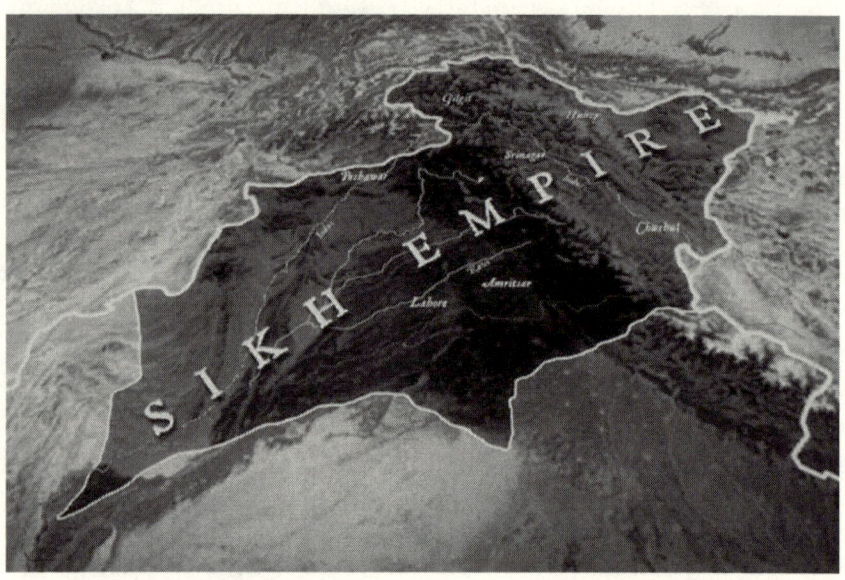

Image 1.2: Map of Maharaja Ranjit Singh's Sikh Empire
Source: Archives of AIM Television Pvt. Ltd.

The Maharaja allowed Gulab Singh complete autonomy over his own army.[6] Their special relationship intensified in 1823 when the Maharaja granted Jammu to Gulab Singh as a hereditary principality.[7] The Maharaja, enamoured by Gulab Singh's brother Dhyan Singh, bestowed the province of Poonch to Dhyan Singh as a hereditary principality as well. In later years, Dhyan Singh would become the Prime Minister of the Sikh Empire.

Sikh governors were employed in the valley of Kashmir to administer the adjoining region. In 1834, Gulab Singh's forces, led by the dynamic Gen. Zorawar Singh, captured Ladakh[8] and the ruling Maharaja was exiled to the village of Stok near Leh.

After Maharaja Ranjit Singh's death in 1839, Zorawar Singh conquered Baltistan and Gilgit. In 1841, his army extended the Sikh Empire till Gartok, near the source of the Indus, and to Lake Mansarovar. In December 1841, a combined Tibetan and Chinese force killed Zorawar Singh and 4,000 of his men near Lake Mansarovar in the Battle of To-Yo. A shrine constructed in his memory, by his enemies, still attracts tourists. Zorawar Singh's foray into Tibet shook the delusions of omnipotence that the Daoguang Emperor of China enjoyed. The mighty Chinese Army had been humbled by the valour of Gen. Zorawar Singh's forces. If the Dogra logistics had not failed him, the entire area around Mount Kailash, replete with water bodies, would have been a rightful part of India.[9]

Around the same time, the Daoguang Emperor's army was defeated in Nanjing, the imperial capital, by a force of the Indian Army led by Maj. Gen. Hugh Gough. Gough later became Commander-in-Chief of the Indian Army.[10] The Daoguang Emperor was forced to sign the Treaty of Nanjing in August 1842, which ended the First Opium War.

Barely a month later, on 17 September 1842, the Qing Emperor of China and the then Dalai Lama of Tibet signed the Treaty of Chushul, with Gulab Singh as a representative of the Sikh Empire, restoring the boundaries of the Sikh Empire to Aksai Chin, a desert plateau between the Karakoram and Kunlun mountain ranges in southern Sinkiang.[11] Gulab Singh was also granted a *jagir* of three villages near Mansarovar. These had originally belonged to the deposed Maharaja of Ladakh. This somewhat ambiguous treaty, drafted in those heady days, would later, in 1949, become the basis of both Indian and Chinese claims to Aksai Chin.[12] In the 1950s, this dispute resulted in the Chinese intrusion into and the annexation of this tract of land.

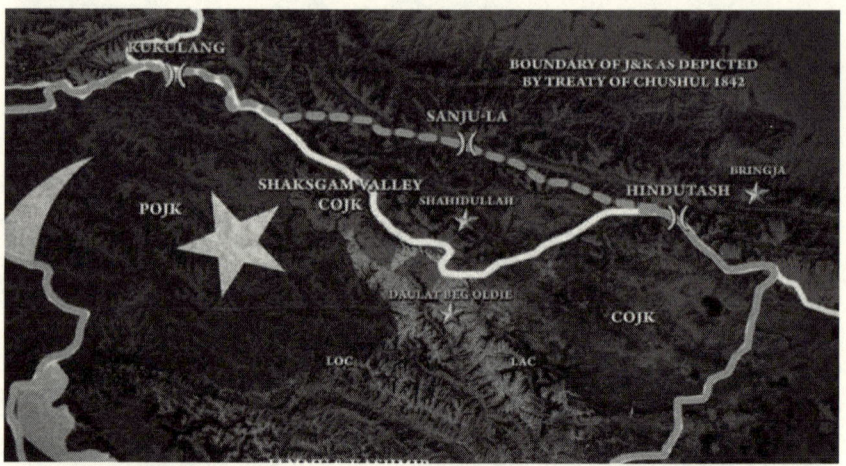

Image 1.3: Map of the boundary of Jammu and Kashmir as depicted by the Treaty of Chushul, 1842

Source: Archives of AIM Television Pvt. Ltd.

The death of Maharaja Ranjit Singh in 1839 plunged the Sikh Empire into instability. This coincided with the untimely deaths of Gulab Singh's two brothers, Dhyan and Suchet Singh, and that of his nephew Hira Singh, who were all prominent functionaries in the Sikh Empire. This paved the way for Gulab Singh to consolidate his position of power within the declining empire. These deaths were concurrent to the demise of all Maharaja Ranjit Singh's sons and grandsons, save his youngest son Duleep Singh. Gulab Singh struck a deep friendship with Col. Henry Lawrence of the East India Company in 1842 and decided to gradually wean himself away from the Sikh Empire.[13]

A master of politics, Gulab Singh's secret alliance with the British led him to refuse the command of the Sikh army. As a result, he was able to stay away from the First Anglo-Sikh War of 1845–46. Gulab Singh's decision was a major tactical and strategic boost for the East India Company and helped tip the power balance in favour of the British, allowing them a tough but assured victory in the battle for Punjab.

After a bitter battle, the British defeated the Sikh forces at the end of February 1846. The British, with the help of Gulab Singh, rapidly executed the Treaty of Lahore on 9 March 1846. This treaty compelled the vanquished infant ruler of Punjab, Maharaja Duleep Singh, to allow Gulab Singh to enter into a separate treaty with the British. The treaty recognised Gulab Singh's independent sovereignty in his existing territories and in any territories sold to him by the British. By all accounts, this was an extraordinary document and Gulab Singh's British ally, Col. Henry Lawrence, was a signatory to it.

The unusual turn of events did not end here. Exactly a week later, on 16 March 1846, the British signed a second treaty called the Treaty of Amritsar with Raja Gulab Singh. In this treaty, the British, who now had conquered the Sikh Empire, sliced off the valley of Kashmir and all territories of the Sikh Empire east of the river Indus and west of the river Ravi, and sold it to Gulab Singh for 75 lakh rupees in Nanakshahi currency, the currency of the Sikh Empire. This was the amount the defeated Sikh Empire had to pay the East India Company as war reparations for the just concluded Anglo-Sikh War. Historians argue that since the Treaty of Lahore specifically mentioned Gulab Singh's name just one week before he received Kashmir via the Treaty of Amritsar, there is enough reason to believe that there was a pre-war arrangement between Gulab Singh and the British over Kashmir.

Further, Raja Gulab Singh received indefeasible and sacrosanct ownership of Jammu and Kashmir and was recognised as the Maharaja of this new political entity. By virtue of the Treaty of Amritsar, the British obtained paramountcy in relation to defence, foreign affairs and communications over Jammu and Kashmir.

Image 1.4: Maharaja Gulab Singh, the first ruler of the Dogra Dynasty (1846–57)

Source: Still extracted from Films Division footage, licensed by AIM Television Pvt. Ltd.

Ranbir Singh: Successor to Gulab Singh

In February 1856, because of his failing health, Maharaja Gulab Singh abdicated his throne in favour of his third and youngest son Ranbir Singh, with the permission of the British. The new Maharaja was able to quell the rebellion in Gilgit and expand the empire to include the principalities of Puniyal, Yasin, Hunza and Nagar. Even though Maharaja Ranbir Singh was an independent and expansionist ruler, he maintained close ties with the British as had his father. He played a crucial role in suppressing the nationalist forces in the First War of Independence in 1857 and, for this, he earned the gratitude of the British. They awarded him the title of 'Grand Commander of the Star of India'.

Ranbir Singh not only built upon the kingdom that he had inherited from his father, but he also expanded his empire to share common borders with Russia, Sinkiang and Tibet. He hobnobbed with the Russians, much to the chagrin of the British, who were always wary of Russian Czar Alexander II's designs on India. This was the era when the long-drawn game of imperial domination in Central Asia played out between Britain and Russia.[14]

In 1846, Maharaja Gulab Singh inherited the tenuous hold of the Sikh Empire on Gilgit. However, in 1852, a tribal rebellion forced his forces to retreat to Bunji on the east bank of the Indus. Ranbir Singh finally recaptured Gilgit in 1860.

In 1861, to the north of Gilgit, in China-controlled Sinkiang, the writ of the Chinese Manchu Emperor Xian Feng collapsed when Sinkiang's Muslims rebelled and severed the only line of communication between this area and metropolitan China. Taking advantage of this situation, Maharaja Ranbir Singh despatched a small force in 1864 across the Karakoram Pass to Shahidullah (Xaidulla) located between Leh and Kashgar. He also established a military post there and informed the neighbouring warlords about it.

Since 1855, during the rule of Maharaja Gulab Singh, the British had been carrying out the Great Trigonometrical Survey of India, thereby surveying every part of the state. Ten years later, the only part that was left to be surveyed was the northeast corner of Ladakh, including the route from Leh to the Karakoram Pass. This job was entrusted to an Anglo-Indian survey official named W. H. Johnson. Johnson held a grudge against the British for their racist attitude towards his Anglo-Indian ancestry. The Maharaja exploited this and offered him post-survey employment if he agreed to carry out some survey to aid the state's diplomatic ambitions.

In 1865, Johnson crossed over to Khotan in Sinkiang from Leh. On his return, he told the Maharaja that the north-eastern border of the state was, in fact, some 100 miles north of the Karakoram Pass. It extended into what, in the absence of field data, was believed to be Chinese territory. The state's border lay within 50 miles of Khotan.

The British were not amused when they figured out that the Maharaja was devising his own militaristic foreign policy. Helpless, they decided to include Johnson's map of the state of Jammu and Kashmir into the official Indian cartographic records. This then became one of the pillars of evidence for India's claim to Aksai Chin.

Pratap Singh Succeeds Ranbir Singh

Upon Maharaja Ranbir Singh's death in September 1885, his eldest son Pratap Singh became the new Maharaja. The full brunt of bearing the British insecurity generated during Ranbir Singh's rule now fell upon the new king. They appointed a Resident to monitor affairs in the state, overruling Pratap Singh's objections to this appointment. Though he improved the state's armed forces, Pratap Singh, like his father, continued to exclude ethnic Kashmiris from the army and the civil services. This calculated and sustained exclusion led to further alienation of the ethnic Muslim-Kashmiri people from their Dogra rulers.[15]

The years before the death of Ranbir Singh had caused a lot of turmoil within the Muslim population in the north-western parts of India and Afghanistan. After June 1878, the Congress of Berlin ended tensions between Britain and Russia; the latter, thereby, turned its sights on Central Asia. Russian envoys descended upon Kabul in July 1878, and the British unsuccessfully demanded the right to do the same from Sher Ali Khan, the Emir of Afghanistan. Despite the Emir refusing the British, they still sent a diplomatic mission to Kabul in September 1878, which was stopped at the border. This eventually triggered the Second Anglo-Afghan War and a British force of 50,000, consisting mostly of Indian troops, invaded Afghanistan.[16] Unable to enlist Czar Alexander's help, the Emir died in September 1879 at Mazar-i-Sharif.

The war finally ended in September 1880 with a British victory. The Second Anglo-Afghan War was, in many ways, a proxy war carried out by the British against the Russians. Consequently, any dalliance of any Indian ruler with the Russians was viewed as an act of treason by the British.

After the death of Maharaja Ranbir Singh in 1885, the British levelled charges of treason against his successor, Maharaja Pratap Singh. This charge was linked to Maharaja Duleep Singh's visit to Russia in 1888. Duleep Singh was the Maharaja of Punjab when the Treaty of Amritsar was signed, and he visited Russia to garner the support of the Russian Czar, Alexander II.

In the same year, a Russian agent, Capt. Gromchevsky, accompanied by a six-man Cossack escort, entered Hunza where its ruler, Mir Safdar Ali, received him as a guest. Ali was a vassal to Maharaja Pratap Singh, which ultimately became the grounds for Maharaja Pratap Singh's suspension from his rule from 1889 to 1905.

First Instance of Central Rule in Kashmir

In February 1889, the British Resident, Col. Parry Nisbet, stripped Pratap Singh of his authority as the sovereign ruler for carrying out treasonable correspondence with the enemies of the British Empire.[17] Col. Nisbet was the first of many British Residents who ruled the state during this interregnum, assisted by a Council of Regency. Though this action violated both the Treaty of Amritsar and the Queen's Proclamation of 1858, there was no appeal made against it in any court of law because it was deemed an 'act of state' and was not subject to the jurisdiction of the courts. The heir to the throne, Raja Amar Singh, Pratap Singh's younger brother, was actively involved in the Council of Regency and exercised great influence in the state during this period. Many historians assert that Amar Singh was actually favoured by Maharaja Ranbir Singh to be his successor, but the law of primogeniture prevented this from happening.

In order to keep the Russians at bay, it suited the British to keep the state in governmental limbo, notwithstanding the 'independence' granted to it via the Treaty of Amritsar. Pratap Singh's diplomatic forays were quelled and, seven years later, in September 1896, the Pamir Boundary Commission protocols were signed, thereby defining the border between Afghanistan and Russia. The Wakhan Corridor which joined Gilgit to Russia was given to Afghanistan and the country now officially became a buffer between Russia and India. In this case, Kashmir was explicitly considered a part of India and its ruler had been dispossessed by the British.

This action of the Government of India in superseding the rule of the Maharaja and dispossessing him of his sovereignty, even though his grandfather Maharaja Gulab Singh had signed the Treaty of Amritsar way back in 1846, was unthinkable even in those times. In post-independent India, this action, in later years, became the basis of the right to invoke President's rule in any Indian state. Such a rule suspends the state's existing legislative assembly and removes the elected government whenever there is a perception of a threat to the state or a breakdown of law and order. In post-independent India, the President's rule has been invoked several times in the state of Jammu and Kashmir.

Image 1.5: Map of the Dogra Empire with a picture of its coat of arms (1846–47)

Source: *Archives of AIM Television Pvt. Ltd.*

The similarities between what the British did and independent India's invoking of the President's rule, are uncanny. In the 19th century, the perceived enemy was Russia and the Maharaja's possible alliance with the Russians was construed by the Government of India to be a threat that was serious enough to warrant the disposition of his rule and sovereignty in Kashmir. In post-independent India, in the 20th and 21st centuries respectively, the enemy in question is Pakistan by itself first and then later as a proxy for China. The political flirtation of successive Kashmiri politicians with separatists, propped up by Pakistan, has, time and again, resulted in the suspension of the democratic political process in Kashmir and in the declaration of the Governor's rule. Today, the threat to the state of Jammu and Kashmir is China, both directly and via its proxy, Pakistan. Indian forces have been engaged in confrontational military policies with the Chinese in the eastern parts of the state for almost two centuries now. Both in 1841 and later in 1962, Indian forces in Ladakh have been defeated by the Chinese, thanks to India's bad logistical tactics. History, unfortunately, tends to repeat itself.

The Government of India's perception of threat from Maharaja Pratap Singh's alleged communication with the Russians carried such gravitas that the dispossession of the Maharaja's rule was held for 16 long years. It was only with the humiliating defeat of Russia in 1905, in the hands of the Japanese Army, that Britain and Russia were persuaded of the need to resolve their differences in Asia. They engaged in talks and the Anglo-Russian Convention of 1907, or the Convention between the UK and Russia relating to Persia, Afghanistan and Tibet, was signed on 31 August 1907, in St Petersburg. The convention sought to remedy the shaky Russian-British relations by solidifying boundaries that identified each nation's respective control over Persia, Afghanistan and Tibet. The treaty delineated each country's influence in Persia and stipulated that neither country would interfere in Tibet's internal affairs. It also recognised Britain's influence over Afghanistan. It was only when these talks reached a determinate stage that the Government of India felt secure enough to restore the Maharaja's rule.[18]

Further Erosion of Pratap Singh's Powers

The restoration of the Maharaja's rule in 1905 was not a reversal of the status quo ante that existed in 1889 when he was dispossessed. Riders were imposed on the Maharaja's authority, and he was effectively ring-fenced by the Government of India.

The Maharaja could not take any consequential decision without the consent of the Government of India's plenipotentiary, the Resident. Furthermore, the British policy of divide and rule was used to the hilt by the Resident, who encouraged Raja Amar Singh to shadow every action of the Maharaja. For his loyalty to the Government of India, Raja Amar Singh was rewarded with the guarantee that his only son Hari Singh, born in 1895, would succeed Pratap Singh as the next Maharaja. This was in line with the principle of primogeniture, given that Hari Singh was a direct male descendant of Maharaja Gulab Singh. Further, given the distrust between Pratap Singh and the Government of India, the latter was never going to endorse any of Pratap Singh's nominees. The combined issue of dispossession, restoration and succession overwhelmed Maharaja Pratap Singh throughout his constrained reign, the issue of succession being the most important of the lot. Apart from Raja Amar Singh, Maharaja Pratap Singh had another younger brother named Raja Ram Singh who died childless. Relations between the two brothers, Pratap Singh and Amar Singh, which were contentious even when Maharaja Ranbir Singh was alive, became worse during the period when the British Resident directly ruled the state, a period which also saw Amar Singh's political ambitions peak. The question of deciding Pratap Singh's successor gained more traction, 1889 onwards. He was childless after having lost his only son in infancy. Visibly shattered after the 16-year-long limbo in his rule, Pratap Singh decided to retaliate after he was reinstated as the ruler of the state in 1905. In 1906, it was rumoured that Pratap Singh intended to adopt a distant male relative ostensibly for religious purposes. Obviously, the larger plan was to exclude Hari Singh from succession. The Government of India took up the case with the Maharaja and pointed out that he should not adopt a distant relative, especially when he had a brother and a nephew. Refusing to comply, Pratap Singh pointed out that that wouldn't be feasible; Amar Singh was too old to adopt a son and Hari Singh, being Amar Singh's only son, could not be adopted under Hindu law. When J. D. Mayne's 'Treatise on Hindu

Law and Usage' was consulted, his argument was annulled. Yet, he insisted on adopting a distant relation, citing religious requirements. He argued that in Hinduism, when one did not have a son, one had to adopt one so that he could perform the annual *shraaddha* or ritual remembrance of his departed father's soul. The Viceroy of India then clearly informed him that the Government of India had decided that Raja Amar Singh and his son, Hari Singh, would be the successors to Pratap Singh's rule.[19]

The embittered Maharaja Pratap Singh never accepted this decision and, despite the Viceroy's communication on the subject, in 1907, he actually adopted Raja Jagat Dev Singh of Poonch, a descendant of Raja Dhyan Singh, the younger brother of Maharaja Gulab Singh. The Government of India, thereafter, wrote to him informing him that this adoption would not affect the rights of Pratap Singh's closest relatives.

While the Anglo-Russian Convention of 1907 secured the British enough to reinstate the Maharaja, the Government of India could not let its guard down for too long. The Russian Revolution of 1917 and the British support to the White Russian armies had re-established the rivalry between Britain and Russia. The embattled Bolshevik regime in Russia that was fighting the pro-Western White Russian armies, during the Russian Civil War, decided to establish the Comintern or Communist International in March 1919. The leaders of Bolshevik Russia announced that the only way they could preserve the revolution was to fight back against the Western powers and spread communism throughout the world via the Comintern.

The obvious corollary of this decision was to take the fight to India, the jewel in the crown of the British Empire. Earlier in July 1918, Maj Gen. Sir Wilfrid Malleson of the Indian Army led an expedition of both British and Indian troops to Turkestan, Russia, during the Civil War. The Indian troops of the 19th Punjab Rifles engaged Bolshevik forces and defeated them at Merv, in what is present-day Turkmenistan. This was the first direct military confrontation between British and Russian troops since the Crimean War of 1853–54. The 19th Punjab Rifles' contingent was reinforced in September 1918 by troops from the 28th Light Cavalry, which was merged into the 7th Light Cavalry in post-independent India. The Indian troops fought at Kaka, Arman Sagad and Dushak but because of the collapse of the anti-Bolshevik forces in April 1919, Malleson was forced to withdraw from Russian Turkestan in April 1919. The reach of the British Empire had finally been extended into Russian soil.

Wary of the British might, the Bolsheviks decided to counter-attack and the Third Comintern organised the First Congress of the Peoples of the East at Baku in September 1920. The Congress specifically aimed at fighting imperialism in Asia. Baku, in Soviet-controlled Azerbaijan, was only 2,000 km from Merv. Tashkent, where the Communist Party of India was formed on 17 October 1920, was only 900 km away from Merv. The Communist Party of India's two main founders of Indian origin were M. N. Roy and Abani Mukherjee.

The seeds of the old British-Russian enmity had now flowered into a new confrontation between the Government of India and Soviet Russia. Kashmir, once again, became the underbelly of this dispute. Abani Mukherjee, an associate of Rash Behari Bose, had already been jailed in Singapore for procuring weapons for use in the Hindu-German conspiracy of 1914–17. The objective of this conspiracy was to foment rebellion in the Indian Army, all the way from Punjab to Singapore. Mukherjee escaped from the Fort Canning prison in Singapore in 1917 and made his way to Moscow. M. N. Roy had also participated in the Hindu-German conspiracy and, escaping from British detention, made his way to Moscow via the US and Mexico.

It was against this backdrop in 1920 that a worried Government of India established the Council of State in Kashmir.[20] This was a successor to the Council of Regency which was dissolved in 1905. After Amar Singh's death in 1910, his son and British-supported heir to the throne of Jammu and Kashmir, Hari Singh, took his father's place as a senior member of the council. His task was to shadow the Maharaja in much the same way his father had done in the past.[21] This further fuelled Pratap

Singh's existing animosity towards Hari Singh, who had literally been foisted upon him by the British. Pratap Singh died in 1925, a frustrated and embittered man who had spent 36 of the 40 years of his rule as a ring-fenced, downsized Maharaja far removed from the glory of his grandfather, Maharaja Gulab Singh.

The wheel had turned a full circle; the Government of India was not confident enough about the loyalty of Pratap Singh and considered him a weak link in the overall strategic challenge that the state of Jammu and Kashmir faced.[22] The government further had no choice but to intervene in the state's functioning; the ruler's autonomy, or even that of an at arm's length relative, could not be an option. This policy towards the state's government continues to be followed today in 21st-century India. Rulers, politicians and civil servants have come and gone, but the Government of India is still the overarching central authority that firmly continues to exercise its control over Jammu and Kashmir. The challenges that the state faces have remained the same and the options that it has to deal with them, have also remained pretty much the same as they were in the 19th century. The succeeding chapters will dwell on the conformity of the arc of history.

Chapter 2

Cloudy Waters

Struggle for the Throne

On 23 September 1925, Maharaja Pratap Singh passed away.[1] Although Hari Singh was in line to succeed the late king, two issues gained currency even as the Maharaja's body lay awaiting its last rites. The state was governed by the Council of State since 1920 and the Resident, Sir John Wood, had to officially recognise Hari Singh as the new Maharaja.[2] But Wood was away on tour in Hunza and his first assistant, knowing Raja Jagat Dev Singh's claim to the throne, decided to directly communicate to Hari Singh that the Government of India recognised him as the new Maharaja. Despite this act of apparent goodwill, far from experiencing a smooth succession, Hari Singh was shocked when the Viceroy's condolence telegram addressed him as Raja Hari Singh instead of Maharaja. This, he feared, put him in the same status as the late Maharaja's adopted son Raja Jagat Dev Singh.

The problem did not end there. According to the rules of succession of a natural heir in the direct line, a prince succeeded his demised father as a matter of course and his succession was recognised by an exchange of formal letters or *kharita*s between the new ruler and the Viceroy of India.[3] The Viceroy had to first recognise and accept the succession of the new ruler and only after that, could the exchange of *kharita*s take place. Hari Singh's succession was peculiar because he was not the late Maharaja's son and was, therefore, not a natural heir in the direct line of succession.[4] His succession had to be both recognised and confirmed[5] by the Viceroy before there could be an exchange of *kharita*s between the two of them.[6] And then, there was the whole concern over the late Maharaja's adopted son, Raja Jagat Dev Singh, who was also a member of the Council of State.

The Government of India never trusted Maharaja Pratap Singh and, by extension, also mistrusted Raja Jagat Dev Singh. They were not willing to take a risk and give the latter the benefit of the doubt because, technically speaking, he was also of the same bloodline, an equally direct descendant of Mian Kishore Singh, the common great-great-grandfather of Jagat Dev Singh and Hari Singh.

Hari Singh's claim to the throne rested on his father Amar Singh's unwavering loyalty to the Government of India and the latter's perception was that he was a much safer bet for British interests. Of course, future events were to prove otherwise.

Hari Singh first began to reveal his autonomous thoughts by objecting to the government's delay in confirming his succession.[7] He believed that his succession had already been endorsed by both the Government of India and Maharaja Pratap Singh, while he was still alive. He did not buy the government's defence of the distinction between the natural heirs in the direct line and the heirs presumptive, and was dismissive of the process and procedures laid down in the law. The British, however, were sticklers for these details. After much deliberation, and obtaining the Secretary of State's consent, the Viceroy finally presented the *kharita* of offerings[8] to Hari Singh[9] on 14 October 1925.[10] For three long weeks, the issue of succession had remained unresolved. Hari Singh's bitterness towards the British and their tardiness began to colour his perception towards them and their interests.[11] The British were stuck on the horns of a dilemma; to them, their chosen domino had displayed a streak of impatience and imperiousness. Could they continue to trust him? They weighed in on the option of Raja Jagat Dev Singh. Though he had supported his adoptive father in the proceedings of the Council of State in order to remain an obedient and faithful son, could he prove to be a more malleable domino?

In the end, the British cast their lot with Hari Singh but only after the Resident, Sir John Wood, privately read[12] out the riot act to Hari Singh and secured his consent to the long-established practice of non-interference in the frontier areas by state officials, and he also agreed that state officials would take no action in Ladakh without consulting the British Joint Commission.[13] But, this episode ended the untrammelled hegemony of the British in the state as Hari Singh kept standing up against the British on several issues, gradually culminating into the events of August 1947 when he thwarted British designs and took decisions that ultimately led to the state being divided between India and Pakistan, along military lines. His actions also resulted in the Congress-led Indian Government deposing him as the ruler of the state, just as the British had done with his predecessor, Maharaja Pratap Singh.

Maharaja Hari Singh inherited a state which had an overwhelmingly large Muslim population; this was a unique political situation where a Hindu ruler was ruling over a Muslim majority. The situation in the rest of India, till the advent of British rule in 1757, had been the very opposite.

Image 2.1: Maharaja Hari Singh, the last Dogra ruler (1925–49)
Source: Still extracted from Films Division footage, licensed by AIM Television Pvt. Ltd.

After Hari Singh's accession to the throne, an organisation called *Anjuman-e-Nusrat-ul-Islam,* founded in 1905 by the Maulvi of Srinagar's Jamia Masjid, started a movement calling for the educational emancipation of Kashmiri Muslims. As a result, many Kashmiri Muslims went to study at universities all over India. In 1931, among the first Kashmiri graduates to return to Srinagar, were Sheikh Mohammed Abdullah, Mirza Afzal Beg and G. M. Sadiq. These young men got politically involved and stood in opposition to the Maharaja's perceived autocracy.[14] What triggered this opposition, were a succession of incidents in Jammu wherein some state government officials had purportedly demolished a mosque. When this news reached Srinagar, it caused public outrage. On 25 June 1931, a Pakhtoon man called Abdul Qadeer made a seditious speech against the Maharaja's rule. Qadeer was arrested and put on trial in Srinagar on 6 June 1931.

On 13 July 1931, while Qadeer's trial was on in the Srinagar central jail, the police opened fire on an unruly mob of Qadeer supporters, killing 22 demonstrators. The agitation then spread throughout the rest of the state. The Maharaja was convinced that a senior minister in his court, a British bureaucrat named Wakefield, was the brain behind this agitation and immediately dismissed him. The Maharaja believed that the agitation was a pre-planned attack on him; a punishment for taking a contradictory stance against the British, at the Round Table Conference in London, in 1930. G. E. C. Wakefield was replaced by a distinguished Kashmiri Pandit, Sir Hari Kishan Kaul, who was made the state's Prime Minister.

The Rise of Abdullah and the Mirwaiz

The agitation throughout Kashmir was spearheaded by two men: the religious leader Mirwaiz Mohammad Yusuf Shah and his protégé, a young schoolmaster called Sheikh Mohammed Abdullah. The agitation led by these two men with the support of other Muslim leaders in the country forced the Maharaja to set up a commission of enquiry that would investigate this violence. The commission, presided over by Sir Bertram Glancy, asked Hari Singh to create a constitution for the state which would enshrine freedom of speech, expression and assembly for its inhabitants. At the same time, Sheikh Abdullah and the Mirwaiz were imprisoned in the Srinagar central jail; their arrest added to their popularity and they found a dedicated population of followers in the state. In 1934, the promised constitution was introduced in the state of Kashmir. This was the first time that the government imposed a constitution upon a princely state. The document guaranteed certain fundamental rights and forced Hari Singh to concentrate on his subjects and their political and economic needs.

Just as Pratap Singh's political freedoms were heavily constrained,[15] Hari Singh's powers were also brought to check by the imposition of the constitution. The introduction of the constitution enabled some of the agitators to act upon and consolidate the power gained from the political mobilisation of 1931. Sheikh Abdullah and Mirwaiz Mohammad Yusuf Shah, while still in prison, orchestrated the establishment of a political party called the Muslim Conference in 1932, which brought together all political forces that opposed the Maharaja's rule. Though the princely state of Jammu and Kashmir now had a legal and lawful political opposition, it was far from entering a perfect democratic arrangement.

Hari Singh's Dogra community and the valley's Sikh population, who had lived there from the time of Maharaja Ranjit Singh's conquest, along with the Hindu Kashmiri Pandits, stood at the receiving end of the ever-growing strength of the Maharaja's Muslim subjects. The political mobilisation of the large Muslim population had established a communal divide. The Maharaja had been outsmarted by the British, who had very deftly engineered a deepening rift in his political power and authority.

However, arising personality differences between Sheikh Abdullah and Mirwaiz Mohammad Yusuf Shah gave the Maharaja some breathing space.[16] Sheikh Abdullah, then a 29-year-old, acquired a progressively cosmopolitan outlook while studying at Aligarh. He made peace with the Maharaja and upon his release from prison in 1933, married the half-Kashmiri daughter of Harry Nedou, the extremely wealthy Croatian proprietor of a chain of hotels in the state. Already enamoured by progressive political ideas, Abdullah's outlook underwent a further change when he met Pandit Jawaharlal Nehru in 1938. Abdullah embraced the political lineage of the Congress party and began to operate the Muslim Conference as an extension of the Congress party in Jammu and Kashmir. His new and progressive ideas clashed with the ultra-conservative religious mindset of the Mirwaiz.

A Divided Muslim Opposition

A split in the Muslim Conference was inevitable given the existing differences between the two leaders. Unable to work together, they finally dissolved the Muslim Conference in 1939. In its place, Abdullah founded the National Conference, a secular and progressive body with policies where Islamic theology gave way to more pressing issues such as land reforms. In 1941, following the announcement of the Pakistan Resolution in Lahore, many Muslims in the state, disgruntled with Abdullah and the secular nature of the National Conference, convinced the Mirwaiz to resurrect the Muslim Conference. The newly resurrected organisation became the trump card for both Mohammed Ali Jinnah and the Muslim League. The National Conference, with its secular agenda, and the Muslim Conference, with its rabidly communal agenda, spearheaded the political struggle against the Maharaja's rule.

Within 10 years, the political opposition to the Maharaja's rule was legally mobilised under two different ideological strains. The British had succeeded in gradually eroding the omniscience of the Maharaja and had ensured the institutionalisation of a process that caused him continuous problems and ultimately unseated him.

The 1934 Constitution lasted only five years. A relentless campaign of protest by the politicians from the mobilised Muslim majority forced the Maharaja to scrap the existing constitution in favour of a new one, in 1939. The crown of thorns that sat on the Maharaja's head never gave him a moment of peace since the 1930 Round Table Conference took place in London.

The British Prepare to Snatch Gilgit

One of the reasons behind the introduction of the constitution in 1934 was to keep the Maharaja preoccupied with political changes in the valley, and to deflect his attention away from the state's northern borders. During this period, in neighbouring Sinkiang, Sheng-ts'ai, a Chinese warlord, had taken control over most of the region.[17] This development was dangerous for the Indian Government because Sheng-ts'ai was in close contact with the Soviets. There was a high chance that Sinkiang would become a Soviet puppet state or be completely absorbed into the Soviet Union.

Image 2.2: Map of Sinkiang's boundary with Jammu and Kashmir

Source: Archives of AIM Television Pvt. Ltd.

The natural barrier of the Karakoram mountains could not keep agent provocateurs from infiltrating into British India and corrupting Indian politicians with the Bolshevik virus; a term used for Soviet or Comintern agents in the period during WWI and WWII. Sheng-ts'ai's main opponent, the Islamic warlord Ma Hu-Shan, was then living in Khotan[18] close to the Ladakh border, and there was a big chance that he would spread his control into northern Ladakh, where there were no Indian Army units stationed and the borders were not defined. Thus, in 1934, the entire state was potentially under threat.

In New Delhi, officials were extremely worried about the intent and actions of Hari Singh. Once again, as in Pratap Singh's time, the northern threat dominated the discourse. Ever since Hari Singh's participation in the Round Table Conference of 1930, serious doubts about his loyalty and cooperation in the event of an emergency worried the government officials. Moreover, the internal situation in Gilgit had deteriorated to a state of diarchy wherein communications and defence forces were handled by the British but the civil government was still being controlled by the Maharaja through his governor.[19]

Interestingly, in 1931, when there were riots in Srinagar, the British were trying to persuade the Maharaja to take on greater financial responsibility for the Corps of Gilgit Scouts, who were the primary defence forces in the region. This was because the global depression had affected the Indian Government's budgets. The Maharaja sat over this proposal until mid-1933 and presented a set of counter-proposals. He was ready to take on the entire financial burden for the defence of Gilgit provided the system of diarchy was terminated and complete authority returned to the governor. Hari Singh's sights were clearly set on exploiting the situation in Sinkiang and using it to his advantage. The British, in the meanwhile, parried the Maharaja's growing political ambitions by acting upon the Glancy Commission's proposal to introduce a constitution in the state, thereby leaving the Maharaja to cope with internal dissent in the valley. The Government of India got the opportunity they were looking for and sought to secure all rights in the region for themselves.

Formal negotiations between the Maharaja and the government began in October 1934, right after the constitution was introduced. The Maharaja was represented by his Prime Minister, Col. Colvin and the Government of India was represented by the Resident in Kashmir, Lt. Col. Lang, assisted by B. J. Glancy, who had forced the constitutional changes upon the Maharaja's rule. On 26 March 1935, the Maharaja leased the entire Gilgit *wazarat*, or kingdom, north of the Indus and all its vassal states to the British for a period of 60 years. The annual lease, a paltry sum of 1,250 rupees, was paid to the Maharaja as a lump sum of 75,000 rupees. On 1 October 1935, the British Political Agent in Gilgit, Maj. G. Kirkbride, took absolute charge of the region.

Thereafter in 1938, the Kuomintang regime in China closed down the Khunjerab Pass (the trade route between Sinkiang and Gilgit) and the Karakoram Pass (the trade route between Sinkiang and Leh). This was because a number of local warlords from Sinkiang were using these passes to escape into the Gilgit region and Ladakh. The two most notable of these warlords were one Mahmud and one Ma Hu-Shan. The British defence forces were now worried—if military refugees could reach Leh via Aksai Chin, up the Karakash River from Khotan, would India not be under serious threat if more such warlords were able to enter Sinkiang?

This question remained unanswered and India paid a heavy price for this ambivalence 24 years later, in 1962. By 1943, during WWII, the British decided to station agents in Central Asia, who would continue to provide them with intelligence from the ground. The latter part of this chapter and the other succeeding chapters will reveal the policies that the British adapted in order to remain a dominant player in the region.

Turmoil in the Valley

Meanwhile, within the valley, political unrest had increased after the declaration of the Pakistan Resolution in Lahore, in 1941. The Lahore Resolution, presented by A. K. Fazlul Huq at the three-day general session of the All India Muslim League in Lahore on 22–24 March 1941, is popularly known as the Pakistan Resolution because it called for independent states based on religion. The Anglo-Soviet Pact made during WWII, and Stalin's subsequent disbandment of the Comintern had provided the Government of India some respite from the perceived Soviet threat to the state. Hari Singh, anticipating the inevitable departure of the British from the subcontinent, needed to broaden his popular support. He sought to do this by appointing one Muslim and one Hindu member from the legislative assembly as ministers in his government. That he even considered doing this, is a reflection of how fast socio-religious equations were changing in the state and how inadequate the state forces were of quelling any Muslim uprisings. Hari Singh chose Mirza Afzal Beg, the deputy leader of the National Conference and a close associate of Abdullah, as the Minister of Public Works and Municipalities. Wazir Ganga Ram was the Hindu minister chosen by the Maharaja.[20] Beg's collaboration with the Maharaja undoubtedly reflected Abdullah's political craftiness and his excellent sense of timing. As WWII drew to a close and Jinnah's demand for Pakistan began to take shape in the form of nationwide communal conflagrations, Abdullah decided to test the waters by rocking the Maharaja's throne. In March 1946, Beg resigned from his ministerial post. At that time, the British Cabinet Mission was in India negotiating with Jinnah and the Congress party about the mechanics for the transfer of power. In May 1946, the National Conference launched the Quit Kashmir campaign against the Maharaja. In incendiary speeches, Abdullah condemned the sale of the valley by the British to Gulab Singh, in 1846.[21] He emphatically declared that this was an invalid act. It, therefore, followed that the Maharaja, as the descendant of the Dogra dynasty, was also an invalid ruler. He insisted that the Maharaja should leave Kashmir immediately and hand over power to the people of the state. It had taken 15 years of British Machiavellian intrigue to unleash the forces that had shaken the seemingly unshakeable rule of Gulab Singh's descendants.

The Poonch Imbroglio

Around the same time, in 1946, trouble was brewing in Poonch, which was a feudatory territory of Jammu and Kashmir. Way back in 1827, Maharaja Ranjit Singh had appointed Raja Dhyan Singh, Gulab Singh's brother, as the Raja of Poonch. Gulab Singh had been appointed as the Raja of Jammu. After the death of Maharaja Ranjit Singh in 1839, Dhyan Singh was assassinated in the September 1843 *coup d'état* against the Sikh Emperor Sher Singh, in Lahore. It is speculated that Gulab Singh had a role to play in this event. Thereafter, Poonch was confiscated by the Sikh Empire on the grounds of Raja Dhyan Singh's rebellion. Poonch was handed over to Faiz Talib Khan of Rajouri and after the signing of the Treaty of Amritsar, it was transferred to Maharaja Gulab Singh by the British. He, in turn, restored Poonch to Jawahir Singh, the eldest surviving son of Dhyan Singh, albeit with the reduced status of a *jagir*, a feudal land grant.

Gulab Singh had cleverly managed to neutralise the potential opposition he and his descendants would have faced from his family. The rumoured circumstantial evidence of Gulab Singh's role in the death of his brother Dhyan Singh, and him demoting Poonch's status down to being a *jagir*, angered the surviving clansmen of Dhyan Singh, who were led by Jawahir Singh and his younger brother, Moti Singh. They petitioned the British, who did not want to annoy Gulab Singh, their trusted ally. In 1852, the arbitrator, Sir Frederick Currie, the British Resident in Lahore ruled that Gulab Singh was indeed the *suzerain*, or the feudal overlord, of Poonch.[22] The *jagir* was further sub-divided into Jawahir Singh's 2/3 share and the remaining 1/3 share of Moti Singh. Later on, in 1859, Maharaja Ranbir Singh and the British levelled a charge of 'treacherous conspiracy' against

Jawahir Singh and dispossessed him of his rightful 2/3 share. This left Moti Singh, his son Baldev Singh and grandson Jagat Dev Singh with a much-truncated *jagir*. The descendants of Raja Dhyan Singh had been marginalised by those of his brother Gulab Singh, and this inter-generational bitterness continued to the era of Hari Singh.

When a beleaguered Maharaja Pratap Singh sought to resist the combined pressure of Raja Amar Singh and his British masters to impose Hari Singh as the heir to the throne, he turned to his marginalised second cousin's nephew, Jagat Dev Singh, and adopted him as his son and heir. Jagat Dev Singh performed the last rites of Maharaja Pratap Singh in 1925 and became the Raja of Poonch in 1928. Hari Singh, however, continued the policy of marginalisation towards the *jagir* and imposed a *sanad*, or a land deed, on him, further implementing several encroachments on his administration. Further, a diarchy was established. Hari Singh appointed a Resident Administrator and more officials were loaned from the state, leaving Raja Jagat Dev Singh's jurisdiction to handle only petty cases. All serious crimes were referred to the courts in Srinagar. The Raja of Poonch's powers were completely diminished and the throne had lost its prestige as well as power.

With the British and the Maharaja both against the Raja of Poonch, and with the residual part of the state being inconsequential because of Maharaja's imposition of heavy taxes, the choices for Raja Jagat Dev Singh were very limited. It can be argued that with rising powers of the Muslim Conference and the National Conference, the clouds of war in Europe and the growing communal divide in the rest of India, the Raja had only one weapon to use against the enemies of his family—the mobilisation and militarisation of the Muslim subjects of the state. Muslims constituted 90 per cent of Poonch's population; they were ethnically different from the Muslims in the larger Kashmir Valley and also spoke Punjabi. Over 30,000 men from Poonch had served in the Indian Army in WWI; they were enlisted as 'Punjabi *Mussalmans*' and were admitted into the Punjab Regiment. In WWII, over 60,000 men from Poonch served in the Indian Army and formed the nucleus of the revolt against the Maharaja, in 1947.

Raja Jagat Dev Singh feared that Maharaja Hari Singh would leave no stone unturned to completely usurp his power. His only option now was to fan the communal unrest and encourage a revolt by the Muslim population against the Maharaja. However, the Muslim population needed a leader and Raja Jagat Dev Singh thought Muhammad Ibrahim Khan, the son of his carpenter, to be the perfect fit. He sent the young man to Lahore to finish his graduation and then sent him to London to get an LLB. Khan then obtained a Bar-at-Law degree from Lincoln's Inn. Sardar Muhammad Ibrahim Khan thereby became Raja Jagat Dev Singh's agent provocateur against the Maharaja and when he returned to India in 1943, he started his career as a Public Prosecutor in Mirpur.

Unfortunately, Raja Jagat Dev Singh died under mysterious circumstances in 1940 and his wife was prevented from taking control of the *jagir* in the name of their minor son, Ratan Dev Singh. She eventually fled to Nepal with her son and two daughters. The *jagir* came under the direct control of Hari Singh, which obviously agitated Sardar Muhammad Ibrahim Khan, who was then studying in London. He planned to avenge the death of his benefactor and the marginalisation of his benefactor's descendants, and in the process, he also wanted to advance the interests of Poonch's Muslim majority, who would now come under the direct rule of the Maharaja.

Hari Singh, keeping in line with the consistent actions of most of his predecessors against the surviving members of Dhyan Singh's family, had unwittingly created what was going to be, in 1947, the pivot for the many-pronged attack on his rule and state. The Poonch family was not the only problem that was going to grow into terrifying proportions.

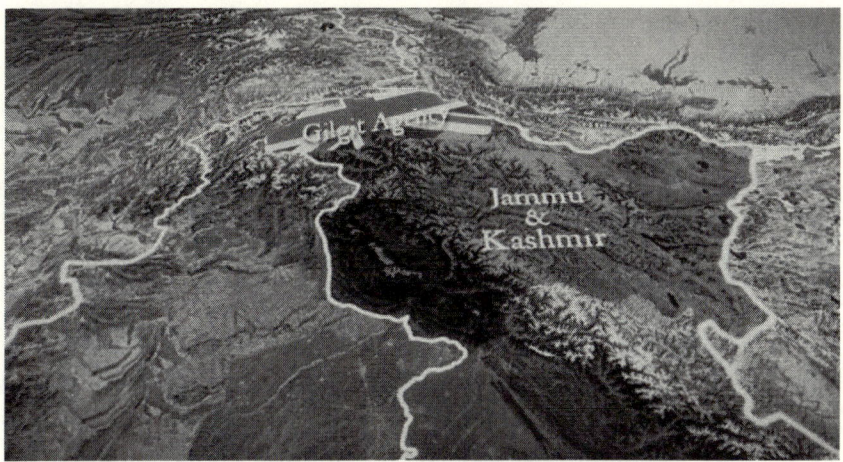

Image 2.3: Map of Gilgit Agency sharing its boundary with Jammu and Kashmir

Source: Archives of AIM Television Pvt. Ltd.

In 1935, Hari Singh's attitude towards the British had prompted them to take over a 75-year lease on the Gilgit Agency.[23] Gilgit was the last outpost of British India before the landmass of Jammu and Kashmir merged with Sinkiang. To the south of Gilgit flowed the mighty Indus as she meandered westwards towards Punjab. To the north of Gilgit lay the Karakoram Range. Of the eight known passes between Central Asia and the subcontinent, six lay within a week's march from Gilgit. From 1935, the leased region was treated as part of British India and was administered by a Political Agent who reported to the officials in Delhi. As a result, the kingdoms of Chitral, Hunza, Nagar Haveli, Puniyal, Chilas Yasin, Yashkoman and Koh-e-Khizr, all vassals of the Maharaja of Kashmir, now came under direct British rule. The newly leased territory was now called the 'Gilgit Agency'.

British Consolidate Gilgit

In early 1943, the British posted a Pushto-speaking Indian Army officer, Capt. William Brown, to the Gilgit Agency, where he spent the next three years. Brown had learnt Pushto at Peshawar while serving with the south Waziristan Scouts during 1942–43. He was appointed as the Assistant Political Agent for Chilas, which is only 90 km from Gilgit. Brown travelled widely throughout the Gilgit Agency, gaining experience and invaluable local knowledge. While in the Gilgit Agency, he learnt Shina, the dialect of the region, as well as some Burushaski, the language of Hunza. In 1946, he was posted to the Tochi Scouts in north Waziristan. In June 1947, he was posted to Chitral as the Acting Commandant of the Chitral Scouts.

Image 2.4: Captain William Brown, Acting Commandant of the Gilgit Scouts
Source: Public Domain

Brown soon became an expert in the language, culture and politics of this region. Though he worked as an undercover army officer, he was clearly much more than that. Brown secured the confidence of the son of the Raja of Nagar Haveli, Raja Muzaffar-ul-Din Shah. The two of them developed a close friendship which was founded upon a common strategic agenda: to deny, at any cost, the accession of the Gilgit Agency and the vassal states to

India. Brown also developed close ties with the ruler of Chitral, the Mir of Hunza, the Raja of Yasin and the Raja of Puniyal. Unfortunately for Maharaja Hari Singh, he remained blissfully unaware of the alliances Brown was forming in the northern tracts of his own state.

One wonders why Brown was posted to the Gilgit region in 1943, in the first place. What were his orders and who was he reporting to? What was the chain of command in the mission he was serving? Was he ordered to secure the complete confidence of the Raja's of the Gilgit Agency and the vassal states, and what was all this groundwork serving? What was the endgame in sight for the British, and what do the British archives reveal about this issue, today?

Image 2.5: Map of all the vassal states of the Maharaja of Kashmir
Source: Archives of AIM Television Pvt. Ltd.

Consequently, 1946 was a watershed year for Maharaja Hari Singh. His state was a composition of five parts: the Gilgit region, Ladakh, Poonch, the Kashmir Valley and Jammu. Each of them was ethnically, religiously and linguistically different from each other. In three of these parts, the Maharaja's personal agendas had empowered three formidable men whose actions, in 1947, were not only going to dismember the state from the consolidated whole that it was in 1946, but would also dispossess him from his rule, and force him into exile. These men, destined to play key roles in the breaking up of the state and the unseating of the Maharaja, were Sheikh Abdullah in the valley, Sardar Muhammad Ibrahim Khan in Poonch and Capt. William Brown in the Gilgit Agency. The tragedy is that apart from Sheikh Abdullah, the Maharaja was completely unaware of the potential upheavals the actions of Sardar Muhammad Ibrahim Khan and Capt. William Brown could cause.

The Maharaja's mind was so occupied with pursuing his own agendas that he had no clue of the trouble brewing right behind his back. He also had no way to foretell the impact that the departure of the British would have on his state. The Maharaja had forgotten that he was able to amass all this power only because the British had swung their weight in his favour, in the battle for succession to Maharaja Pratap Singh's throne. He forgot that it was only because of his father, Raja Amar Singh's continued demonstrative loyalty towards the British that he got his throne. The Maharaja forgot that his predecessor, Maharaja Pratap Singh, paid a very heavy price for trying to establish his independence from British control.

If the Maharaja had thought through his moves in advance and chosen to study the works of the great Indian political scientist, Chanakya and followed his directives, he would never have pursued his personal vendetta against Raja Jagat Dev Singh of Poonch. He would have handled the British with finesse rather than imperiousness. He would have never permitted xenophobia to get out of hand and prevented the British from establishing a constitution. Chanakya's *Arthashastra* lays down the virtues of an intelligence network that informs kings and rulers not only about the plans and actions of adversaries but also about discontent within their own population.

Most importantly, he never grasped the reality that while it may have seemed fashionable and heady to employ British advisors and officials, ultimately their loyalty would always rest with the British crown.

Chapter 3

Emerging Ripples

The year of 1946 saw the playing out of different levels of political intrigue that contributed to a rapid churn of events which ultimately, in 1947, led to the break up of Maharaja Hari Singh's kingdom of Jammu and Kashmir. To begin with, the Prime Minister of the state, Ram Chandra Kak began to exploit the differences that arose between Sheikh Abdullah's National Conference and Mirwaiz Mohammad Yusuf Shah's Muslim Conference. Kak's deft political intrigue largely isolated the Muslim Conference from the Quit Kashmir movement. While Kak placed the state under martial law and arrested almost the entire top leadership of the National Conference and hundreds of its workers, he spared the Muslim Conference his wrath. Sheikh Abdullah, following an arrest and a three years' imprisonment sentence for sedition, escaped to Punjab, leaving the National Conference leaderless and in disarray. To outside observers like Pandit Nehru, it seemed that all popular support in the valley resided with Abdullah, since the Mirwaiz appeared to be out of touch with the popular political sentiment. Nehru, however, failed to read the fine print. Kak had also arrested Muslim Conference leader Chaudhry Ghulam Abbas, so that it would not appear that Abbas was in support of the Maharaja.[1] This deft action politically neutralised the Mirwaiz and facilitated Abbas's takeover of the Muslim Conference.

Image 3.1: Ram Chandra Kak, Prime Minister of Jammu and Kashmir (1945–47)
Source: Creative Commons

An emotional Nehru decided to personally rally around his protégé and close friend, Sheikh Abdullah. He first tried to persuade Kak to release Abdullah and when this failed, he decided to pay a visit to Kak in Srinagar and try and get him to agree. While crossing into Kashmir from Punjab, on 21 June 1946, Nehru was detained in Uri Dak Bungalow, under Kak's orders. This was a personal affront to Nehru, which made him very resentful; he resolved to bring Kak and the Maharaja down.[2] With Viceroy Lord Wavell's intervention, Nehru reached Srinagar a month later, in July 1946. He visited Abdullah in prison and attended one of his many trials. The Maharaja, however, declined to meet Nehru because he was very displeased with Nehru's powerful clout with the British, which had forced him to permit Nehru's entry into his state. The differences between the Maharaja and Nehru were to grow wider in the years to come.

In 1944, Kak engineered Jinnah's visit to Srinagar and got him to mediate between the Muslim Conference and the National Conference in an effort to unite the two warring factions that were both working towards the same intrinsic goal. However, Jinnah was unsuccessful and ended up endorsing the Muslim Conference as the only sincere representative of the suffering

Muslim masses of the state. This helped Kak introduce the nascent idea of Pakistan to the Maharaja.

Looming Threats

But in 1946, the state's security faced newer threats. Tibet had *de facto* independence and was one of the countries that shared a border with Jammu and Kashmir. In order to secure India's borders, the British Government was willing to provide military support to Tibet. In the same year, the British Government officials prepared a confidential memo entitled, 'Appreciation of the scale of direct military assistance which could be provided in support of Tibet'.[3] According to this memo, Russia and China were potential threats to India's security. The memo proposed a line passing through Chamdo, Nagchuka, Garyarsa and Leh, and opined that any invasion by Russians or Chinese from south of this line would prove to be highly dangerous for India's security. The area south of this proposed line was to be the buffer zone between India and the two expansionist powers of Russia and China. This memo emphasised on the crucial role the state of Jammu and Kashmir played in maintaining India's military defence. Before this memo was written, India's Secretary of External Affairs, Sir Olaf Caroe, had stated that the Gilgit-Kashgar boundary was the only direct contact point between India and China, and that no other contact points should be added. Caroe was made the Governor of the NWFP, succeeding Sir George Cunningham in late 1946. Thereafter, he was succeeded by Cunningham, on 15 August 1947, when Cunningham was reappointed the Governor of the province, by the new Pakistani Government.[5]

Divide and Rule

The Maharaja decided to hold elections to the state's assembly in January 1947. The population in the valley was divided in their allegiance between the National Conference and the Muslim

Conference. With the National Conference boycotting the elections and the Maharaja's government keeping the remainder of the seats unfilled because of nomination screening, the Muslim Conference won 15 seats and secured the largest elected representation in the assembly. Kak had thus successfully quelled the residual slim chances of goodwill between the National Conference and the Muslim Conference. The quarrel he engineered between Abdullah and the Mirwaiz had gone against the original mandate of unity within the Muslim upsurge against the Maharaja. Glancy's constitutions of 1934 and 1939 had created an electoral system that, while legalising dissent and political activity, only permitted the electoral participation of 10 per cent of the population. Further, this system was vulnerable to extreme manipulation and corruption, especially in the matter of nominations.

The political polarisation in the state was now complete. The National Conference allied with the Congress party and the Muslim Conference allied with the Muslim League. The former had almost total control in the Kashmir Valley while the latter was dominant in the Jammu province, especially in the western districts of Mirpur, Poonch and Muzaffarabad. However, both parties held ambiguous positions on the accession of the state. The National Conference demanded that the common people of Kashmir should decide on accession. The Muslim Conference was generally inclined to support accession to Pakistan but in September 1946, it passed a resolution in favour of an *azad*, or free, Kashmir. This change of stand was engineered by Kak and allowed the Maharaja to hedge his bets till the bitter end. The Hindus, who were mostly confined to the Jammu province, were organised under Rajya Hindu Sabha led by Prem Nath Dogra. Nehru believed that Dogra was financed by the Maharaja. The Jammu Hindus mostly regarded the Maharaja as their leader and gave him total support.

Meanwhile in Poonch, after the death of Raja Jagat Dev Singh in 1940, Maharaja Hari Singh appointed a guardian for his minor son, Shiv Ratandev Singh, and used the opportunity to integrate the Poonch *jagir* into the state of Jammu and Kashmir. The Rajmata,

Jagat Dev Singh's widow, took the young heir and fled into exile in Nepal, fearful of their lives. Poonch became a district of Jammu that was administered by the officers of Jammu and Kashmir. This resulted in Poonch's loss of autonomy and subjected its people to the increased taxation levied by the Kashmir state, both of which were resented by the people. Sardar Muhammad Ibrahim Khan led the people of Poonch to protest against measures; he was a protégé of the late Raja Jagat Dev Singh.[6]

Khan, who was biding his time as an agent provocateur while serving as the Assistant Advocate General of the state, resigned from his job and secured a Muslim Conference ticket to fight the assembly elections in 1947. Kak was very pleased that a non-valley, British-educated Muslim, who ostensibly shared his strategic overview, would be a member of the legislative assembly and would likely be gullible enough to be manipulated by him. Little did Kak know that the seeds of revenge and rebellion had already been planted in Sardar Muhammad Ibrahim Khan's mind by Raja Jagat Dev Singh. Sardar Muhammad Ibrahim Khan won the election from Bagh Sudhanoti constituency and returned to Poonch after attending the assembly session in March–April 1947. The time was ripe to seek vengeance and a motive presented itself. By his own account, Khan was thoroughly convinced that there was a conspiracy brewing between the state forces and the RSS, so he politically mobilised the people of Poonch and set in motion a chain of events that would lead to the formation of Azad Kashmir some months later.

Further Control of Gilgit

Up in the highlands of Gilgit-Baltistan, there was a development in 1943. As described in the previous chapter, the news of Soviet troop movements and infiltration in the Hindu Kush region compelled the Government of India to take the Gilgit subdivision on lease from Maharaja Hari Singh in 1935. They merged the Gilgit sub-division with the districts of Puniyal, Koh-e-Khizr, Yasin and Yashkoman and the state of Chitral. The whole conglomeration was called the Gilgit Agency, which came under the absolute control of the political agent based in Gilgit. In 1943, Lt. Col. E. H. Cobb took over as the Political Agent and he enforced his power through an armed force of 800 men, called the Gilgit Scouts. The Commandant and all the top officers were British. In effect, the Commandant was, for all practical purposes, the military advisor to the Political Agent. The force was divided into platoons and billeted at strategic locations throughout the agency. Lt. William Brown was appointed adjutant of the scouts in 1943 and was based in Gilgit. Thereafter, he was promoted to Captain and spent one year as the Assistant Political Agent in Chilas.

The winds of change blowing through the state in 1946 saw Col. Roger Bacon OBE take over as the Political Agent in Gilgit. At the same time, Capt. William Brown was transferred to Waziristan in the NWFP in November 1946 as an officer in the Tochi Scouts. It was here that he met Jock Mathieson who was later to serve as his assistant in Gilgit.[7] Was there a hidden agenda in these seemingly routine and innocuous moves?

Image 3.2: Sir George Cunningham, Governor of NWFP

Source: Flickr Account of Dr Ghulam Nabi Qazi

In 1946, Sir George Cunningham ICS was the Governor of the NWFP,[8] and was perhaps the most well-informed British civil servant to have served in NWFP. He was fluent in Pushto and Hindko and was a proponent of the Forward School that advocated an aggressive stance by the Government of India at its frontiers. He strongly believed in Pax Britannica and presumed that despite Indian independence, the Gilgit Agency would continue to be a British administered leasehold property, somewhat like Hong Kong. It provided the British with a vital listening post in Central Asia. Before he resigned as the Governor of NWFP, Cunningham recommended one of his most trusted officers from the NWFP, Lt. Col. Roger Bacon, to take over as the Political Agent in the Gilgit Agency. This was ostensibly to the prepare the vassal rulers of the Gilgit Agency for the changes that were likely to take place after the transfer of power, and to ensure their continuing loyalty to the British rule.

Lt. Col. Bacon was to sit out the period of transition in Gilgit, waiting for some coherence in British policy. After Sir George Cunningham left for the UK in 1946, it is speculated that he spent a lot of time in confabulations with Lord Hastings 'Pug' Ismay and the former Prime Minister Winston Churchill.[9] They discussed the future of post-British India and the preservation of British interests. Lord Ismay was a seasoned Indian Army officer who as Churchill's Chief Military Advisor during WWII. It was necessary for George Cunningham to transfer his powers to someone who could chaperone his plans through the upcoming turbulence. Many believe that the red line of the Indian Partition was finalised in 1946, between Churchill, Ismay and Cunningham.

Image 3.3: Lord Hastings Ismay, Chief Military Advisor to Churchill
Source: Wikimedia Commons

Therefore, at the beginning of 1947, Sardar Muhammad Ibrahim Khan in Poonch, Lt. Col. Roger Bacon in Gilgit and Sheikh Abdullah and Prime Minister Kak in the valley, were positioned as the emerging poles of dissonance within the Maharaja's rule. For reasons best known to himself, Kak was pursuing a pro-Pakistan agenda and sought to irrevocably manoeuvre the Maharaja to accede to Pakistan. Lt. Col. Bacon's agenda was to preserve British interests at any cost and to achieve this, he had to hold on to the Gilgit Agency for the time being. Sardar Muhammad Ibrahim Khan's agenda was to destroy the Maharaja's rule and lead Poonch to accede to Pakistan. Sheikh Abdullah's agenda was to overthrow the Maharaja and replace him. Nehru's agenda was to secure the entire state for the Indian Union, securing a land bridge for India's access to Central Asia and thereby also defying the two-nation theory [10].

The stage was set for all these people to play their cards in 1947.

Chapter 4

Swelling Crests

The year 1947 was a very challenging year for British Prime Minister Clement Attlee's government. The weather began to take a turn for the worse in January 1947 as heavy snowfall covered south-east England; this was the worst weather the country had seen in the 20th century. The whole country was plagued by months of power cuts and most big cities experienced a gas scarcity. There was a breakdown in the public transport system and all of this added to a widespread national gloom.

Image 4.1: Clement Attlee, Prime Minister of UK (1945–51)
Source: Creative Commons

The public sector borrowing requirement took a big jump and there was tremendous pressure on the country's finances. Britain's transition to a welfare state, as promised by Attlee, required the diversion of resources in order to establish the social services, universal secondary education and the National Health Service. However, the country's global commitments began to falter. It decided to abandon the fight against communism in Greece and pulled back from supporting the Turkish economy. Britain agreed to transfer the Palestinian Mandate to the UN by June 1948. This date also coincided with the transfer of power in India to a successor government or joint governments if that were to be the case.

A Crumbling Empire

The empire was beginning to crumble. In an unprecedented move, the RAF mutinied in 1946.[1] There were a series of demonstrations and strikes at several dozen RAF stations in India and South-east Asia in January 1946. The protests arose from slow demobilisation and poor conditions of service following the end of WWII. The mutiny began at the RAF's Drigh Road station in Karachi and later spread to involve nearly 50,000 men over 60 RAF stations in India and Ceylon, including the then-largest RAF base at Cawnpore (now, Kanpur) and far-off RAF bases such as Singapore.

This contagion set the precedent and instigated subsequent mutinies undertaken by the members of the Indian Air Force first and then the navy. In February 1946, 78 out of a total of 88 ships mutinied in Bombay and Karachi.[2] Lord Wavell, the Viceroy of India at that time, conceded that both the mutinies considerably undermined the power of British authority in India. The Indian Army soldiers who revolted in Singapore in 1942 consolidated to form the INA, under the leadership of Subhash Chandra Bose. The INA had fought the British Army in Burma and north-eastern India and lost. However, an irreparable trust deficit had been created and British could no longer trust the officers of the Indian Army to sustain and preserve British rule in India. Further, IB intercepts of radio broadcasts ostensibly made by Bose in December 1945 and January 1946[3] struck fear in British intelligence circles and made them fear the consequences of Bose's army attacking them.

In the midst of all this turmoil, Attlee's cabinet took a decision in February 1947 to wind down all the country's overseas commitments that would prove difficult to sustain in the future.[4] British shipping through Suez had to be protected, along with the bases in Aden, Hong Kong and Singapore. There was a growing communist insurgency in both Malaysia and Indonesia and India's Congress party was objecting to the use of Indian troops to fight in these countries as well as in the Middle-East. The emerging Cold War in Europe entailed diversion of resources to protect western Europe and to develop a British nuclear deterrence. Something had to give way. Weighed against all of these responsibilities, the jewel in the crown of the British Empire, India, would have to be abandoned.

This panoply of events on the world stage proved to be too much of a burden for Attlee's government and they decided to find a candidate for Viceroy of India; someone who would replace Wavell and handle the winding up of the British Raj in India. Attlee offered the job to King George VI's cousin, Lord Louis Mountbatten. No historian has provided a plausible reason for this appointment. Mountbatten had always dreamt of serving as First Sea Lord of the Royal Navy[5], a post he took charge of, in 1955, and held for four years. In Britain's naval history, Mountbatten and his father were the only father and son duo to ever serve on this post. Till his retirement in 1965, Mountbatten served as the UK's Chief of Defence Staff. He was the longest-serving professional military officer in the British armed forces.[6]

No historian has examined whether Churchill, Ismay and Cunningham influenced Attlee in his decision to appoint Mountbatten, who was a member of the British royal family and a former commander of British forces in South-east Asia, as the last Viceroy of India.[7] Could this task have been entrusted to a safer pair of hands? Was there anyone safer than a member of the British royal family and a distinguished military man to handle this delicate task? Did Churchill brief Mountbatten before he accepted the job? Was Lord Ismay's appointment as Mountbatten's Chief of Staff, Churchill's idea? Was Ismay Churchill's way of making sure that Mountbatten toed the Churchillian line to the hilt?

Mountbatten Opens His Account

Mountbatten arrived in India to take over as the Viceroy, on 22 March 1947. By this time, the Government of India had a clear idea as to what Maharaja Hari Singh intended to do after the transfer of power in June 1948. If possible, he would prefer to opt for independence from India.[8] He already had bad blood with Nehru, and Sheikh Abdullah continued to be a thorn in his side. The Maharaja needed to free himself from the slow strangulation that was on offer as Kashmir was forcibly propelled towards political reform. Kak had his eyes set on striking a deal with the emerging state of Pakistan. In his dispatch from Srinagar on 14 November 1946, the British Resident in Jammu and Kashmir reported as much.

It had been a major objective of the British policy, from the 19th century, to insulate the state of Jammu and Kashmir from Russian influence. After the start of the Cold War, the possibility of Subhash Chandra Bose's refuge in the Soviet Union and the Soviet presence in Sinkiang posed to be potential threats to the Gilgit lease and the security of Jammu and Kashmir, thereby threatening the stability of the post-independence government in the rest of the subcontinent. All these interests would be best served if Jammu and Kashmir was prevented from being the site of further foreign policy experiments. Resolute control over the state was clearly called for and many in the British administration believed that India was better equipped to exercise this control, than Pakistan.

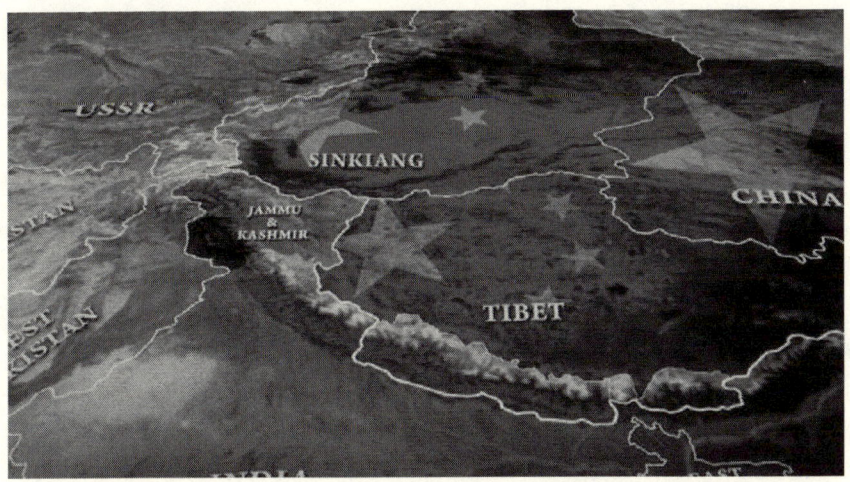

Image 4.2: Map of Chinese presence in Sinkiang and Tibet
Source: Archives of AIM Television Pvt. Ltd.

On 29 April 1947, Mountbatten displayed that he was well aware of the complications of the Gilgit lease when he advised Lord Listowel, the Secretary of State for India in the British Government, on the future of the lease. At this point, the date for the transfer of power was still known to be June 1948. In a startling departure from the Cunningham-Ismay line, Mountbatten recommended that the entire area of Gilgit be returned to the state of Jammu and Kashmir before June, perhaps as early as October 1947. Listowel agreed and Nehru, too, concurred when consulted. Jinnah was not asked for his opinion.

Why did Mountbatten take this new decision? Did Attlee tell him to rescind the Gilgit lease as the overburdened British state could no longer continue to bear the costs associated with maintaining it? Or was Mountbatten influenced by reports from the British Political Agent in Kashgar, Michael Gillett who had informed the officials in New Delhi about the Ili rebellion in Sinkiang? This was a Soviet-backed revolt against the Chiang Kai-shek-dominated Kuomintang Government of the Republic of China, in 1944.[9] The outbreak of this Government in November 1944 quickly spread to the two northern districts of Chugachack and Altai. Gillett observed that the rebels had received considerable help from the Soviets. A measure of peace was negotiated in January 1946, through Soviet mediation. However, the autumn of 1947 saw a complete change in things—the Ili rebels took control of Ili, Chugachack and Altai, thereby isolating these regions from the rest of Sinkiang. As late as the summer of 1948, Gillett's successor, Eric Shipton continued to express the hope of travelling to Ili from Kashgar. However, this was politically impossible. Support from the Soviets also saw the Kirghiz and Tadjik uprising in the south of Sinkiang; this uprising, known as the Sarikol Rebellion, took place in the autumn of 1945. The rebels threatened Kashgar, captured Kaghilik and attacked Yarkand. Further north, Aksu was attacked and portions of the Urumchi-Kashgar highway were occupied. The Sarikol rebels had also cut off the approach from India, going as far east as the Karakoram Pass in Ladakh. All courier services between Gilgit and Kashgar were stopped.

In these circumstances, it would be difficult to make a case for transferring the responsibility of defending Gilgit to Maharaja Hari Singh. It was largely to keep the area out of Hari Singh's hands that the Gilgit lease had been secured in the first place. Yet here was Mountbatten apparently abandoning this vital outpost and handing it back to Hari Singh. This was a paradox which only made sense on the assumption that the new lessees of the Gilgit lease would be based not in Srinagar and Jammu, but either in New Delhi or in Karachi.

Did Mountbatten run the developments in Sinkiang past Ismay? Did Ismay accept the inevitability of the rapidly changing Central Asian dynamic? Was there a split in the opinions of these men? If Mountbatten had been willing to let Pakistan be the guardian of the Gilgit Agency and the high passes of the Karakoram, he could well have left the Gilgit lease alone. The original contract was between the state of Jammu and Kashmir and the Government of India and the lapse of paramountcy upon the transfer of power had nothing to do with it. There was no reason why it would lapse automatically in October 1947 or earlier. For added safety, the extension of the lease could have been carried out by a simple standstill agreement which would ensure that even if Jammu and Kashmir acceded to Pakistan, the tenancy created as a consequence of the lease would also pass to Pakistan.

Was Ismay convinced by Mountbatten's reasoning? Did Mountbatten overrule him and secure the consent of an overburdened Attlee to rescind the Gilgit lease? Did this action of Mountbatten propel Ismay to sound out Col. Roger Bacon to start planning for the execution of the Gilgit rebellion? Did Ismay also set in motion the return of Sir George Cunningham's third term as the Governor of NWFP from 15 August 1947? Did Ismay take Jinnah into partial or complete confidence about a top-secret plan to invade Jammu and Kashmir if it acceded to India? Was Cunningham a part of this plan? After all, Jinnah did invite Sir George Cunningham in July 1947 to take over as the Governor of NWFP. This appointment cannot be viewed in isolation of the facts emerging.

On 4 June 1947, Mountbatten announced 15 August 1947 as the deadline for the transfer of power, instead of sticking to the earlier target date of 30 June 1948.[10] Why did Mountbatten spring this surprise? Mountbatten was a shrewd man and there was no way that he could have not known that his Chief of Staff, 'Pug' Ismay had a different viewpoint. Did the advancement of the date for the transfer of power have anything to do with Ismay's planning for an alternative plan to give Pakistan control of Kashmir rather than India?

For Mountbatten, there remained the complex problem of the future intentions of the two big states of Jammu and Kashmir and Hyderabad, which had indicated an interest in being an independent state after Partition. Mountbatten made it abundantly clear that he was personally unhappy about the prospect of independence for either. On 9 June 1947, he announced that he was instructing the British residents in both states to urge the rulers to make no announcements about independence until he had had the opportunity to visit them and discuss the matter.

Mountbatten, accompanied by Lady Mountbatten and Lord Ismay, arrived in Srinagar on 17 June 1947 and was back in New Delhi six days later. During these crucial six days, his aim was to engage in detailed parleys with Hari Singh and Kak. Mountbatten asked Nehru to prepare an exhaustive briefing note on Kashmir for him that would provide him with talking points for the ensuing discussions. While in Srinagar, Mountbatten was frustrated because Hari Singh was unwilling to engage in any serious discussions with him; the Maharaja had picked up the gossip about Nehru's friendship with Edwina Mountbatten and his extraordinary closeness to the couple while Jinnah was kept at arm's length by the Mountbattens. To Hari Singh, Lord Mountbatten was merely a votary of Nehru's views on the future of the state. He did not allow Mountbatten to visit Sheikh Abdullah in prison, even with Nehru's intervention. Lady Mountbatten found it impracticable to meet Begum Abdullah and Mountbatten made no attempt to visit another of the Maharaja's political prisoners, Chaudhry Ghulam Abbas, or to seek the views of the Mirwaiz. He did, however, engage with Kak. Mountbatten is believed to have said to Kak that the state of Jammu and Kashmir would have to accede to either India or Pakistan, as it would have great difficulty protecting its security on its own.[11]

Ismay's Treachery

What did 'Pug' Ismay do? Ismay, fluent in both Urdu and Punjabi, is reported to have conferred with the Maharaja in Punjabi and with Kak in Urdu. His conversations are not a part of the official record. What did he discuss with Kak and the Maharaja respectively? Did Mountbatten get independent intelligence feedback about these vernacular discussions? We can safely infer that not only did Ismay meet Col. Bacon in Srinagar, but he also met Maj. Gen. Scott, Chief of Staff of the Jammu and Kashmir state forces. It is obvious that the issue of the state forces manning the Gilgit Agency would have come up in these conversations since the lease was likely to be rescinded before the transfer of power on 15 August 1947. In that event, who would be the Political Agent? Would the Gilgit Scouts accept a non-British officer? Maybe a Muslim one, but certainly not a Hindu officer. Where would Maj. Gen. Scott source such an officer from?

Sensing some skulduggery afoot, on his return to Delhi, Mountbatten announced that the Gilgit lease would be rescinded on 31 July 1947. This set the proverbial cat amongst the pigeons as far as Ismay was concerned. Col. Bacon immediately summoned Maj. Brown who was then stationed in Waziristan as a major with the Tochi Scouts.[12] In Waziristan, Brown had sounded out Capt. Jock Mathieson and primed him to become his deputy in Gilgit if and when the eventuality arose. During the first week of July 1947, Maj. Brown met Col. Bacon, who had convinced Maj. Gen. Scott and the Maharaja to appoint British officers as Commandant and Deputy Commandant of the Gilgit Scouts until a more 'suitable' arrangement was arranged. Both of these officers would report to the Kashmir state-appointed Political Agent or Governor. The selected officers were to be Brown and Mathieson.[13]

This arrangement had a hidden subtext—both these British officers would have to resign their respective commissions with the British Army. What was the need for this, unless Col. Bacon had some questionable tasks in mind for these officers when he spoke with Maj. Brown? What were these questionable tasks and what were the assurances and incentives offered to these young men to quit their coveted commissions? Col. Bacon wanted these young men to operate at an arm's length from the British Government in their private capacities as private mercenaries. Ismay was worried that if it ever came out that serving British officers had participated in a conspiracy to execute the Gilgit Rebellion and defeat the objectives of the British Parliament, there would be a monumental scandal. Ismay was only too aware of the impact of the 1946 RAF mutiny.

It is obvious that Bacon wanted the preservation of the Gilgit Agency under Pax Britannica and the method by which this could be effected, despite Partition, would be to make the Gilgit Agency an agency of the NWFP, directly under its governor. On Partition, Sir George Cunningham was to take over as the Governor of NWFP.[14] The preparations would then be complete.

Having obtained Brown and Mathieson's consent, Bacon flew back to Srinagar the very next day to swing these appointments. Indirect endorsement of their acceptance came in the form of an urgent wireless message from the Inspector General of the Frontier Corps; Brown was asked to reach the Bala Hisar Fort, Peshawar. At the fort, the IG presented a way out for Brown if he wished to reconsider this assignment. Brown, however, stuck to his mission. On 29 July 1947, Brown boarded a Harvard trainer aircraft and flew to Gilgit. That this was possible so fast reveals that the conspiracy to execute the Gilgit Rebellion was thought out well in advance, had key British players and intended to defeat the Viceroy's intent of nudging the Maharaja to accede to India on or around 15 August 1947.

The conspirators in key places appear to at least be the following:

1. Lord Hastings Ismay, Chief of Staff to the Viceroy of India, Lord Mountbatten
2. Sir George Cunningham, Governor Designate, NWFP
3. Maj. Gen. Scott, Commander-in-Chief Jammu and Kashmir state forces
4. Col. Roger Bacon, Political Agent, Gilgit Agency
5. Brig. D. H. J. Williams, Indian Army at Peshawar
6. Ram Chandra Kak, Prime Minister of Jammu and Kashmir
7. Maj. William Brown, Commandant Designate, Gilgit Scouts
8. Capt. Jock Mathieson, Dy. Commandant Designate, Gilgit Scouts
9. Mohammed Ali Jinnah
10. Abdul Qayyum Khan, Chief Minister, NWFP, from 23 August 1947

The following day, the Raja of Puniyal, the Governor of Koh-e-Khizr, one Ishkoman from the Khuswaqt family of Chitral and Raja Mehboob of Yasin had a series of closed-door meetings with Col. Bacon and Maj. Brown. All of these men were made privy to the events that were to unfold if Hari Singh acceded to India.

While this conspiracy was being put in place, what were Lord Mountbatten and Nehru doing? Undoubtedly, Mountbatten had guardedly discussed his apprehensions about Srinagar and the layers of intrigue shrouding it. There is available evidence that Mountbatten shared his apprehensions with Nehru and Sardar Patel and sensed some trouble brewing in Gilgit. Between the three of them, Mountbatten, Nehru and Patel persuaded Mahatma Gandhi into meeting with the Maharaja in Srinagar as a final effort to persuade the Maharaja to accede to India.[15]

Hari Singh Gets Back Gilgit

On 1 August 1947, a day after the Gilgit lease was rescinded, two significant events happened in Jammu and Kashmir.[16] Up in the north in Gilgit, an Avro Anson aircraft landed at 10:00 AM. The first to disembark was Maj. Gen. Scott, followed by the Governor Designate Brig. Ghansara Singh and Capt. M. Said of the Jammu and Kashmir state forces. The next day, the ceremonial handover was completed. Maj. Gen. Scott, Col. Bacon and Maj. Brown reportedly fine-tuned the various options for the Gilgit Rebellion as news came through of Gandhi's arrival in Srinagar the previous day.

Gandhi arrived in Srinagar on 1 August 1947 by road via Rawalpindi. According to A. M. Watali, who retired in 1987 as the IG of the valley and who, as a teenager, was an eyewitness, Gandhi arrived in a convertible whose hood was drawn down. Thousands of people had collected in what is now the Batamaloo bus stand, and the crowd continued up to where the Badshah Bridge now stands. From the bus stand till the Old Secretariat, and right up to the Maharaja's palace on Gupkar Road, there was a sea of people. They were only shouting one slogan, *'Baghi Abdullah ki jai'*, 'All Hail, Abdullah!' Watali saw Gandhi covering his ears because the reverberations of this continuous chant were too uncomfortable to bear. It was a spontaneous upsurge of popular support for Abdullah. A visibly moved Gandhi experienced personally the kind of popular support that Abdullah enjoyed in the valley. But was Gandhi aware that this volume of public support for Abdullah was only restricted to the valley?

With great difficulty, the driver of Gandhi's car drove him to the house of Seth Kishorilal in the Barzulla suburb of Srinagar, where he was to stay. Later in the evening, around 5:00 PM, Gandhi drove up to the palace and met with the Maharaja and the Maharani.[17] He appeared to have impressed upon the Maharaja to release Sheikh Abdullah from prison, remove Kak from his position and swiftly make up his mind about accession. As dusk descended, the palace and the city were celebrating the return of the Gilgit Agency to the rule of the Maharaja. Gandhi, it appeared, frowned on this celebration and curiously observed and prophesied that the Gilgit Agency would ultimately be snatched away. Gandhi's curious observations only underscored his knowledge of what was brewing in the highlands. However, Mountbatten, Nehru and Patel were helpless unless the Maharaja acted.

Hari Singh turned a deaf ear to Gandhi's foreboding on the Gilgit Agency, finding false comfort in Maj. Gen. Scott, Premier Kak and Brig. Ghansara Singh's assurances. Hari Singh never granted any of Gandhi's wishes and never issued orders to release Abdullah from prison. Nehru and Mountbatten felt that maybe the Maharaja was apprehensive because Kashmir would have no land link with prospective Indian territory, post the transfer of power. What could Nehru and Mountbatten do to catalyse the Maharaja from his state of nervous inertia?

Currently, all land routes connecting Kashmir to the Indian mainland, through parts of Punjab, were likely to fall in Pakistan. However, if the three eastern *tehsils* of Gurdaspur district were to be awarded to India by the Punjab Boundary Commission, then the accession of Jammu and Kashmir to India would be possible, provided the Maharaja cast his lot with India.

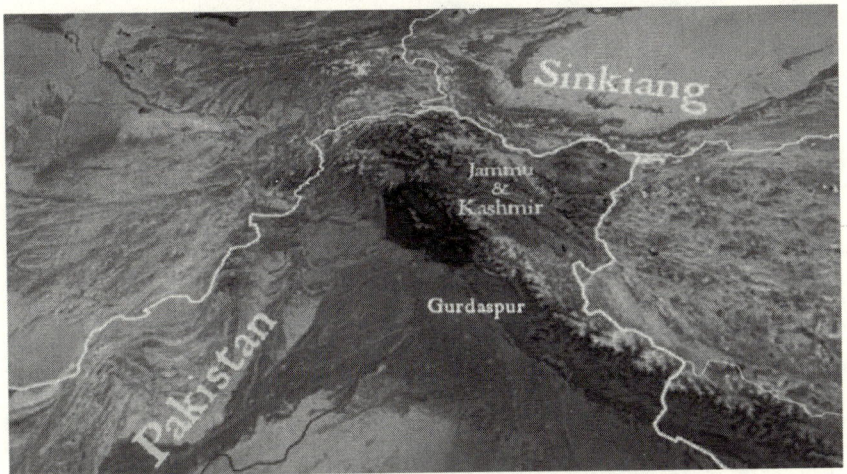

Image 4.3: Map of Gurdaspur's location
Source: *Archives of AIM Television Pvt. Ltd.*

On 8 August 1947, a provisional map was released by the Punjab Boundary Commission that showed the three eastern *tehsils* of Gurdaspur district falling under India, even with their major Muslim population.[18] On 12 August, the final award by the Punjab Boundary Commission was not only restricted to the three eastern *tehsils*, but India also got rewarded with Ferozepur and Zira *tehsils*, on grounds of accessibility to good irrigation. Between 8 and 12 August, when the final award was made, the Maharaja took the first tangible step towards accession to India, when on 11 August he sacked Premier Kak. After his sacking, Kak was arrested at Srinagar airport while boarding an aircraft with his English wife, Margaret. It is said that both the IG Police Richard Powell and Maj. Gen. Scott assisted him in this foiled attempt at escape.[19] An enraged Maharaja completely isolated him by placing him under house arrest. It appears that the Maharaja's resolve was also strengthened by his wife and her brother Nishchant Chand Katoch, who had lobbied for accession to India and the sacking of Kak. So, by 12 August 1947, the Maharaja had travelled one-third of the way to fulfilling Gandhi's wishes.

At the same time, Ismay was in radio contact with Col. Bacon who had now taken over as the Political Agent in Peshawar.

Bacon, in turn, was in radio contact with Brown in Gilgit. Plans were being crystallised to stage a *coup d'état* in Gilgit, with as little bloodshed and disturbance as possible. The goal was to get the whole Gilgit Agency to accede to Pakistan.[20] The code name of the operation was to be 'Datta Khel'.

Col. Bacon's former Parsee radio operator called Limbuwala was to use one-time pads to communicate with another trusted member of Col. Bacon's team, wireless operator Donaldson. Limbuwala had spent many years in Kashgar, Sinkiang as a radio operator and cipher clerk at the British Consulate. He was married to a girl from Kashgar and was, in all probability, actually employed by MI 6, as was Donaldson.

The operationalisation of Datta Khel was contingent upon Maharaja Hari Singh acceding to India. Maj. Brown was strategising his best options.

Prime Minister Kak's government was now replaced by one led by Maj. Gen. Janak Singh. Maharaja Hari Singh was now busy with getting India and Pakistan to sign standstill agreements with his state.

Sheikh Abdullah was freed from prison and was contemplating his next moves. Sardar Muhammad Ibrahim Khan was in the hill station of Murree in West Punjab, preparing for the Poonch uprising.

Sir George Cunningham was waiting to be sworn in as the third-time Governor of NWFP. Cunningham had been placed by Ismay and Churchill for a purpose; he had the ability to successfully motivate frontier tribesmen to invade Kashmir.[21] In the period just before the transfer of power, almost every tribe on the frontier was asking him to let them go so that they could go ahead and kill Sikhs. Pleased with his hold over the tribes of NWFP, Cunningham wrote, 'I would only have to hold up my little finger to get a *lashkar* of 40,000 or 50,000.'[22] Cunningham found that internal tribal dynamics and local political manoeuvring determined who went to Kashmir. NWFP Chief Minister Designate, Khan Abdul Qayyum Khan, and Muslim League supporter, Pir of Manki Sharif, lobbied Pashtuns for the

Kashmir invasion. These were Pashtuns from Mardan and Swat. Some were Pushto and Hindko speakers. Others were Mahsud, Afridi, Mohmand and Bajaur tribesmen. It was quite a motley crew. Abdul Qayyum Khan and the Pir of Manki Sharif were the two recruiting agents deployed by Cunningham[23] to raise his ragtag army of tribesmen that would, in the years to come, lay the grounds for sustained and never-ending militancy in Jammu and Kashmir.

Chapter 5

Lashing Waves

On the midnight of 14/15 August 1947, when Jawaharlal Nehru, the first Prime Minister of the Indian Dominion was reading out his famous 'Tryst with Destiny' speech in Parliament House in New Delhi, what was happening in Maharaja Hari Singh's palace in Jammu and Kashmir?

Hari Singh's Dilemma

The Maharaja was in a quandary. After he had sacked his Prime Minister, Ram Chandra Kak, on 11 August 1947, he discovered that both the IG Police, Richard Powell IP, and the Commander-in-chief of Jammu and Kashmir State Forces, Maj. Gen. H. L. Scott, were a party to helping Kak and his British wife Margaret escape Srinagar.[1] If the Maharaja could not trust his own Police Chief and Commander, how was he going to preserve the writ of his rule? It is no surprise that hardly a month later, on 24 September 1947, Maj. Gen. Scott relinquished his command. In a few weeks, the Maharaja sacked IG Police Powell, days before the Pathan invaders reached the borders of the state. It is believed that the Maharaja had received intelligence reports about Powell's involvement with his Pakistani counterparts in Muzaffarabad and Rawalpindi. Upon his sacking, Powell left for Rawalpindi via Muzaffarabad, and in no time at all, he allegedly joined the Pakistan security apparatus as an advisor.

The cadres of the Muslim Conference were getting very restive, particularly after Kak's sacking. There were daily demonstrations in Srinagar while the Maharaja installed Maj. Gen. Janak Singh as the new Prime Minister on 12 August 1947. Brig. Rajinder

Singh was appointed the Chief of Staff on 24 September 1947. The Maharaja also relied on a trusted coterie of friends whom he used as a sounding board. This included Ram Lal Batra, who was made Deputy Prime Minister; Swami Sant Dev[2] who became the Maharaja's spiritual advisor and the Maharaja's close friend, Victor Rosenthal. These people were clearly inadequate for the task at hand. How would Jammu and Kashmir survive as an independent entity from 15 August 1947? When two trusted officers of that state are sacked because of their divided loyalties, days before a massive invasion of the state, what would be the level of anxiety and insecurity of the ruler?

The team of Janak Singh and Batra neither had the skill of Kak, nor did they have the kind of relationship with Scott and Powell that Kak enjoyed. The mere fact that both these British officers had assisted Kak in his aborted escape from Srinagar, confirms that despite being professionals, they could not have held the Janak Singh-Batra duo in the same esteem that they held Kak in. Therefore, from 12 August 1947, both Janak Singh and Batra were relatively ineffective in dealing with law and order, and external security.

Neither Nehru nor Jinnah had reached a decision on the prospect of the state of Jammu and Kashmir remaining in a state of limbo till the moment of the transfer of power. In fact, after the removal of Kak and the obvious mistrust towards both Scott and Powell, it became clear that the new, weakened political leadership of the state was ripe for exploitation.

The Standstill Agreements

During his June visit to the state, Mountbatten had suggested the need for the state to secure a Standstill Agreement with both India and Pakistan.[3] Such an agreement would enable the state to continue to enjoy the existing trade, communications and service arrangements it had enjoyed within British India. On 12 August 1947, the first thing Janak Singh had to do was to send telegrams to both the emerging dominions of India and Pakistan, proposing parallel standstill agreements with both of them. The telegram sent to the Government of India stated that Jammu and Kashmir would welcome a standstill agreement with the union of India on all matters that presently existed between the state and the outgoing British Indian Government. It suggested that the existing arrangements should continue till the deciding upon and the formal execution of fresh arrangements. These arrangements, according to the Treaty of Amritsar of 1846, comprised the use of Indian forces if there was internal rebellion or invasion by a foreign government.

On 15 August 1947, Pakistan agreed to sign a Standstill Agreement and under this agreement,[4] the Pakistani Government assumed charge of Jammu and Kashmir's postal and telegraph system and also agreed to supply the state with foodstuffs and other essential commodities. However, the Government of India demurred. If the Government of India had signed the standstill agreement, could it have come to the aid of the state without having to use the device of the Instrument of Accession, in case the state faced either an internal rebellion or external? Did Mountbatten cancel the Gilgit lease so it would not endure if the Standstill Agreement had been signed with India, as he expected? Did the loophole of the absence of a standstill agreement with India activate Lord Ismay and his team into action?

We are already aware of the conspiracy behind Datta Khel. Was the invasion of the state by the Pashtun tribesmen on 22 October 1947, under the aegis of Operation Gulmarg, actually the part of a combined plan to invade the state, overthrow its leadership and absorb it into Pakistan by force? For many years, the operations Gulmarg and Datta Khel have been assumed and marketed to be independent and isolated operations. But, it can be argued that parallel coincidences do not exist in reality and that both of these actions were part of the same grand design. While there is no written archival record to substantiate this observation, let us examine the circumstantial arguments and attempt to join the dots.

We know that the trigger for kick-starting Datta Khel was the accession of Jammu and Kashmir to India, by virtue of the state signing the Instrument of Accession. We also know that the installation of Sir George Cunningham as the Governor of NWFP was integral for both the aforementioned operations to be carried out. We also know that the mobilisation of tribesmen for the invasion, by using the cutouts of Khan Abdul Qayyum Khan and the Pir of Manki Sharif, could not have happened until Abdul Qayyum Khan became the Chief Minister of NWFP on 23 August 1947. Only after 23 August 1947 and after receiving Sir George Cunningham's blessing, could Abdul Qayyum Khan and the Pir of Manki Sharif start mobilising the tribal *lashkars*. This process would definitely take at least three to four weeks.

Treachery in NWFP

Most historians are unaware that Sir George Cunningham had been cleverly planning for the Partition and the transfer of power since 1944. In 1944, blessed by Cunningham, who was then serving his second term as the Governor of NWFP, a frontier committee was formed under Lt. Gen. Sir Francis Tucker and its task was to recommend a new frontier policy. This committee recommended that regular Indian Army troops should be withdrawn from the Razmak, Wana and Khyber Pass garrisons and be replaced with scouts and *khassadars* (tribal levies).[5] Sir George Cunningham and Sir Olaf Caroe both recommended immediate implementation of these recommendations. The immediate effect of this was to remove all Hindu and Sikh army officers and soldiers from the NWFP and have the northern frontiers of India only defended by the Muslim staffed-Frontier Scouts and Frontier Constabulary.

In 1944, the Indian Army's Khojak Brigade on the Baluchistan frontier was disbanded. In March 1945, the Indian Army's Tal Brigade was disbanded and some of its units were assigned to the Kohat Brigade. In April 1946, Indian Army Commander-in-Chief, Field Marshal Sir Claude Auchinleck, presided over a high-level conference at Peshawar. It was attended by Governor NWFP, Sir George Cunningham, the Political Agent to the Governor of Baluchistan, the British consul at Kabul and senior military and civil officers. A unanimous decision was reached to replace regular troops in all tribal areas with scouts and *khassadars*. It was to be a gradual withdrawal in five phases and to be completed over a course of two years. It was against this background that the Pishin Scouts were raised, and a decision was also made to raise the Central Waziristan Scouts and to retrain the Malakand Battalion. The Khyber Rifles was re-raised on 26 April 1946.[6] The recruiting pool was to be drawn from the wartime-raised Afridi Battalion. Lt. Col. Muhammad Sharif Khan, aka Sharifo (5/10 Baluch Regiment), was appointed the Commandant of the Khyber Rifles. *Khassadars* were to be trained and disciplined, in order to make them a reliable partner of the scouts. To achieve this objective, in 1946, a new position called District Officer-in-charge was created to take charge of *khassadars*. In 1946, in north Waziristan, about 2,000 *khassadars* were put under the command of the new District Officer, Frank Leeson.

On 23 July 1947, the General Officer Commanding of the Northern Command, Lt. Gen. Sir Frank Messervy issued orders for reconstitution of his command. This plan involved the removal of 14 battalions deployed on frontier defence. Four battalions of the Zhob Brigade were also withdrawn and levies took their place. Three battalions from the Tal Brigade were removed and replaced by Frontier Scouts and *khassadars*. Four battalions from the Gardal Brigade were to be withdrawn in two phases: on 15 August and on 1 October 1947. One battalion stationed at Malakand was removed earlier in July 1947. The Wana and Kohat brigades were also reduced in size. The decision of the gradual withdrawal of Indian Army troops from the frontier was made by Field Marshal Auchinleck, long before the Partition of India and the process was already underway at the time of independence.[7]

Was Auchinleck making these significant changes at the behest of Lord Ismay, who was then Chief Military Advisor to Churchill? Both Ismay and Auchinleck were fluent in Punjabi and no British officer would have thought of tapping into their phone calls or conversations. The proof that the British state was involved in Operation Gulmarg comes from a rather unusual chain of events. In Bannu, which was a district of the northern frontier of India, the Political Agent in August 1947 was Arthur Dredge. Dredge worked very closely with the Brigade Commander of the Indian Army's Bannu Brigade, Brig. C. P. Murray. On 19 August 1947, Murray was at Mir Ali Mirali, which is a frontier settlement 41 km away from Bannu. Dredge was the only British officer at work, that day in Bannu. Murray was visiting Mir Ali Mirali to review the troops of the 1/8 Punjab Regiment. This battalion had arrived from Bannu in February 1947 to relieve the 14/9 Jat Regiment; it was commanded by Lt. Col. L. J. E. Kealey.

The Plucky Major Kalkat

A Sikh officer, Maj. Onkar Singh Kalkat, was in charge of the brigade in the absence of Brig. Murray. Both Murray and Kalkat were essentially waiting to hand over the charge of the brigade to Brig. Mian 'Ganga' Hayauddin (4/12 Frontier Force Regiment) and Maj. Muhammad Hayat respectively. On 20 August 1947, a courier arrived carrying a demi-official letter from Gen. Sir Frank Messervy at General Headquarters in Rawalpindi. As he was authorised to do so, Maj. Kalkat opened the letter. Attached to the letter was an appendix entitled, 'Operation Gulmarg—The Plan for the Invasion and Capture of Kashmir'. The day for the commencement of the operation was 20 October 1947.

At first, Maj. Kalkat thought of speaking about the contents of the letter with Dredge, but then decided against it. The troubled Kalkat called up Murray and related his startling discovery. Murray reached Bannu the very next day, on 21 August 1947, and was also very disturbed after reading the letter. Murray realised that Kalkat's life would be in danger if people came to know that he knew about the contents of the Messervy letter. Murray ordered Kalkat to act normally and wait for the handing over to take place on 5 September 1947. Meanwhile, through a network of Muslim friends, which included the District Commissioner of Mian Wali district, Kalkat dispatched his wife and infant son to safety, in India. He was left alone in Bannu, waiting to hand over charge. After that was done, the new Brigade Commander, Brig. Hayauddin discreetly moved Kalkat to house arrest in the Dalipgarh Fort in Bannu. Maj. Kalkat had been overheard talking to Brig. Murray by the head clerk at the brigade headquarters; he had betrayed Kalkat to Pakistani military intelligence. However, some of Kalkat's faithful Muslim soldiers, apprehending that he would be killed, hatched a plan to smuggle him out of the fort and the town on the night of 22 September 1947. They drove him to the Bannu railway station in a truck, from where he took a narrow-gauge train to Mari Indus, a major railhead 150 km away. Mari Indus was the location where Hindus and Sikhs leaving for India by train, got together.

However, early next morning, the duty officer discovered that Kalkat had escaped, he was soon traced to the town of Mari Indus. The British had established a big Army Service Corps depot at Mari Indus to serve troops stationed in Bannu, Tank, Kohat and Waziristan. Maj. Kalkat immediately went to the depot and reported to the British Base Commander that he planned to go to India, after having handed over charge in Bannu. He feared for his life and, despite urgent requests from Bannu asking for his return, the British Base Commander refused to hand him back. The kind British officer provided Maj. Kalkat with a rucksack full of provisions and armed him with his own service weapons. Finally, Kalkat boarded a goods train bound for Amritsar and concealed in one of the bogeys, he finally reached Amritsar and made haste to Delhi, arriving there on 18 October 1947.

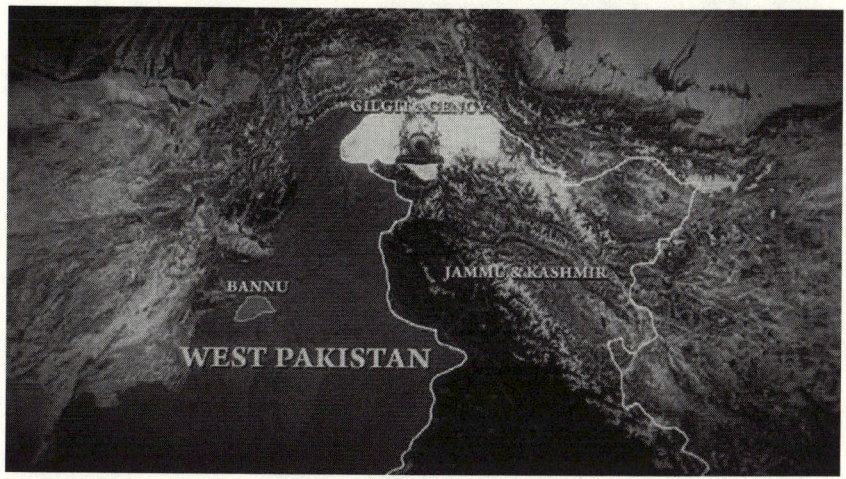

Image 5.1: Bannu district in erstwhile NWFP
Source: Archives of AIM Television Pvt. Ltd.

That same day, he met Maj. Gen. Kulwant Singh and Maj. Gen. P. N. Thapar and briefed them about the information he had about Operation Gulmarg. Both Thapar and Singh were unconvinced, but were duty-bound to take him to meet the Defence Minister, Sardar Baldev Singh, on 19 October.[8] The invasion was three days away. A sceptical Baldev Singh asked the army's Intelligence Directorate to verify Kalkat's account. However, the British-staffed Intelligence Directorate paid no heed to Kalkat's account and no action was taken!

Deception and Disinterest

The Intelligence Directorate's reaction has to be assessed in the perspective of other warning signals on the impending invasion that were being flagged in other areas. On 15 October 1947, the new Prime Minister of Jammu and Kashmir, Justice Mehr Chand Mahajan, met a group of Hindu and Sikh refugees who had reached Srinagar, by crossing the border at Domel. They reported that they had seen large concentrations of tribal Afghans or *Kabailis* in the area around Abbottabad and Man

Shera. The air was rife with rumours that they were a part of an invasion plan of the Kashmir Valley. On Mahajan informing him of this development, the Maharaja cabled Attlee but there was no reaction of consequence. The Maharaja followed this missive with another written communication on 18 October 1947, this time to Pakistan's Governor General Jinnah and Prime Minister Liaquat Ali Khan with information about border incursions, subversion of Muslim troops in the state's forces and the other violations of the standstill agreement.

On 18 October 1947, British officers and bureaucrats, holidaying with their families in the valley, were given emergency evacuation orders.[9] The very next day, on 19 October 1947, 20 RAF buses and trucks from Rawalpindi and Peshawar carried these passengers away from Srinagar to Rawalpindi via Baramulla, Uri and Muzaffarabad. The Maharaja himself was surprised and offended by this unexplained exodus. Clearly, an invasion was imminent. However, the Maharaja was unable to be decisive. To make matters worse, the same day, Liaquat Ali Khan wrote to Mahajan admonishing the state for trampling on the rights of the state's Muslim majority. This was followed by Jinnah's letter to the Maharaja on 20 October 1947, proposing an end to the acrimony and inviting the Maharaja to send Mahajan to Lahore for amicable talks that aimed to settle matters. The Maharaja declined. The following day, the Maharaja and Mahajan made a flash tour of Mirpur district to assess the extent of infiltration along the borders, following the fall of Fort Owen.

In the light of these fast-moving developments in the state, it seems incredible that Defence Minister, Sardar Baldev Singh not only discounted Maj. Kalkat's accounts but also chose to bury his head in the sand. The extent of British perfidy and complicity in a grand overall plan to annex the state of Jammu and Kashmir can now be understood and better accepted on the basis of these facts. It was to be complemented by the complacency of Indian politicians like Sardar Baldev Singh. It is only after the invasion had started in full swing that the import of Kalkat's warning was taken seriously and Kalkat was taken before Nehru on

24 October 1947, to relate his account.[10] Nehru was reportedly livid at Baldev Singh, Thapar and Kulwant Singh, but it was now too late. In later years, Kalkat wrote a book called *The Far-flung Frontiers*, detailing his experiences. Field Marshal Manekshaw, then a Brigadier in the military operations directorate, wrote the foreword to this book and never contradicted Kalkat's arguments. Manekshaw also wrote a foreword to Maj. Gen. Bajwa's book *The First Kashmir War 1947–48*, and again confirmed this thesis.[11]

Hari Singh Under Pressure

The slow erosion of the Maharaja's control over his own territories was now on in full swing. It was clear that Maj. Brown and the Gilgit Scouts were the real power in the Gilgit Agency. Notwithstanding the termination of the lease and the installation of Governor Ghansara Singh, the Maharaja's writ was a rapidly fading flame. The situation in Poonch was no different. During the course of September 1947, the Poonch uprising acquired a formal command structure. Sardar Mohammed Ibrahim Khan had escaped from Srinagar at the end of August and made his way to Pakistan. There he managed to set up a base at the hill station of Murree, only 33 km from Poonch, where he became the initiator and controller of an unofficial command post. Weapons were collected, many of them ancient muzzle-loaders, ammunition was prepared and supplies were smuggled across the Jhelum into Poonch and Mirpur, where he had fathered a military organisation of demobilised Poonch soldiers. Soon, a number of Muslim officers in the Jammu and Kashmir state army deserted the Maharaja and joined this force. They were soon followed by volunteers from Pakistan including several former Muslim INA officers who were looking for action. The most famous of these was Maj. Zaman Kiani a former trusted assistant of Netaji.[12] He was, more or less, the main Military Commander under Sardar Muhammad Ibrahim Khan. The funds for this organisation were provided by Mian Iftikharuddin, a wealthy Muslim League politician from Punjab, who was a confidant of Jinnah.¹³ By early October, this force had gained control of almost the entire Poonch district except for the town of Poonch that was still being garrisoned by the Jammu and Kashmir state forces. Flush with his success, Sardar Muhammad Ibrahim Khan proclaimed the formation of a provincial Azad Jammu and Kashmir government in Pallandri, a township in Sudhanoti district, on 24 October 1947.¹⁴

The same day, the invasion force of *Kabailis*, now led by Col. (later Major General) Akbar Khan of the Pakistan Army who had adopted the invasion *nom de plume* of Gen. Tariq, had taken over Muzaffarabad and Uri. The *Kabailis* had destroyed the electricity sub-station at Mahura, which supplied power to Srinagar. The city was plunged into an eerie cloak of darkness. Of their own volition, the raiders got sidetracked in an orgy of rape, plunder and loot at Baramulla. Though the road to Srinagar was open and lay undefended, the short-sighted *Kabailis* ignored the orders of their commanders took to behaving like barbarians. Only when the town had been stripped of its money, firearms, jewellery, women and boys, was their thirst satisfied. It was their stay at the prosperous town of Baramulla for three crucial days that gave the Maharaja the shock that was finally able to shake him off his inertia. Even the arrival of the Pir of Manki Sharif could not detach the *Kabailis* from Baramulla. Only when this loot had been collected, divided and dispatched to the tribal areas in NWFP, would their advance to Srinagar be resumed. There is no doubt that the ranks of the *Kabailis* were buttressed by units from the Frontier Corps and Frontier Constabulary. However, their lack of disciplined leadership was their Achilles' heel. If the original version of Operation Gulmarg had been retained, as was the plan of Operation Datta Khel, the invasion force would have been led by British mercenaries who had resigned from their commissions from the Frontier Corps, Frontier Constabulary and the political department. This entire force would have been in uniforms and headgear a little different from the clothing of the ordinary tribesmen. It is our guess that because of the snafu concerning Maj. Kalkat in Bannu, all British mercenaries were asked to stand down. This is what explains the difference between success and failure of the invasion. It is also in line with the blueprint of Messervy's Operation Gulmarg that Kalkat had read in Bannu.

When the Maharaja appealed for help to New Delhi, he was asked to sign the Instrument of Accession, before any help was sent. Meanwhile, near New Delhi, the largest peacetime air armada of 100 planes was being organised by the Government of India to fly off hardened fighting units of the Indian Army to Srinagar, once the Instrument of Accession was signed. This happened in Jammu on 26 October 1947. Sir V. P. Menon, Principal Secretary to Sardar Patel, flew into Srinagar on 25 October and instructed the Maharaja to leave for Jammu. The Maharaja wanted a 'limited accession' of the state to India only with regard to defence, foreign affairs and communication. The Maharaja felt unprotected ever since he had been betrayed by his army and police chiefs. He wanted the protection of the Indian Army but still wanted to retain his hold on the state. Menon flew back to New Delhi with Sheikh Abdullah as sunset descended on Srinagar. That night, the Maharaja's entourage left Srinagar for Udhampur with the gold idol of the presiding deity, Lord Vishnu from the Gadadhar Temple in Srinagar. According to Sheikh Abdullah, as the caravan of cars drove into Udhampur, the Maharani sat clutching the idol with the car's hood down.[15] This picture of the Maharani made all of the Dogra onlookers at Udhampur very angry. Meanwhile, Menon landed in Jammu and obtained the Maharaja's signature to the Instrument of Accession on the morning of 26 October 1947.[16]

Accession

There was a twist in the execution and acceptance of the Instrument of Accession. Lord Mountbatten accepted the accession but added a caveat to it—this was the Indian Government's promise to ratify the accession by means of a plebiscite seeking the consent of the people of the state, regarding the accession. Why did Mountbatten enter this caveat? Why did Nehru and Patel accept it? Was this a last-ditch attempt by Ismay and his gang to keep the issue of Kashmir alive in international forums forever? It appears that Mountbatten had relented to the dictates of the British deep state and forcibly yanked Nehru and Patel along.

At this point, one cannot but wonder how and why the standstill agreement between Jammu and Kashmir and the Dominion of India remained unsigned, and who were the principal votaries who voted against it? If this agreement had been signed at independence, the Indian Government could have come to the aid of the Maharaja much earlier. Perhaps people were told that by signing the agreement, India would be taking a step towards recognising Kashmir's sovereignty and independence. The lack of a standstill agreement did not hinder the Maharaja of Patiala, in the first fortnight of October 1947, to dispatch a battalion of infantry and a battery of mountain artillery to Kashmir. When Indian troops, led by Lt. Col. D. R. Rai, landed in Srinagar on 27 October 1947, they found Patiala gunners guarding Srinagar airfield, where they had been in control since 17 October.

Gilgit Erupts

At the same time, frequent cipher messages were being exchanged between Col. Bacon in Peshawar and Maj. Brown in Gilgit. Because of what happened with Kalkat,[17] the British mercenaries had to stand down and the opportunity to cleanly take over Srinagar and the entire valley had been lost. *Pax Britannica* had clearly failed, and they had to resort to the use of communal arms to achieve its ends. Col. Bacon was concerned that matters in Gilgit would get similarly messy. On 28 October 1947, Brown received word that the Mehtar of Chitral was mobilising forces to join Maj. Brown's proposed joint command, that would offer stiff guerrilla resistance to an expected ascent by the Indian Army towards Gilgit. Similarly, the forces of the Wali of Swat had entered Tangir and were posted on the borders of the Gilgit Agency. On 29 October 1947, at the instructions of

Col. Bacon, Brown readied for the execution of a bloodless coup by providing Governor Ghansara Singh a chance to step down with a promised safe passage out of Gilgit. On 30 October 1947, he proposed this to Ghansara Singh saying that the alternative option was for him to hold a referendum in the Gilgit Agency. This would be along the lines of the referendum suggested by Mountbatten for the entire state. That way, Ghansara Singh could continue to govern the province till the requisite authority took over. Singh disagreed as both these options not only offended his Dogra pride but also counted as acts of treason against the Maharaja. As a result, Brown had no choice but to put into execution Operation Datta Khel on the night of 31 October 1947.

Brown laid siege to the Governor's residence that night and after a fierce gun battle, Ghansara Singh and his staff were outnumbered and forced to surrender. The next morning, on 1 November 1947, Brown sent cipher messages by radio to Abdul Qayyum Khan and Col. Bacon informing them that he was now *pro tem* administrator of Gilgit. Brown's message to Abdul Qayyum Khan was carefully worded and dispelled the notion that the *coup d'état* had been performed at the instigation of the British Government. Now that power had passed to Brown, it had to be held and preserved until it could be passed on to the Government of Pakistan and permanently secured in their favour. Further, plans had to be implemented on how to keep the Indian Army at bay.

Maj. Brown had no remorse. He had committed treason against the state of Jammu and Kashmir after taking an oath to uphold the state's constitution and the rule of the Maharaja. He had drawn generous pay and allowances and had confiscated a reported amount of £60,000 of the state's funds lying in the treasury at Gilgit.[18] There are unsubstantiated indications that this sum could have been much more. He had deserted, mutinied and instigated the Gilgit Scouts to mutiny, and had ordered the scouts to finish off large parts of the Maharaja's forces by deceit. Since the state of Jammu and Kashmir had acceded to and been accepted by India, which was then a dominion of the British

Empire, his actions had amounted to waging war against the king and was an act of high treason. Not only Maj. William Brown, but his subordinate officer Capt. Jock Mathieson, Col. Roger Bacon, Sir George Cunningham, Gen. Sir Frank Messervy, Lord Ismay and many others had committed high treason against the throne. This is the irony behind the operations Gulmarg and Datta Khel.

On 4 November 1947, an imprisoned and humiliated Brig. Ghansara Singh signed a surrender order drafted by Maj. William Brown. Thereafter, Brown exchanged numerous radio messages with Col. Bacon about the military challenges created by the Indian Army's presence in the state. The Burzil Pass was the weakest link on the Astore Road to Gilgit from Harmosh near Kargil. This position was reinforced. In the event of the Indian Army taking this route, guerrilla action would be launched between Astore and Ramghat. More scouts would have to be urgently recruited and trained; they were drawn from the Chitral, Hunza and Ishkoman forces. Contact was made with Gen. Tariq instructing him to secure the Gurez Valley to prevent an Indian force that was coming up the Burzil route. In fact, a year later in November 1948, Brig. Kanhaiya Lal 'Bagga' Atal, Commander of the 77 Para Brigade had taken Kargil and was ready to go up the Astore Road to Gilgit. He had signalled to the Northern Command Headquarters, asking for permission to do so.[19] The permission was never granted. Why?

Pakistan Takes Gilgit

Back in Gilgit on 11 November 1947, Maj. Brown received a cipher message from Col. Bacon in Peshawar informing him that a representative from Pakistan would be arriving on 16 November to relieve Brown of his command. Bacon wanted all the Rajas and Mir's of the Gilgit Agency to be in Gilgit to meet this representative of the Pakistan Government. On 16 November, at exactly 10 AM, a Harvard aircraft of the Royal Pakistan Air Force, flown by Squadron Leader Ahmed, landed in Gilgit and delivered the new Political Agent Mohammad Alam. Alam had been thoroughly briefed by Col. Bacon in Peshawar before flying to Gilgit. Earlier, he was a Sub-collector or *tehsildar* in NWFP. The handover was formalised on 17 November 1947 and the Pakistani flag was slowly run up on the flagstaff, reaching the pole-head on the last bar of 'God Save the King'. Thereafter, as per Col. Bacon's instructions, over the next week, plans were put into place for formalising recruitment of additional scouts, organising their training and ensuring their equipment: from wireless radios, automatic weapons to pack mules. On 24 November 1947, Col. Bacon ordered Brown to appear at Peshawar for briefings. The same Harvard aircraft piloted by the same Squadron Leader Ahmed flew Brown to Peshawar, on 25 November 1947. On landing in Peshawar, Brown was driven up to Khyber House, the residence of Col. Roger Bacon. After being debriefed by the Colonel, the two of them then drove across to the Government House to meet the NWFP Governor, Sir George Cunningham for the most important debriefing. Brown was asked to prepare a detailed report along with maps of ground positions. He was also met by Charles Duke, the British Deputy High Commissioner in Peshawar and former Political Agent in south Waziristan. Duke was also given a copy of the Brown report and this was forwarded to Whitehall.[20]

Col. Bacon also called his old friend from Sandhurst, Lt. Col. Iskander Mirza, who was Pakistan's Defence Secretary and later, Pakistan's President, and asked him to fly into Peshawar to meet Brown. Brown and Bacon both briefed Mirza. A British mercenary who had waged war against the king had come in from the cold and was warmly received back in the folds of the British deep state. Such was the treachery at hand in the execution of all of the variants of operations Gulmarg and Datta Khel.

This story has an interesting postscript. After his return from Gilgit in 1947, William Brown was appointed to the Frontier Constabulary, the police force of the NWFP in Pakistan, in which he served in various capacities for the next two years. In July 1948, William Brown was awarded the Member of British Empire (MBE) by the King-Emperor with an unspecified citation. The act of awarding Maj. Brown an MBE, even though he had not only resigned his commission in the army but also that he had waged war against the King-Emperor, was one of the enduring paradoxes of British rule in the Indian subcontinent. This final act confirms that both operations Gulmarg and Datta Khel were the brainchildren of the British deep state and this confounded legacy continues to haunt the Government of India even today. Furthermore, it is highly unlikely that the ghosts of Ismay and Cunningham are going to be exorcised for quite some time.

Chapter 6

Temperamental Tides

The first week of October 1947 found the Pakistani Government sending Dr Muhammad Din Taseer and Shaikh Sadiq Hasan to convince Sheikh Abdullah to support Jammu and Kashmir's accession to Pakistan. The Pakistanis were worried that the Maharaja had signed a deal with Abdullah and accession to India was on the cards. Abdullah did not strike a deal with them. He saw no role for himself in a Kashmir which was in Pakistan. Shortly thereafter, Abdullah flew to Delhi on 14 October, and stayed with Nehru.[1]

Other Pakistani agent provocateurs like Gilgit-born K. H. Khurshid, who was the Private Secretary to Jinnah, was also in Srinagar plotting against the Maharaja. As we have seen, mobilisation of the Pashtun tribesmen or *Kabailis* took place under the joint leadership of NWFP Chief Minister, Abdul Qayyum Khan and the Pir of Manki Sharif. Mian Iftikharuddin was the Pakistani puppet master controlling the actions of Sardar Muhammad Ibrahim Khan in Murree.

The tentacles of the Pakistani political machinery extended to the Kashmiri press corps as well. By 7 October 1947, the Maharaja introduced press censorship in the state and ordered the newspaper *Kashmir Times* to stop publishing any news on the state's accession. In protest, the newspaper suspended publication altogether. *Kashmir Times* was owned and published by Abdul Rahman Mittha in Srinagar, who was a fervent advocate of the state's accession to Pakistan. Since he was not a resident of the state, Mittha was served with an expulsion order and sent over to Pakistan via Kohala. In Pakistan, he joined Sardar

Muhammad Ibrahim Khan and started living in Murree. Sardar Muhammad Ibrahim Khan appointed Mittha as the Director of Public Relations of the Azad Kashmir Government, even before the said government was announced.

Another journalist, G. K. Reddy, who was the Resident Editor of *Kashmir Times* in the 1940s, also served as the Correspondent for the Associated Press in Srinagar.[2] He used to report to its Lahore chief, Malik Tajuddin. Reddy was detained at Domel near Muzaffarabad for 10 days in mid-October 1947. After that, he was transported to Kathua, escorted by the military, and expelled from the state at the Pathankot border. The same day, he drove straight to Lahore and reported the whole story to Malik Tajuddin. News of the expulsion of Mittha and Reddy was flashed on Pakistan press outlets and announced on the radio. Sardar Muhammad Ibrahim Khan promptly appointed Reddy as the Deputy Director of Public Relations of the Azad Kashmir Government. While in Lahore, on 21 October 1947, Reddy received a phone call from Lt. Col. Alavi, the Public Relations Officer of the Pakistan Army, who stated that the Ramkot post of the Jammu and Kashmir Government was being attacked that night. This news, he demanded, should be published as coming from the Azad Kashmir Headquarters in Pallandri. Reddy was also told that all further news of invasion would come from the Army Headquarters in Rawalpindi, but Pallandri is the place that should be mentioned in all press releases. Reddy hated the Maharaja, and this prompted him to give a detailed interview on 26 October 1947 to the Lahore-based daily *Civil and Military Gazette*, where he described the 'mad orgy of Dogra violence' against Muslims in Jammu.

Endgame for Hari Singh

Little did Maharaja Hari Singh know that the crimson-coloured leaves of the valley's Chinar trees would end up being a metaphor for the blood of all those slaughtered in the state, by the machinations of all of these agent provocateurs and their Pakistani masters.

On 26 October 1947, if Maharaja Hari Singh had taken a reality check, he would have been dismayed. He had already signed the Instrument of Accession with India; the postscript of this deal was the legitimisation of the political transition of Sheikh Abdullah into a position of political power in the state. After the appointment of Mehr Chand Mahajan as the Prime Minister, strong winds were rattling the locks of Sheikh Abdullah's prison cell. As Mahajan began to come to terms with the complexities of his office, he discovered that the Maharaja, through Deputy Prime Minister R. L. Batra, was in serious negotiations with Sheikh Abdullah on the nature of his release. The Maharaja was a beleaguered man and options were fast running out for him. These negotiations culminated in the release of Sheikh Abdullah on 29 September 1947. However, some weeks prior to his release, Abdullah was shifted from the Bhadarwah Jail of the Doda district in Jammu to the Badami Bagh cantonment hospital in Srinagar. For a few days, in the hospital, Abdullah had a regular visitor in the Maharaja's brother-in-law, Nishchant Chand Katoch.[3] These meetings were to prepare Abdullah for his audience with the Maharaja. A technicality demanded that Abdullah offer the Maharaja *nazar* or a tribute of gold coins. Abdullah had none. Thereupon, one Shyam Sunder Lal Dhar gave him some gold coins which he, in turn, presented to the Maharaja. It appears that some sort of deal was struck between the two men as a few days later Abdullah was formally released, along with other National Conference leaders. The Muslim Conference leaders, however, remained in jail.

For the Maharaja, this was a great comedown since he had to now do business with the very man who had challenged the legitimacy of his rule. For Abdullah, his borrowed gold coins not only bought him his freedom, but also a seat at the high table with the Maharaja. The middle-class shawl maker's son had come a long way in his political struggle.

If the Maharaja had reflected on his actions from the time he was positioning himself to succeed his uncle, the Late Maharaja Pratap Singh, to the throne, he would have gathered that his opposition to British hegemony had cost him dearly. His great-grandfather, Gulab Singh, had been the beneficiary of British indulgence. Prior to admitting him to the privileges of a separate treaty, they elevated him to the status of Maharaja at Amritsar on 15 March 1846, during a state ceremony.[4] It was on this occasion that Gulab Singh stood up, joined his hands in an expression of gratitude to the British and declared himself to be their *zar kharid ghulam* (a bought slave).[5] It was on the next day, 16 March 1846 that the British entered into the Treaty of Amritsar with Gulab Singh, through which he became Maharaja of Jammu and Kashmir.

Contrary to his great-grandfather's tact and guile in dealing with the British, the Maharaja's desire to be independent of British hegemony paved the way for the conditions that led to Sheikh Abdullah's rise to power and for the Maharaja to now be forced to uneasily share power with him. Further, the British not only engineered the operations Gulmarg and Datta Khel to sequester parts of the valley and the entire Gilgit Agency from his rule, but they also planted treacherous British officers in his state forces, who betrayed him at key milestones in his struggle to keep his head above the water.

Further, the Maharaja holding on to the long-standing blood feud between his family and the family of his great-grandfather's brother Raja Dhyan Singh of Poonch, had caused the secession of the areas of Poonch, Mirpur and Muzaffarabad led by Sardar Muhammad Ibrahim Khan, the protégé of Raja Jagat Dev Singh. This was now functioning as Azad Kashmir.

For Maharaja Hari Singh, his world lay in tatters. Little did he know that the unravelling of his state was not going to stop here but was going to continue as his position and power were going to be continually eroded. If he had thought carefully, he might have adopted a different position by willingly aligning himself with his new overlord—the Government of India under Nehru.

It was the consequence of these misjudgments made during these trying times that on that fateful day of 26 October 1947, the Maharaja had signed away what remained of the state that had been welded together by his crafty ancestor, Maharaja Gulab Singh. That very day in New Delhi, in a meeting attended by Mountbatten, Nehru, Patel, Baldev Singh, Batra, Menon, Abdullah, Mahajan and the army chief and IAF chief, a decision was made to provide Indian military assistance in return for the accession and for the agreement, demanded by Nehru, that the Maharaja would entrust to Sheikh Abdullah the task of forming an emergency government under Prime Minister Mahajan. The said meeting, on 26 October 1947, was attended by several people, some of whom were members of the cabinet defence committee. The Indian cabinet had established a defence committee on 30 September 1947; it consisted of both Indian and British members. The Indians were Prime Minister Jawaharlal Nehru, Deputy Prime Minister Sardar Vallabhbhai Patel, the Defence Minister Sardar Baldev Singh, the Finance Minister R. K. S. Chetty and a minister without portfolio, Sir Gopalaswami Ayyangar. The British side consisted of Lord Mountbatten and the three British Commanders-in-Chief of the armed forces. At this stage, Mountbatten took the chair. Some would say that the presence of Ayyangar is interesting; he had been the Prime Minister of Jammu and Kashmir in 1937–43 and had the reputation of being a tough taskmaster. It has been suggested that his presence in the cabinet, which he joined at the very end of September 1947, was directly related to the Kashmir problem. It may be significant that Nehru regarded Ayyangar as the only former Prime Minister of Jammu and Kashmir who had enjoyed a tolerable working relationship with Sheikh Abdullah. Ayyangar was to succeed Sardar Baldev Singh as the Defence Minister, a year later in 1948.

The very next day, on the morning of 27 October 1947, the IAF's air armada began to airlift battle-hardened Indian troops to Srinagar. The first wave, led by Lt. Col. V. R. Rai, disembarked and immediately reinforced the airfield's defences, which were under the Patiala state force's control. Within a few days, at least 35,000 Indian regular troops were involved in the defence of the valley.

Sheikh Abdullah's First Taste of Power

With the Maharaja having already left Srinagar for the relative safety of Jammu,[6] the morale of Srinagar was very low. If the Indian Army had not arrived by 27 October 1947 and taken charge, anything could have happened in the power vacuum. Sheikh Abdullah, who was in New Delhi, confirmed to both Nehru and Mahajan that he supported the accession. This now paved the way for the creation of a power diarchy in the state. On 30 October 1947, the Maharaja appointed Sheikh Abdullah as the Chief Executive Administrator with Mahajan continuing to function as the Prime Minister. Abdullah's long journey that started in 1931, with his political agitation against the autocratic rule of the Maharaja, had now resulted in the Maharaja appointing him the *de facto* Prime Minister of the state. The Maharaja, now having accepted Abdullah as a political representative of the Muslim majority in his truncated and disintegrating state, opened the way for Mountbatten to play his next card. The argument for plebiscite was to ascertain what the public wanted. Given that the overwhelming population of the state was Muslim and a communal conflagration was in progress in the state and in the neighbouring state of Punjab, the apprehension in the minds of both Nehru and Patel was that without Sheikh Abdullah on their side, a single comprehensive plebiscite would tilt the scales towards accession to Pakistan. This would include giving both Jammu and Ladakh, where Muslims were in a minority, to Pakistan. The combined numbers in these two regions would be insufficient to fight the Muslim majorities in the valley, the Poonch belt and the Gilgit Agency. Both Nehru and Patel were unsure if Abdullah wanted to accede to Pakistan. They wanted to be sure that he was on the side of accession to India, so that he could bring in the votes from the valley, the Gilgit and Poonch in a plebiscite. Therefore, it was necessary to both lure and reward Abdullah with political power so that the majority in the state voted for India, if ever a plebiscite was called for.

Mountbatten understood this reality very well and his major contribution to the Maharaja's accession may well have been to formally introduce the requirement for a plebiscite and to persuade both Nehru and Patel of its desirability. This was Mountbatten's answer to the pressure that he was subjected to, by the British deep state, to frustrate the accession of the state to India. When in his radio broadcast on All India Radio, on 2 November 1947, Nehru confirmed that the fate of Kashmir is ultimately to be decided by the people, and that the pledge India had signed to have a referendum would be fulfilled. Patel may well have been uneasy about the consequences of handing over political power to Abdullah, and he may have preferred an unqualified accession by the Maharaja to India. However, Nehru cast his lot with Mountbatten and Patel was overruled, India accepted the principle of the plebiscite. By giving Abdullah the plebiscite card, Nehru had institutionalised its use to prove that the Instrument of Accession was not final in itself.

It is clear that accession meant different things to different people. For Sardar Patel, accession meant that Jammu and Kashmir would become a part of India beyond all doubt, not least to guarantee the security of the northern frontier. For Nehru, accession was a means to challenge the two-nation theory by creating a secular state within the Indian Union out of a Muslim-majority province, albeit through the efforts of Sheikh Abdullah. For Mountbatten, accession, with the twist of the plebiscite, meant that the British deep state could consolidate the gains of Operation Gulmarg and execute Operation Datta Khel, thereby reinforcing the need for a plebiscite to ultimately legitimise their actions.

Sardar Patel Outmanoeuvred

For Patel, the perception of the security challenges facing post-Partition India coincided with the perception of the security challenges facing British India. There was no difference as India had inherited the mantle of power from the British Raj, notwithstanding the creation of the Dominion of Pakistan and its sequestration from the body of India. The Department of External Affairs of the Dominion of India sent a memorandum on 25 October 1947 to British Prime Minister Clement Attlee. This memorandum heavily relied upon the conceptual and strategic conclusions drawn from two other documents generated from the Indian Government that we have spoken of in the third chapter of this book. The first document, in the form of a memorandum, was written by Sir Olaf Caroe, the then Secretary of External Affairs, on 19 September 1945, in reply to certain queries raised by the new British Foreign Secretary, Ernest Bevin.[7] The second memorandum[8] was written in 1946 when the British General Staff prepared a top-secret memo entitled, 'Appreciation of the scale of direct military assistance which could be provided in support of Tibet'.

Geopolitically, as mentioned in the Department of External Affairs' memorandum of 25 October 1947, India was just about to suffer a major defeat, just like the defeat of the British in Afghanistan, in 1841–42. The Gilgit Agency, which was the key to the defence of the western end of the northern frontier, the crucial zone where Afghanistan, Russia and China meet, was almost slipping away from the control of Jammu and Kashmir. It seemed like it would formally be placed under the flag of Pakistan, in less than a week's time. Consequently, India's north-west frontier had been pushed several hundred miles to the east and a century of British strategic planning (which included the sale of Kashmir to Gulab Singh in 1846) had been undone. The real goal of the military intervention which began on 27 October 1947 was to gain control over not the valley of Kashmir but the Gilgit Agency. The memorandum of 25 October 1947 makes it clear that the state of Jammu and Kashmir was of fundamental importance to India and that had nothing to do with the fact that it was Nehru's ancestral home. The legal merits of the Maharaja's Instrument of Accession were also not the main reason for the state's significance for India. It was the symbol of India's status as the true successor to the British Raj.

The announcement of this memorandum, possibly inspired by Sardar Patel, was in congruence with the interests of the British deep state. However, unless Patel was made the Prime Minister of India, the British deep state could not be sure that India could be relied upon to deliver on Britain's strategic interests. That was the paradox which caused the anxiety for the British to immediately execute Operation Datta Khel, in order to thwart the realisation of Patel's strategic vision for the defence of the Dominion of India.

The Indus, that flowed through Ladakh, was extremely important for the survival of the people of Pakistan. The corollary of Operation Datta Khel was that the takeover of the Gilgit Agency would provide Pakistan a means to outflank India in the race for Ladakh and the waters of the Indus.

Only a week after the memorandum of 25 October 1947 was sent to Attlee, Mountbatten and Ismay flew to Lahore to discuss the Kashmir crisis with Jinnah and Liaquat Ali Khan.[9] This summit was inconclusive. Ismay was put in the uncomfortable position of opposing the party line of the British deep state. Liaquat Ali Khan visited New Delhi in December 1947 and Mountbatten, Nehru, Baldev Singh and Ayyangar followed him to Lahore. For a plebiscite to happen, Pakistan needed the Indian Army to withdraw and then have a 'neutral' caretaker government to replace the Mahajan-Abdullah diarchy. By now, post-Operation Datta Khel, the Government of India was convinced that the Pakistani Government had officially sponsored both the operations. During the last two months of 1947, the Indian Army succeeded in breaking the backs of the raiders and securing Srinagar. On 1 January 1948, India put forth its case before the security council of the UN.

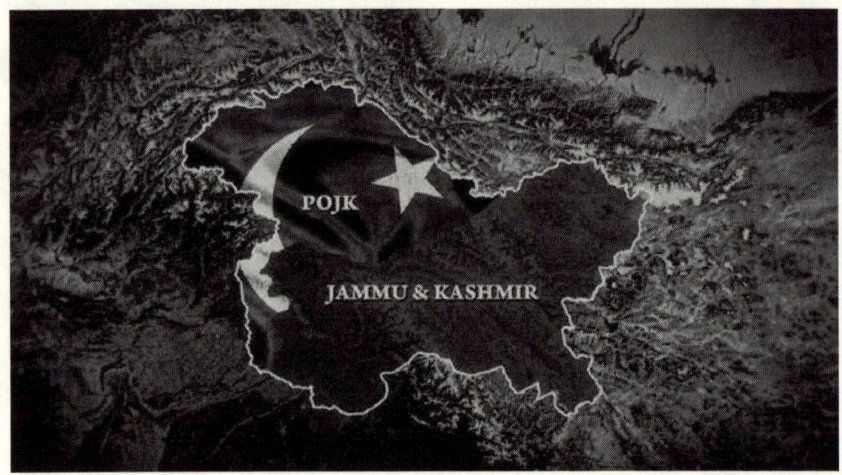

Image 6.1: Pakistan Occupied Jammu and Kashmir
Source: Archives of AIM Television Pvt. Ltd.

The British Hand

Throughout 1948 the fighting continued unabated. Gen. Rob Lockhart, the Indian Commander-in-Chief, was pro-Pakistan in his outlook, as was[10] his successor, Gen. Bucher. All through 1948, Bucher would moderate military decisions not only because of possible political repercussions, but also because he believed that the Kashmir conflict potentially brought communism to the doorstep of the subcontinent.[11] He also empathised with Pakistan's vital need for Kashmir in terms of defence, water supplies and the need to control the NWFP.

These two generals were strongly supported by the West Punjab Governor, Sir Robert Francis Mudie. Mudie attended school with Sir George Cunningham and Gen. Rob Lockhart and after they reunited in India, they were all a part of the British deep state that thought it necessary for Pakistan to retain a post-Partition presence in the part of India that contained Kashmir and the NWFP.[12] Mudie anticipated three threats to Pakistan's existence,[13] namely the Afghan-Russia threat, the India-Abdul Ghaffar Khan threat and the conflict in Kashmir. He was of the view that Pakistan was the only barrier to the spread of communism in the subcontinent. Another famous officer of the Pakistan Army, Maj. Gen. W. J. Cawthorn, founder of Pakistan's ISI very lucidly voiced all the British strategic fears arising from the Kashmir dispute. His speech in London's Chatham House in 1948 has him arguing that Pakistan could not afford to have a hostile India by the western borders of Jammu and Kashmir. It would bring the Indian Army within 30 miles of the Pakistan Army Headquarters in Rawalpindi, right behind its vital north-south communication line. It would give India control over the waters of Chenab, Jhelum and Indus rivers, and would put India in direct contact with Afghanistan, Chitral and Swat. There was already speculation that the Indian National Congress and the Young Afghan Party were jointly encouraging the Pashtunistan idea. It would also provide India with a land border with the USSR.

On 11 February 1948, Lt. Gen. Douglas Gracey took over as Pakistan Army Chief from Gen. Frank Messervy. He was faced with India's spring offensive expected in March 1948, which the British viewed as a decisive thrust against Pakistan's jugular. Both the British generals, almost comically, orchestrated the adoption of mutually defensive positions. In his memoirs, Lt. Gen. Loftus Tottenham, who was a Division Commander in the Pakistan Army during this war, stated that the Kashmir war was strange in that it was fought under several restrictions. The prevalent attitude was to hit the Indians hard but not too hard, otherwise, they knew that there would be all kinds of unsavoury consequences. The same view prevailed on the other side. It was a shadow boxing competition with both boxers fighting while on a leash.

In early May 1948, the British High Commissioner in Pakistan, Laurence Grafftey-Smith informed Whitehall of the presence of Pakistan Army troops in Kashmir.[14] Of greater concern was his revelation that two British officers in the Pakistan Army, Lt. Col. Milne and Capt. Skellon, were operating in Kashmir with Gen. Gracey's approval.[15] He also reported that three Pakistani battalions were present in Kashmir and the opposing

Indian commanders were aware of this and were continuing to avoid a direct engagement. Intriguingly, Gen. Gracey had personally informed Gen. Bucher about the officers being present.[16] Whitehall worried that this could prove to be a big embarrassment, if the information leaked out. However, one month later, in June 1948, the presence of Pakistani troops in Kashmir was evident beyond any doubt.[17] Two dominions of the empire were at war with each other and there were British officers pitted against one another.

British Foreign Secretary, Aneurin Bevan decided not to take any action. Their defence secretary and the chiefs of staff committee also kept mum.[18] The reason the British were playing possum was very clear—if India asked British officers to step down, the Pakistan Army would be crippled because of the lack of senior officers.[19] In India, Gen. Bucher put a lid on this issue and acquiesced to compromising on India's interests. He also toned down the plans for offensive operations and use of the Royal Indian Air Force, which was proposed by Indian generals.[20] Bucher was clearly a Trojan horse in the Indian Army who, in hindsight, deserved to have charges of high treason filed against him.[21]

In London, the Foreign Office was primed to resolve and resist all Indian enquiries on this subject by bluffing and presenting every argument that they could muster. The reason for this was that Gen. Gracey was stubbornly opposed to stepping down and was not bothered about embarrassing the British Government in the process.[22] Gracey's zealousness had no boundaries. In July 1948, Whitehall was further shocked to learn that a dozen British officers from the Pakistan Army were fighting in Kashmir.[23] India, on the other hand, was restrained by Gen. Bucher as he was anxious about going into direct combat with Pakistan. He used his influence to stop moderating and diminish the initiatives of Indian commanders on the field and at the planning level.[24] Mountbatten encouraged Bucher, along with Air Chief Marshall Elmhirst, to remain in personal touch with Nehru and manipulate him from taking any aggressive action that might put Pakistan at risk.[25]

Gen. Bucher constantly harped on having military operations that are linked to political policies.

However, Gen. Gracey's aggressive policy soon faced repercussions. One of the British officers in the Pakistan Army fighting in Kashmir, Maj. R. E. Sloan was killed on Saturday 10 July 1948 in the Tithwal sector while commanding 71 Field Company, Royal Pakistan Engineers.[26] Whitehall strove to hush this mishap.[27] Secretary of State for Commonwealth Affairs, Philip Noel-Baker advised Attlee against enforcing the stepping down of officers, and argued that it would remove the influence of moderation by India and it would be impossible for Pakistan to run its army without British officers.[28] Noel-Baker was supported by Grafftey-Smith who delivered assurances that no British officer would be posted on actual battlefields in Kashmir, thereafter.[29]

As a result, Attlee turned down Nehru's request for a stand-down of British officers by arguing that all errant British officers who had participated in the fighting would be recalled immediately. Gen. Gracey was made the scapegoat by Whitehall who called him names and charged him with disloyalty to the British crown. Quite a performance indeed!

A month later, in August 1948, Nehru once again requested a stand-down. This time, the request was routed through the Chancellor of the Exchequer, Stafford Cripps and Ismay. Both Noel-Baker and Bevin argued that the Pakistan Army would disintegrate without British officers. Pakistan was not only in the frontline against Soviet expansion but also held great leverage in the Muslim world. Furthermore, the UN which was now playing a significant role in the Kashmir conflict, viewed all British officers as a great stabilising influence.[30] By this time, the Indian armed forces had less than half of the 800-odd British personnel who were working for the Pakistan armed forces. Lastly, the treasonous link between Generals Bucher and Gracey would have snapped had the stand-down been declared. Therefore, Attlee refused Nehru's request, citing a combination of desperation and disillusionment in Pakistan, defiance by British officers there, Muslim hostility and communist profit. Four months later, for a third time, Nehru raised the issue of a stand-down with Attlee, and received his third successive refusal, this time communicated via the British Defence Secretary. By now, the entire rank of British officers in the Pakistan Army was fully engaged in the war.

Meanwhile, to buy time, the British Government commissioned the Templer Report. In November 1948, this report confirmed that 440 British officers served in executive positions in Pakistan as opposed to the 230 Britons in India.[31] This imbalance was exacerbated by Gen. Bucher's relative detachment from the war as against Gen. Gracey's hands-on involvement in it. The choices before the British, now, were to stand down or ceasefire. Nehru was fed up with the state of affairs and had announced the replacement of Gen. Bucher by Gen. Cariappa, the first Indian general of the Indian Army.[32] Bucher worked hard to secure a ceasefire on 1 January 1949, a mere 15 days before he relinquished his office.

Gen. Bucher and his accomplice in Pakistan, Gen. Gracey had thwarted the Indian Army's ambitions of recapturing all of Jammu and Kashmir.[33] The entire war had been a mockery and had only enabled Pakistan to hold on to the Muzaffarabad-Poonch belt and the Gilgit Agency, purely as a result of British perfidy and treachery.[34]

Chapter 7

Stormy Seas

Protracted negotiations for a ceasefire in Jammu and Kashmir between generals Bucher and Gracey gained currency with the Templer Report. The fear of a collapse in the Pakistan Army intensified the pressure on the need for the ceasefire. Their dream of a complete takeover of the state through proxy forces in Pakistan now lay in tatters. The ceasefire brokered by the two British generals was agreed to by both the countries and finally came into effect on 1 January 1949. The terms of the ceasefire, as laid out in a UN resolution of 13 August 1948, were adopted by the UN on 5 January 1949. This required Pakistan to withdraw all its forces from the entire state including the Poonch-Muzaffarabad belt and the Gilgit Agency while allowing India to maintain minimal military strength in the state, so as to preserve law and order. On full compliance of these conditions, a plebiscite was to be held to determine the future of the state.

To Pakistan, the plebiscite and these conditions were a shattering blow. This had been a considerable gamble for the British and the Pakistanis; had Pakistan lost, then not only would Azad Kashmir have disappeared into Sheikh Abdullah's empire, but it was inevitable that India would have done everything in its power to displace Pakistan from the Gilgit Agency and to regain control over the entire northern frontier. Both sides, however, at the outset, converged on one point of great importance—the state of Jammu and Kashmir would be treated as a whole; there was no question of holding separate plebiscites in the various regions that had been combined by Gulab Singh and his successors into a single polity under Dogra rule.

Sheikh Abdullah's emergency government was announced by the Maharaja at the end of October 1947; it was a 'peculiar diarchy'. Mahajan was still the Prime Minister but effective political power lay in the hands of a cabinet presided over by Abdullah and his National Conference associates—Bakshi Ghulam Mohammed, Mirza Afzal Beg and G. M. Sadiq. These men were answerable to no elected assembly and their relationships with Mahajan and the Maharaja, who represented a dying regime, were far from cordial. India, by virtue of Nehru's repeated declarations that Abdullah represented the true voice of the Kashmiri people, could do little at this stage to control the actions of its own nominee.

Concurrent events soon demonstrated that Sheikh Abdullah, for all his opposition to the Maharaja and to Jinnah, was no subservient follower of India. His regime had, from the outset, showed signs of being a potential dictatorship and was soon seen to be exhibiting a form of arbitrary and extreme government, so much so, that it would be difficult for even Nehru to defend. Fortunately for Nehru's reputation, the military situation in the state and the rhetoric of Indo-Pakistan arguments distracted attention from what Abdullah was really up to. But, his actions were all too apparent to those directly involved in Kashmiri affairs. Within six weeks of having been entrusted with the state's administration, Mahajan began complaining to Sardar Patel that the state government reminded him of Nazi Germany, run by gangsters and he added that he wished to be, in no way, associated with it. The sooner he was out, the better.[1]

The state high court had been prevented from functioning effectively. Large numbers of officials in the Maharaja's old administration, including the governor of Jammu, had been detained. Abdullah had appointed several of his friends as senior officials without consulting Mahajan. National Conference workers were selling trade concessions and renting out state transport vehicles without any interference from the government. Members of the Muslim Conference, whom the Maharaja had arrested, were left languishing in captivity.

Abdullah Becomes Numero Uno

On 5 March 1948, Mahajan finally vanished from the scene and with him, vanished the last hurdle in Abdullah's path to head an interim government. This was an interim regime which was to function till such time as constitutional provisions were made for a more formal system of administration, backed by some kind of a popular mandate. As head of this interim government, Abdullah continued to reveal his true colours. These were characteristics of his personality and behaviour to which Mahajan had already drawn the attention of Sardar Patel. They now began to bother Nehru and he could no longer ignore them.

The Maharaja also announced the formation of a constituent assembly in order to legitimise the new regime in Jammu and Kashmir. Interestingly, the Maharaja's proclamation had made it clear that the constituent assembly would also be a national assembly; it would be a legislature which would then proceed to create a constitution to validate its own existence. Even without a constitution, it could function as a fully sovereign body, within the parameters of the relationship with India, whatever exactly those might turn out to be. On 29 October 1947, the very day on which Abdullah began his emergency government, the Maharaja of Mysore, having acceded to India, set up a constituent assembly to draft a constitution for his state. The Mysore Assembly promptly passed a resolution that the state's constitution should be essentially what would then be framed by the Constituent Assembly of India for states of Mysore's class. Such a constitution was duly proclaimed by the Maharaja of Mysore on 25 November 1949 and it followed the pattern for what was called Part B states, as set out in Article 371 of the Indian Constitution. These were all former princely states that were to be treated on the same basis as the former provinces of the British Raj. The Maharaja of Kashmir was clearly following the Mysore model.

But Abdullah had very different ideas about what state constitutions ought to look like. He was not prepared to accept the Mysore model. Consequently, there existed considerable anxiety in New Delhi, Srinagar and Jammu about what he would do if he were pressed on the matter. He might even, for example, decide to opt for Pakistan, which would completely disprove Nehru's claim of Abdullah being the embodiment of the Kashmiri people's desire to remain in India. He was permitted an extraordinary degree of latitude in the process of establishing machinery for the devising of a constitution for the Jammu and Kashmir Constituent Assembly.

It would not be far from the truth to argue that from the Indian point of view, late October 1947 onwards, Abdullah was what is sometimes called a loose cannon. This view was reinforced when from 5 March 1948, Mahajan disappeared and Abdullah became the undisputed leader, with the pompous title of the Prime Minister of a 'popular' interim government, amidst considerable publicity. The departure of Mahajan marked the end of the final, albeit tenuous, link between the new regime and a form of government which had some roots in the previous constitutional arrangement. In a very real sense, Abdullah was now an absolute ruler and it was clearly in the interest of the Government of India that some fresh constitutional checks be devised. These would have to involve not only the structure of the internal government of the state but also the state's formal relationship with the Indian Union. The need for these checks arose because of Abdullah's written vision for Kashmir, which was first published in 1944.

In his 1944 *Naya*, or New, Kashmir proposals, which were drafted by Oxford-educated communist ideologue Baba Pyare Lal Bedi (father of Bollywood actor Kabir Bedi), Sheikh Abdullah articulated his vision for the conversion of Jammu and Kashmir into an independent state, which he liked to describe as a South Asian Switzerland. This state could perhaps exist in alliance with the newly independent India but would not be an integral part of it. This remained a dominant theme in his discourses right up to his death in 1982. Abdullah's Kashmir would be secular but it would also be dominated by a Muslim majority and would thus acquire a strong Islamic sheen. Abdullah's acclaimed secularism could well have been a misunderstood version of what can only be described as a variety of Kashmiri nationalism. He argued, on a number of occasions, that just as Kashmiri Islam was different from the Islam of Jinnah's Pakistan, so was Kashmiri Hinduism; it was more Kashmiri than Hindu. In other words, the Hindu minority in the state had more in common with the Muslim majority than it had with the Hindus elsewhere in the Indian subcontinent. It was an outlook that derived itself almost entirely from an interpretation of the situation in the valley. It ignored the composite state founded by Maharaja Gulab Singh. For the Dogra's, the Muslims of the valley were colonial subjects ruled by a Hindu Jammu elite aided and abetted by the Pandit community. For Abdullah, on the other hand, the non-Muslims of Jammu and Ladakh were the colonial subjects of a Kashmiri elite recruited from the ranks of the National Conference, with which only some Pandits collaborated.

On the economic front, Abdullah was committed to social reforms along the lines pioneered by the Soviet Union. One of the first priorities was land reform. This would ultimately lead to Sheikh Abdullah enforcing a revolution in the landholding pattern of the state, in March 1953, which involved the setting up of collective farms. The largest landholding now permitted was just under 23 acres. All this fell under the aegis of the Big Landed Estates Abolition Act introduced by him. All this was accompanied by a great deal of direct governmental involvement within the industrial sector and the distribution of industrial products. Further, Sheikh Abdullah set up a planning system modelled on the Soviet five-year plans. The first Kashmir Plan provided for extensive irrigation works and for the construction of a tunnel under the Bannihal Pass, which would keep the crucial line of road communication between Jammu and Srinagar open throughout the year. Finally, the new regime made it clear that it would welcome no argument or organised opposition—it retained powers of detention and suppression of hostile press comment which clearly was in conflict with the democratic protestations of the state's new overlord, the Government of India.

Abdullah's repeated and long periods of incarceration in the Maharaja's prisons, 1931 onwards, resulted in the articulation of a very strong demand from the National Conference, during the Quit Kashmir agitation of 1946, to abolish the rule of the Dogra dynasty.[2] This demand was treasonous and the top leadership of the National Conference was arrested that year. Subsequently, however, the Maharaja may have hoped that, given his reconciliation with Abdullah in September 1947, Abdullah would let bygones be bygones. Further by acceding to India, the Dogra ruling family may have persuaded itself that it stood a better chance of staying in power than it would have by joining Pakistan. If the Maharaja believed both of these hypotheses, he was soon to be disillusioned.

Abdullah Alienates Nehru

Nehru must have been dismayed to discover that Abdullah had distinctly ambivalent views about the potential the state of Jammu and Kashmir would have with India and the larger world. Abdullah said many things to many people at different times, but careful analysis can reveal certain consistent threads in his actions and policies during the first phase of his government, which ended abruptly in August 1953. Most of these consistencies re-emerged during the government's second phase from 1975 until his death. These were sometimes paradoxical—Abdullah cannot be accused of profound and logically rigorous political thought. They did not, on the whole, coincide with the kind of ideas the seat of government at New Delhi deemed to be appropriate to the chief official of an Indian state.

In his seminal PhD thesis submitted to the University of Southampton, Rakesh Ankit has revealed that T. G. Sanjeevi Pillai, Director of IB, wrote a top-secret note to Nehru on the rampant presence of communists, and their conspiracy to stage a coup, in Kashmir, on 5 August 1948.[3] It was a damning critique on the Abdullah regime and dwelt on the manifestation of communism under its protection. Abdullah's actions were generating serious concerns in London as well. There were grave concerns about the spread of communism under Abdullah's rule. Whitehall read Abdullah's *Naya* Kashmir manifesto for a socialist Kashmir and realised that Grafftey-Smith's warnings about Abdullah's communist leanings were not unfounded. In June 1948, Noel-Baker had been informed about the peculiar makeup of the National Conference's leadership. By December 1948, Whitehall developed the view that Abdullah's involvement with local Indian communists and his constant contacts with the Soviets explained the steadily rising communist influence in Kashmir.

From the initiation of his premiership on 5 March 1948, Abdullah embarked upon a systematic campaign to publicly humiliate and vilify the Maharaja. The state seemed to be like a driverless truck that was propelled by its own momentum. Abdullah had a single-point agenda and that was the Maharaja's removal. There was a total deadlock in the state between the Maharaja and Abdullah's government and in this highly tense atmosphere, Sardar Patel invited the Maharaja, his wife and son to New Delhi, in April 1949.[4] On 29 April 1949, Sardar Patel told the Maharaja that while Abdullah was pressing for his abdication, Patel felt it would be good if the Maharaja and the Maharani left the state for a few months. Patel argued that this was in the national interest, in view of the complications arising from the UN-sponsored plebiscite proposals. In the interim, Patel proposed that Yuvaraja Karan Singh should be appointed the Regent to carry out the Maharaja's duties and responsibilities in his absence. The die was cast. The Government of India stepped in to depose yet another Maharaja in its long history of interference in the administration of the state. The Maharaja never returned to his state and stayed in New Delhi *en route* to his new home in Bombay. From New Delhi, he issued a proclamation, on 20 June 1949, appointing Yuvaraja Karan Singh as the Regent.[5]

Image 7.1: Pandit Nehru with Yuvaraja Karan Singh, 1949
Source: Wikimedia Commons

Meanwhile, there were other developments taking shape overseas, which would have a strong bearing on matters in the state. Rakesh Ankit, in his cited thesis, reveals that the Soviet news agency, TASS, in a report dated 6 July 1949 openly warned the world about Anglo-American aggression against the USSR through Gilgit. The report also highlighted the suppression of communists in Pakistan and spoke at length about the anti-feudal Abdullah and his petty-bourgeoisie overlord in New Delhi, Prime Minister Nehru.[6] By February 1949, two dossiers were prepared on Abdullah and his associates on the basis of the British Residents' reports from 1942 to 1947 and a *Trud* (a Russian newspaper) article dated 29 September 1949.[7] These were added to a memorandum the newly appointed ISI Chief, Maj. Gen. Cawthorn, had prepared in January. In this, he had claimed the presence of 2,300 communists in Kashmir. Further, reports from the MI5 security liaison officer in New Delhi estimated that there were at least 100,000 communists in India, of which 1,500 were in prison. Over June and July 1949, the fear of a red fog over Kashmir deepened when Liaquat Ali Khan accepted an invitation to visit Moscow.[8] This left senior British civil and military officials serving in Pakistan and even Attlee[9] worried, as they could not fail to notice the growing bitterness in Pakistan towards Britain and the Commonwealth.[10] The dominant British presence in India and Pakistan through 1947–49 affected the war and diplomacy in Kashmir. London knew that supporting India could destroy Pakistan and with it, the agenda of the British deep state. It also believed that a Muslim Pakistan would stand against Soviet Russia more than a non-aligned India; but, the British also admitted that it could not afford to totally alienate India given the country's many economic investments and military ties. Each of these concerns came together when deciding on the issuance of stand-down orders to British officers serving in Indian and Pakistani armies and what should've been the 'party line' at the UN. This approach aroused the Soviets, who were historically clued into Kashmir from much before than is credited for. The Kashmir dispute had embarked upon a spell of internationalisation that would remain intact throughout the 20th century.

The Americans Get Interested

In December 1950, the CIA prepared a note on communist personalities and activities in Kashmir that named B. P. L. Bedi, his wife Freda, G. M. Sadiq, Mirza Afzal Beg, Mohiuddin Kara and Dhanwantri.[11] It highlighted the editorial line taken by publications like *Noor*, *Uplift* and *Burj*, which were allegedly funded by the Soviet and Czech embassies in New Delhi. It was especially concerned about the Bedi's, whom it had earlier called the 'leading light' of communism in Sheikh Abdullah's administration. The Bedi's were instrumental in keeping the 'inner core' of Abdullah, Bakshi and Sadiq intact. Deeply involved in the 'nationalisation' of land as well as textbooks, Bedi, however, disturbed the New Delhi Government as much as he was bothering Washington and London.

In January 1951, Col. Coblentz of the US Army and the acting chief of UN's Kashmir Observers returned to Washington after serving there for two years and told the state department that the Abdullah regime, which according to Coblentz had 'no following' and survived on 'intimidation', represented 'the nearest thing to turning over the state to the communists'.[12] He was convinced that the ministers of communication and education in Abdullah's cabinet were communists. Meanwhile, the British Government sent to Washington Grafftey-Smith's report on Kashmir impairing the 'buttress against communism' in south Asia.[13]

Simultaneously, Henderson's military attaché too submitted a memorandum reiterating the usefulness of air bases in Kashmir.[14] Senior British and American military men in the Middle East were arguing that 'political and military considerations could not be separated in Kashmir'.[15]

Earlier, the constituent assembly in India was drafting the Constitution of India, under the leadership of Dr Babasaheb Ambedkar, known in the annals of history as the father of the Indian Constitution. The Indian Constitution, as it finally emerged in January 1950 from the constituent assembly (in which the state of Jammu and Kashmir was allocated four seats, just as it was in due course to have four seats in the Lok Sabha), gave to Jammu and Kashmir what can only be described as a peculiar position, which was unique among Indian states. While the state was deemed in Article 1 to be an integral part of the Indian Union, it was given, by Article 370, a special status by means of 'temporary provisions with respect to the state of Jammu and Kashmir' which effectively limited the powers of the Indian Union Parliament there to the three 'matters specified in the Instrument of Accession governing the accession of the State to the Dominion of India', namely defence, external affairs and communications, and all this was to be confirmed in Article 152 of the 1956 amended version of the constitution where, in the section dealing with Indian states, it was specified that the expression 'State' 'does not include the state of Jammu and Kashmir'. Apart from the three powers reserved to the Centre, everything else would be the concern of whatever form of government the Jammu and Kashmir Constituent Assembly might decide to create. Article 370 (originally 306-A) was drafted by Gopalaswami Ayyangar in close consultation with Sheikh Abdullah.

Had it not been for Sheikh Abdullah, it is probable that Article 370 would have been much more clearly defined. It would have been quite possible to arrange, subject to popular ratification, that the state of Jammu and Kashmir would eventually have a constitution just like that of the other Indian states of the same class. This was the previously mentioned 'Mysore model'.

Meanwhile, in July 1950, a restless Abdullah, who found Pakistani intransigence was delaying the adoption of the UN suggested plebiscite, decided to whet the appetite of his popular base in the state by sending a proclamation to the Regent, Yuvaraja Karan Singh, requesting his signature. This proclamation announced the abolition of *Jagirdari* (the feudal land grant system) and of landlordism, both without offering any compensation. These populist measures were ideologically leftist and also communal in that they would adversely affect the non-Muslim population of the state. The Regent demurred and referred the matter to the Government of India. This incensed Abdullah, who took to the streets and announced measures that were patently illegal without the consent and signature of the Regent. At the same time, Abdullah began articulating his vision of independence for the state and its freedom from the yoke of the Maharaja, who was legally still the ruler. This culminated in the move to convene a constituent assembly for the state as part of a broader political strategy to make the question of plebiscite redundant.

When the provisions for elections for a constituent assembly for Jammu and Kashmir were formally announced by the Regent on 30 April 1951, it was clear that the assembly would concern itself with broader issues than merely devising a constitution for the state. It would also decide, once and for all, the future of the Dogra dynasty and would determine whether landowners and holders of land rights would (or, as Sheikh Abdullah wished, would not) be compensated for their losses under the land reform measures that had already been put to effect.

In August 1951, elections to the proposed Jammu and Kashmir Constituent Assembly had been conducted under a proclamation issued by the Regent.[16] The only effective opposition group, the Praja Parishad in Jammu, boycotted these elections. Consequently, 72 of the 75 members were elected unopposed on the National Conference ticket and no Praja Parishad members were elected because the nominations for all 27 of its candidates had been rejected. The boycott was to protest the rejection of the nominations of the Praja Parishad candidates. The newly constituted assembly was not a fair representative body. The fairness of the election was certainly open to challenge. Unlike the old 1939 Jammu and Kashmir state constitution, based on universal adult suffrage, both the compilation of electoral rolls (which had already begun in 1949) and the registration of nominations were supervised, with great care and efficiency, by Sheikh Abdullah's partisans. Less than 5 per cent of the potential electorate actually voted.

By mid-1951, the mélange of the various populist economic measures forced by Abdullah, his coterie of communist advisors and his public pronouncements, convinced the US State Department that the state of Jammu and Kashmir was the first port of call for both the Soviets and the Chinese communists in the subcontinent. Abdullah and his associates were believed to be in constant touch with Moscow and Beijing. Jammu and Kashmir, alongside West Asia and South-east Asia, was an ideal site for Soviet intervention and communist subversion. India's stubbornness on the Kashmir issue and its posture of international non-alignment did not help the US. President Truman and the Secretary of State, Dean Acheson tried to gauge how long they could let the Kashmir issue remain a Commonwealth matter, especially within the context of the deteriorating British prestige over all of its former colonial possessions.[17] One of the things holding them back was UN representative Frank Graham's mission on Kashmir that was carried out over the months of July,[18] August and September 1951. Its failure, following the earlier failures by the Canadian Gen. McNaughton, US Admiral Chester Nimitz and Australian jurist Owen Dixon, prompted the CIA to remind the state department that the position of

Kashmir will decide the final scene of the political drama over Sinkiang. The Chinese PLA controlled most of Sinkiang by the spring of 1950 and the only organised resistance the PLA encountered was from Osman Batur's Kazakh militia and from Yulbar Khan's White Russian and Hui troops who served the KMT's Republic of China. Batur had pledged his allegiance to the KMT and was killed in 1951.

The British Consul in Kashgar, Eric Shipton left in October 1948 after handing over charge to his deputy Allen Mersh. Mersh was of Anglo-Indian descent and had opted for Pakistani citizenship. He remained in charge till 1949, when he abandoned the post. The consulate was back in Indian control after Capt. R. D. Sathe took charge. In early 1950, the British consul in Urumchi was expelled for his links with Yulbar Khan and he took refuge in the Indian consulate in Kashgar. Shortly thereafter, Capt. Sathe also left Kashgar, never to return.

In his dispatches to the US State Department in December 1951, the new American Ambassador to India, Chester Bowles wrote that in the coming years, the danger from China to Jammu and Kashmir was likely to be much greater. In fact, Bowles found Nehru's political views replete with contradictions on communism and he seemed irritatingly stubborn on Kashmir.[19] Things changed dramatically when on 17 January 1952, Soviet Ambassador Jacob Malik made a speech in the Security Council accusing America and Britain of brazen, imperial intervention in Kashmir. The American delegation to the UN interpreted this speech as a definition of the Soviet stand on a number of issues. The Soviets could simultaneously favour the communists in the 1952 first general elections in India and harm Pakistan and India but also Egypt. The British added that it also reflected the Soviet desire to support an independent Kashmir under the leftist Abdullah. Abdullah's remarks to Selwyn Lloyd, the British Minister for Foreign Affairs, about his vision of independence for Jammu and Kashmir and his indifference towards the Soviet threat, further confirmed that his ideas were completely contrary to those of Whitehall.[20]

By the end of January 1952, it was clear that Malik's attempt to create greater uncertainty over Soviet intentions in Kashmir only benefitted Abdullah and the communists. The British foreign office concluded that while the Soviets were certainly not hoping to win Pakistan's sympathy, they also seemed to have overlooked that Nehru was against the communists and was concerned about internal communism in India. He also vehemently opposed the idea of an independent Kashmir.[21] Willi Nedou, Begum Jehan Abdullah's uncle, who was Sheikh Abdullah's Liaison Officer in Paris, had told the British that Abdullah was seeking Soviet support for his dream.[22] The state department interpreted Malik's speech within the framework of Soviet aims of laying the groundwork for an eventual communist coup in Kashmir. Further, they believed that the Soviets were clandestinely supporting the Chinese campaign in Kashgar of 'liberating' Gilgit and Ladakh. The aim was to create a circle of red in an almost unbroken line from Indo-China to Afghanistan.[23]

Nehru's Disillusionment with Abdullah

Meanwhile, Nehru was also trying to contain the rebellious Abdullah. On 17 June 1952, a National Conference delegation led by Mirza Afzal Beg, including D. P. Dhar and Mir Qasim, all of whom were the communists/crypto-communists in the Abdullah regime, arrived in New Delhi for talks with Nehru. Exactly a month later, on 17 July 1952, Abdullah joined in accompanied by Bakshi Ghulam Mohammed, G. M. Sadiq and Maulana Masoodi. On 24 July 1952, an agreement was reached between Abdullah's group and Nehru. This is often referred to as the Delhi Accord, and this was the third accord on the future of the state; the first accord was the Instrument of Accession and the second accord was the replacement of the Maharaja by the Regent.

Abdullah was now emphatic that the state, while it was a part of the Indian Union, also enjoyed certain unique privileges within that union. Most important was the issue of landownership and he insisted on ensuring that the citizens of the state had rights relating to landownership which were denied to Indian citizens from outside the state. The exceptional authority of the constituent assembly was recognised. The power of the President of India to declare a state of emergency could only be exercised in the state at the request or with the concurrence of the state government. The state would also have its own flag, though this would not exclude the use of the Indian Union flag in the state. Special arrangements were laid down for the election of the head of the state, the Sadr-e-Riyasat, who would be recommended by the constituent assembly to the President of India for confirmation. Both the President of India and the Chief Justice of the Supreme Court could concern themselves with the state's affairs only in certain circumstances. The essential point, made crystal clear by Abdullah, was that in the state of Jammu and Kashmir, unlike all the other states in the Indian Union, the residuary powers mentioned in the Indian Constitution were not to be vested in the centre but in the state. All of these would be defined by the constituent assembly in due course.

Sheikh Abdullah may have been the new king of the valley, but it was soon evident that he was not very revered in either Jammu or Ladakh. As a result of this reality, Nehru was trying to figure how to best maintain the cohesion of the empire Gulab Singh built.

In 1952, despite the later annexations by the Chinese, Ladakh was the largest district in Jammu and Kashmir. It was of enormous geopolitical importance as it served as a route to Sinkiang, and was alternative to the Gilgit Agency.[24] When by the end of 1948, it had become clear that Ladakh would remain within India, there were Ladakhi leaders who advocated an independent relationship with the government in New Delhi that was not routed through the Government of Jammu and Kashmir. Thus in 1949, Chhewang Ringzin, who presided over a body calling itself the Buddhist Association of Ladakh, submitted a memo to Nehru which advocated that Ladakh be integrated with Jammu or east Punjab, in order to either become an Indian state in its own right. The memo argued that one consequence of the accession crisis of 1947 had been the annulment of the Treaty of Amritsar of 1846. Sheikh Abdullah had got Kashmir. In law and equity, Ladakh had reverted to its previous relationship with Jammu established in the 1830s. In other words, the Ladakhi people wanted to be rescued from Sheikh Abdullah. In 1952, the abbot of the Spituk Monastery, Kushok Bakula, who was widely accepted as the Ladakhi equivalent of Abdullah and was also a member of the Jammu and Kashmir Constituent Assembly, returned to these demands in a meeting with Nehru. He complained about the injustices of the Sheikh Abdullah regime and hinted that if matters did not improve, Ladakh might seek to secede from India and join Tibet. He, however, made it clear that Ladakh was quite prepared to cohabit with Jammu Hindus but it needed to be, in some manner, separated from Srinagar. Bakula was increasingly unhappy about what appeared to be a Muslim domination of the region. These Ladakhi grievances were also communicated to Karan Singh during his visit to Leh in the latter part of 1952.

Serious opposition to Abdullah's regime developed in Jammu where non-Muslim political activity was dominated by the Praja Parishad. This political movement was launched at the end of 1947 by Balraj Madhok with the support of many members who had worked for the RSS and enjoyed close links with the charismatic President of the newly launched Bhartiya Jana Sangh, Dr Shyama Prasad Mookerjee. Dr Mookerjee was originally a congressman who had held the portfolio of industry and supplies in Nehru's dominion cabinet from 1947 to 1950. The Praja Parishad view, shared by Dr Mookerjee, was that Jammu and Kashmir's political evolution, under the guidance of Sheikh Abdullah, would increasingly drift away from incorporation into the Indian Union and move towards the creation of what might be called a mini-Pakistan, an Islamic, autonomous state. In Jammu and Kashmir, Dr Mookerjee commented that there were, or would soon be, 'two constitutions, two flags and two heads of the state in one country', and this 'cannot be tolerated'.[25]

The Delhi Accord greatly alarmed the Praja Parishad. Under the leadership of Prem Nath Dogra, a campaign of extra-parliamentary opposition to Abdullah's regime began in the autumn of 1952. Essentially a Hindu middle-class movement, it had been particularly disturbed by Sheikh Abdullah's land reforms and increasingly came to see the ruling National Conference both as an Islamic communal party and as a cover for the extension of communist ideology. It sought the separation of Jammu from the valley, either as a state in its own right or as part of Punjab. It advocated the abolition of Article 370 of the Indian Constitution and the termination of the special status of the state of Jammu and Kashmir. Its thinking had certainly been influenced by the suggestions made in 1950 by Sir Owen Dixon, gaining Nehru's initial interest, saying that there might be, as part of the plebiscitary process, some kind of partition of the state.

Notwithstanding these grave differences that the regions of Ladakh and Jammu had with Abdullah's regime, on 17 November 1952, Sheikh Abdullah announced the end of the Dogra dynasty. The Maharaja was replaced by a constitutional head of state, the Sadr-e-Riyasat, who was to be elected for a five-year term by the legislative assembly or, in the first instance, in the absence of such an assembly, by the constituent assembly. Karan Singh was elected the first such head of state, and so the Dogra's managed to retain some foothold in the corridors of power of the polity that Gulab Singh had created.

From the perspective of the West, there were no positive aspects to close liaison between the Russians and Abdullah in Kashmir. The hope was that Nehru's tough internal battle with the communists would convert him into a cold warrior. The people at London were unsure whether Abdullah was a communist or merely a political opportunist with left-wing leanings. Abdullah taunted his detractors by pointing that they tarred him with many brushes, primarily the communal and the communist brush. His cabinet had several active communist party-card holding members, the most prominent of them being G. M. Sadiq.[26] The CIA was very concerned about Sadiq's upcoming trip to Moscow in November 1952, which he claimed was for medical reasons. It was rumoured that it was actually a combination trip designed to enable his debriefing by his Soviet handlers.[27] For the US State Department, the only redeeming feature of Abdullah's tactical romance with the Soviets was that it made Nehru retain a strong hold on Abdullah[28] since Nehru would not tolerate any overt Soviet intervention in Kashmir. The CIA, in fact, desired to take advantage of Abdullah's dependence on India. They wanted to use the Ladakh-Tibet trade mission of 1953 to gather intelligence in Sinkiang, which was on the verge of being overrun by the PLA.[29]

In November 1952, the Praja Parishad leader, Prem Nath Dogra, and one of his close associates, Sham Lal Sharma, were detained on the orders of Abdullah's interim government. In the spring of 1953, the situation in Jammu grew tense, with the Praja Parishad *satyagraha*. The Abdullah regime retaliated with considerable violence, dispersing crowds with police *lathi* charge and numerous arrests. Dr Mookerjee helped organise this agitation and in May 1953, he set out for Jammu where he proposed to investigate the situation. He was arrested at the state border by the Jammu and Kashmir state police that reported to Abdullah. Mookerjee was taken to Srinagar where, on 23 June 1953, he died under detention. His demise attracted wide publicity in India where the affairs of Jammu and Kashmir always managed to become the subject of public debate. It was widely believed that he had been murdered.

Abdullah's controversial role in Mookerjee's death was being scrutinised with increasing anxiety by the Government of India. The Director IB B. N. Mullick believed that Mookerjee's death, whatever its causes, was the last straw and demanded intervention. Karan Singh and D. P. Dhar, a young member of Abdullah's administration, teamed up with Abdullah's deputy, Bakshi Ghulam Mohammed and decided to bring the crisis to an end by removing Abdullah from power.

By now, Nehru who had earlier called on Sheikh Abdullah in Srinagar in May 1953, had concluded that his old friend was out of control. Abdullah had repudiated the tailor-made 1952 Delhi Accord and was insisting on a status for the state that could only lead to secession from India. Nehru did not oppose the plan to depose Abdullah, nor did Maulana Abul Kalam Azad, who had also visited Sheikh Abdullah in Srinagar in July 1953.

Was Sheikh Abdullah really working for the independence of his state as Nehru earlier believed? B. N. Mullick was probably nearer to the truth when he observed that Abdullah was not actually planning to take the state into Pakistan, but was looking for a semi-independent status where the Indian Government would protect him while he would benefit economically from the tourism industry and other sources, free from the interference of the Hindu-dominated government in New Delhi.

What the IB discovered was that Abdullah was a part of a National Conference working committee, set up as part of the constituent assembly, along with other leading figures in his administration. They all sought radical solutions to the Indo-Pakistani dispute over Kashmir, which was now entering its sixth year. The committee had before it a wide range of possibilities including the accession of the state of Jammu and Kashmir to Pakistan and the establishment of its total independence. In addition, it was examining a variety of plebiscitary devices such as the wily compromises thought up by Sir Owen Dixon in 1950, which were all previously rejected by Abdullah. The working committee, however, came to no conclusions. Nevertheless, its very existence was extremely alarming to Nehru.

Karan Singh Comes of Age

A concerned Sadr-e-Riyasat, Dr Karan Singh, flew down to New Delhi in the third week of July 1953 to see Nehru. Nehru was a changed man with respect to his outlook towards Abdullah. He was ready and willing to take the bull by its horns before it caused any irreparable damage. There was a pronounced rift in Abdullah's cabinet on 7 August 1953; Abdullah was left with only Beg's support. Abdullah forced a showdown by asking Pandit Ram Lal Saraf, leader of the dissenters to resign. Saraf refused to resign and angered Abdullah even further by firing off an accusatory letter accusing Abdullah of treason. This was followed by a memorandum sent to Abdullah on 8 August 1953 by other cabinet dissenters—Bakshi Ghulam Mohammed, G. L. Dogra and Pandit Ram Lal Saraf. A copy of this memorandum was marked to Dr Karan Singh. Abdullah decided to go to Gulmarg later that day and dropped in to speak to Dr Karan Singh. During the meeting, he declared his intention to seek external help to pressurise the Indian Government to grant the state of Jammu and Kashmir independence.[30]

After Abdullah's departure, a distraught and worried Karan Singh called in D. P. Dhar and Brig. B. M. Kaul, who was the state's military advisor. They came to the conclusion that Abdullah had to be dismissed. Bakshi Ghulam Mohammed was called in and he only agreed to participate in the coup if Abdullah was arrested in the process, thereby rendering him politically ineffective. Dr Karan Singh was now about to face the first major political battle of his career; it was ironic that it was his father who had released Abdullah from imprisonment in September 1947 and acquiesced thereafter, clearing the way for him to take over power in the State. Exactly six years later, Karan Singh was now deposing Abdullah from the same seat of power and sending him back to jail. Life had run a full circle and the Maharaja had been partially avenged by the crown prince.[31]

Maj. B. S. Bajwa, ADC to the Sadr-e-Riyasat, accompanied by a police party, was sent to Gulmarg to arrest Abdullah in the early hours of the morning of 9 August 1953.[32] Abdullah and his wife were driven out to Udhampur and were detained at the Tara Niwas guest house. Karan Singh, thereafter, swore in Bakshi Ghulam Mohammed to replace Abdullah. The Indian Army and allied security forces in the state were placed on alert and various other security measures, including press censorship, were announced. Under the new administration of Bakshi Ghulam Mohammed and with the fall of Abdullah, the Praja Parishad agitation in Jammu died away. The death of Shyama Prasad Mookerjee had been avenged. The arrest and detention of Sheikh Abdullah provided the Government of India quite a few years of relative calm.

The summer of 1953 was truly a summer of discontent. Abdullah's dismissal and arrest in August was an intensely debated milestone in India's relations with the state.[33] This milestone was the culmination of a period of double distrust that was symbolised by the defeated US democratic presidential nominee Adlai Stevenson's meetings with Abdullah between 1–3 May 1953. Stevenson and his aides met with Abdullah and his cabinet, where they discussed the creeping influence of communism in Kashmir.[34] Apparently, Abdullah had asked Stevenson for US aid to build Kashmir.[35] After Stevenson left Kashmir for Pakistan,[36] the left-wing Indian press led by *National Herald* and Rusi Karanjia's *Blitz* accused him of having promised US funds to convince Abdullah of the supposed American idea of an independent Kashmir.[37] This set of fateful meetings and attendant publicity added to the collective compulsions that prompted Nehru to agree to Abdullah's dismissal and arrest.

The reportage of the Abdullah-Stevenson summit was replete with ironies. First, to Stevenson, Abdullah had sounded entirely partial to India.[38] Then, the Indian Ambassador to the US, G. L. Mehta said that no responsible person in the Government of India believed that Stevenson had encouraged Abdullah.[39] Finally, the Indian IB had become convinced by March 1953 that Abdullah's National Conference was in cooperation with the communists.[40] After Abdullah's dismissal, it kept a close eye on the spread of communism in Kashmir. It conducted enquiries in the education, and information and broadcasting departments of the state government and was convinced that the trends were no longer as bad as they were under Abdullah.[41]

In hindsight, it is now clear that Moscow had known that Abdullah's position was under threat for quite some time. Baba Pyare Lal Bedi had met the *TASS* Correspondent in India, N. Pastukhov, whose report had reached Soviet Foreign Minister in April 1953. Bedi had also discussed the challenges of implementing agrarian reforms in Kashmir and warned about the religious chauvinism of the Jan Sangh, Hindu Mahasabha and Praja Parishad in Jammu; all parties that he said were 'inspired by US imperialism'. Nehru, Bedi argued, may or may have allied with the Soviet Union but there was no way that he would openly declare an alliance with the Anglo-US bloc. This is why the American influence in India was restricted to these conservative parties. Finally, Bedi had made it clear that communists in Kashmir should no longer contact Abdullah. Instead, they should use Abdullah to expose the Anglo-US game in Kashmir. Right-wing elements began to gain strength and the communists in Kashmir were in a bad shape in every way. They were numerically small, politically untrained and, under G. M. Sadiq, tactically error-prone.[42] This report helps to understand why Moscow did not bat an eyelid on Abdullah's removal.

Chapter 8

Emerging Abyss

The year 1953 was very ominous for Jammu and Kashmir. Apart from the crisis involving Sheikh Abdullah, there was a new crisis brewing with respect to the Chinese. Claude Arpi, a China expert accessed a declassified CIA note dated 15 July 1953,[1] which dealt with the Chinese communist troops in west Tibet and contained a detailed investigation of the planned road construction from Sinkiang to Tibet and Ladakh. It reported that in 1952, the 2 Cavalry Regiment, commanded by Han Tse-min, had its headquarters at Gartok, the main trade centre in western Tibet. The report noted that the regiment had 800 camels and 150 men garrisoned at Rutok, near the Pangong Lake that Tibet shared with Ladakh.

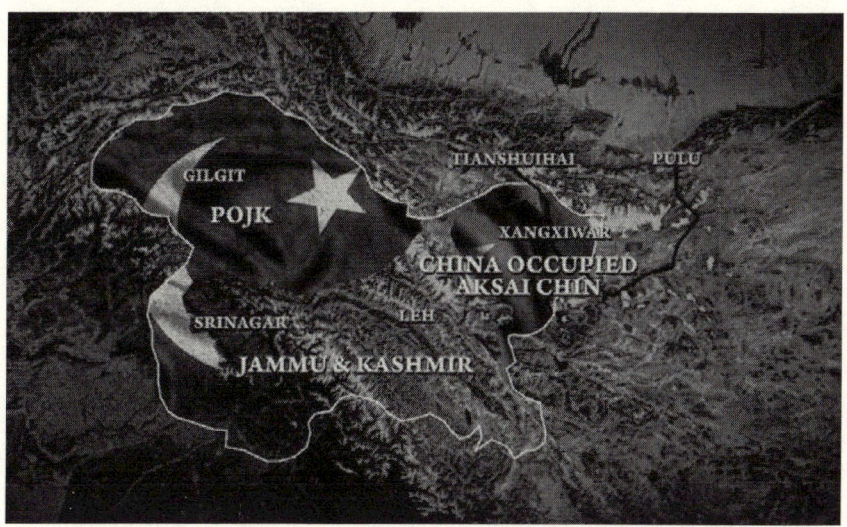

Image 8.1: Roads through Aksai Chin Area in 1953
Source: Archives of AIM Television Pvt. Ltd.

China Encroaches into Ladakh

The report also reveals that another PLA regiment was stationed on the Tibetan side of the Tibet-Ladakh border, near Koyul in the Indus Valley. According to the US document, the 2 Cavalry's Commandant announced the Chinese intention to build new roads in the area. The planned roads would run from Rutok to Keriya, south of the Taklamakan Desert in Sinkiang, on the eastern edge of the Aksai Chin. Also planned, was a motorable road from Khotan to Suget Karaul that would end at Vanjilga at the western end of the Aksai Chin. The road from Khotan to Rutok was slated to be completed in June or July 1953. According to Urumchi radio, it was completed on time, said the CIA note. The latter road is clearly what got to be called the Aksai Chin Road, now known as Highway 219. Back then it was probably not suited for heavy vehicles, but the road was upgraded by 1957 to allow passage of heavy vehicles.

The sources of this report are not clear. What is relatively unpublicised is that Capt. Rajendra Nath of the Indian Army's 11 Gorkha Rifles led the first clandestine reconnaissance mission into Aksai Chin in 1952, after the Chinese intrusion.[2] His report is still classified. It is not known whether his report was shared with the CIA and if it was a part of the CIA report.

It is also reported that a secret protocol was signed in July 1949, in New Delhi, between the US Secretary of State, Dean Acheson and B. N. Mullick, the IB Chief.[3] The protocol involved intelligence sharing between India and the US on China. In the light of both the CIA report and the army headquarters' Intelligence Directorate's information from the ground, it is difficult to comprehend if the CIA had actually shared any information with the IB or whether the army decided to keep this vital information from the IB. Was the IB Director aware of these facts? Did he know where India's frontier lay? Why then, did the Government of India sign the Panchsheel Agreement with China in 1954? Why did India surrender its consulates in Kashgar in Sinkiang and Gartok in Tibet? The Chinese local Commander,

Han Tse-min, asserted that when these roads were completed, the Chinese communists would close the Tibet-Ladakh border and use it to trade. This is what happened a year later, soon after the infamous Panchsheel Agreement was signed. The CIA document even mentions Han declaring that the Chinese communists in Sinkiang were telling people that Ladakh belongs to Sinkiang.

The Chinese had followed their annexation of Sinkiang and Tibet in 1949–50 by annexing a large chunk of Aksai Chin. They sought to overturn the Treaty of Chushul, signed in 1842, between the Sikh Empire in India and the Guofeng Emperor of the Manchu dynasty in China. The Treaty of Chushul was regarded by Mao Tse-Tung as an 'unequal treaty' and they sought to slowly annex back Ladakh from India. This creeping annexation of Aksai Chin introduced a new dimension into the Kashmir saga. There is no record of why the highly unequal Panchsheel Agreement was signed without settling the issue of the India-China frontier and the Chinese annexation of Aksai Chin to build the road linking Sinkiang and Tibet.

In 1959, the Pakistani Government became concerned over Chinese maps that included areas the Pakistanis considered their own. While Pakistan's President Ayub Khan persisted in his efforts towards an Indo-Pakistani military rapprochement, he started pursuing a policy of revisiting the Chinese frontier claims. If China did not intend to penetrate the Karakoram barrier and intrude into the territory of West Pakistan, there would be a diplomatic advantage in establishing closer relations with Beijing. The first overtures to China began in 1959 and led to an agreement between Pakistan and China to construct the Karakoram Highway, also known as the Friendship Highway. The survey of the physical route started in 1959 and the highway traversed through the Gilgit Agency. It became apparent that unlike India, China was offering Pakistan a hand of friendship and in return wanted a part of the Gilgit Agency, specifically the Shaksgam Valley, which Pakistan had annexed from the erstwhile ruler of Jammu and Kashmir. What China sought from Pakistan was a settled border, just as it did with its other neighbours like

Nepal, Burma and the Mongolian People's Republic. Thus, on 15 January 1961, the Pakistan Foreign Minister, Manzur Qadir, was able to announce that Pakistan and China had agreed, in principle, to demarcate their common border. This border, of course, ran through places that were all a part of the erstwhile state of Jammu and Kashmir, which Pakistan had annexed in 1947–48.

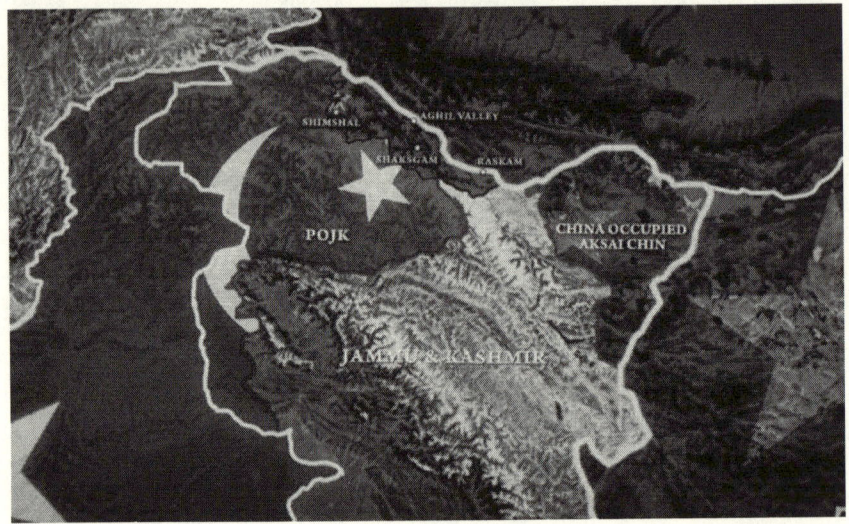

Image 8.2: Pakistan ceded Shaksgam Valley to China
Source: Archives of AIM Television Pvt. Ltd.

By the end of 1962, the overture to China began to make very important changes to the basic structure of Pakistan's diplomacy. Zulfikar Ali Bhutto, then Pakistan's Minister for Industries and shortly to be Foreign Minister, argued that Pakistan's alliance with the US, by means of membership of CENTO[4] and SEATO[5], had yielded no real dividends in terms of settling the Kashmir dispute in Pakistan's favour. US military aid to Pakistan had, in no way, been able to diminish the Indian hold over the valley. There appeared, therefore, an opportunity to play the China card against India. Such a move served directly to balance the depreciating value of Pakistan's American alliance. As Sino-Indian relations deteriorated, the US' inclination towards counting India as an anti-China nation, increased. It could not have escaped the notice of Ayub Khan and his advisors that relations with China could align India, if only tacitly, with the West. They should've also noticed that the US would do nothing to discourage such an alignment. Indeed, to woo India, it was quite possible that America would cease to show much sympathy for Pakistan over its loss of control of Jammu and Kashmir.

From 1899 until the independence of India and Pakistan in 1947, the British maps' representation of the border of Jammu and Kashmir kept varying. In March 1899, Sir Claude MacDonald wrote a diplomatic note that proposed a new border between China and British India that would run through the Karakoram's and Kashmir; this line is now known as the McCartney-MacDonald Line and it still forms the basis of the border between Pakistan and China. The note proposed that China should relinquish its claims to suzerainty over Hunza and in return, Hunza should relinquish its claims to most of the Taghdumbash and Raskam districts. It also said that the border would broadly follow the main Karakoram crest dividing the watersheds of the Indus River and the Tarim River but would also pass through a Hunza post at Darwaza, near the Shimshal Pass. The Chinese did not respond to the note and the British took that as acquiescence. The McCartney Line was modified in 1905 to include, within India, a small area east of the Shimshal Pass and to put the border on the Oprang Jilga River and a stretch of the Shaksgam River.

After Pakistan voted to grant China a seat in the UN, the Chinese withdrew the disputed maps in January 1962, agreeing to enter border talks in March. Negotiations between the nations officially began on 13 October 1962 and resulted in an agreement signed on 2 March 1963 by foreign ministers, Chen Yi of China and Bhutto of Pakistan. The agreement resulted in the surrendering of 13,000 square miles of territory by Pakistan to China.[6] This was the world's most heavily glaciated region with around 250 glaciers. The Sino-Pak Boundary Agreement of 2 March 1963 gave rise to bitter resentment in India and it is probable that it contributed to the failure of the 1963 US-brokered Indo-Pak negotiations on Kashmir.

The series of Indo-Pak talks on Kashmir, brokered by the US, started on 27 December 1962 in Rawalpindi.[7] On the eve of the talks, Pakistan announced that it had reached an agreement with China on their common border in Kashmir. Despite India's sense of betrayal by this Sino-Pak deal, the Kashmir talks went on for six sessions. The third round of talks in Karachi between 8–10 February 1963 was the most critical. Pakistan articulated that they wanted all of Ladakh (a majority Buddhist area) and all of Jammu (a majority Hindu area). The talks broke down at this point.

Pakistan's trade with China over the Shaksgam Valley, which it had wrested from Maharaja Hari Singh through the Gilgit rebellion, was because of the realisation that the Chinese claim to the area, as a traditional trade throughway linking Sinkiang with western Tibet, had more currency because of the numerical superiority of the PLA.[8] The Chinese had shown in Korea that they were willing to sacrifice waves of troops in order to hold on to their perceived strategic positions. Ayub Khan decided that it is better to befriend China and simultaneously use its help against India. The contradictions were obvious. Pakistan, which was a member of SEATO and CENTO, both anti-communist blocs, was cosying up to communist China. Funnily enough, Pakistan had been chosen by the British deep state as the inheritor of British India's northern frontiers just so that it could guard itself against communist penetration. Now Pakistan was ceding vital strategic territory to communist China.

Despite Nehru's public posture of pursuing a rapprochement with the Chinese, the Indian Army continued to send cross-border reconnaissance patrols into Tibet. The second mission was in 1958 and was targeted at collecting evidence about the Chinese highway-building activity in Aksai Chin. Two separate teams were sent across the border: one was an IB team led by Karam Singh and the second was an army team led by Lt. Iyengar. While the IB team returned safely, the army team was captured and interrogated for almost two months.[9] Thereafter, in 1960, the IAF's 106 Squadron called Lynxes conducted several reconnaissance flights over Aksai Chin using Canberra PR 57 aircraft.

These aerial reconnaissance flights were grudgingly authorised by a timid Ministry of Defence after two significant border clashes between the PLA and the Indian Army. The first incident took place in August 1959 at a place called Longju, where there was a firefight between the Indian Army and the PLA. Thereafter, in October 1959, an IB patrol was ambushed by the PLA. Many men were killed and injured and the IB survivors were captured and tortured. The Chinese released them, much later, in November 1960.

The Forward Policy

By the end of 1960, the Indian Army Chief, Gen. Thimayya, had ensured that the army was cognizant of the Chinese threat and recognised it. In May 1961, after Gen. Thimayya retired, Chinese troops occupied a pass in Aksai Chin called Dehra Compass and established a post on the Chip Chap River. The Chinese, however, did not believe that they were intruding upon Indian territory. In response, the Indians launched a policy of creating outposts behind the Chinese troops so as to cut off their supplies and force them to return to China. This has been referred to as the Forward Policy. There were eventually 60 such outposts, including 43 that lay to the north of the McMahon Line. The initial reaction of the Chinese forces was to withdraw when the Indian outposts began to advance towards them. However, this appeared to encourage the Indian forces to accelerate their Forward Policy even further. In response, the PLA adopted a policy of 'armed coexistence'. In response to Indian outposts encircling Chinese positions, the Chinese forces would build more outposts to counter-encircle these Indian positions. This pattern of encirclement and counter-encirclement resulted in an interlocking, chessboard-like deployment of Chinese and Indian forces. Despite the leapfrogging encirclements by both sides, no hostile firing occurred from either side, as troops from both sides were under orders to fire only in self-defence.

The Forward Policy had no impact on the Chinese and only strengthened their resolve to respond with stronger troops against the Indian outposts. On 20 October 1962, Chinese artillery fire commenced across Ladakh around Daulat Beg Oldie, the Chang-Chemo and Galwan valleys; the Spanggur gap between Pangong Lake and the Spangur Lake; and at Demchok. The Chinese were looking for greater strategic depth to build the Aksai Chin highway. On 18 November 1962, the Chinese began the battle for Chushul and its airfield. Chushul was strategically located and provided road access to Leh. Despite occupying the heights overlooking the airfield, the Chinese couldn't take down Chushul. Having achieved their strategic objectives, the Chinese declared a unilateral ceasefire on 20 November 1962.

India had been served a crushing psychological defeat from which it still has to recover. The military defeat put into perspective Nehru's delusionary and patronising policy towards China. He simultaneously feared and belittled China through crafty moves which only irritated Mao and forced him to strip Nehru of his international prestige and self-respect. Patel's caution about China was peremptorily disregarded and the opportunity to check China's rise and pre-empt the emerging Sino-Pak alliance was lost. Krishna Menon's disastrous choice of Gen. P. N. Thapar as Indian Army Chief over Gen. Thimayya's choice of Lt. Gen. Thorat provided Nehru with a convenient scapegoat. Gen. Thapar, who was related to the Nehru family by marriage, was told by Nehru to be the fall guy of this disaster. Thapar's good-natured personality was unequipped to argue down the Krishna Menon-Nehru duo that shrouded itself with the cloak of superciliousness every time Thapar trudged into the South Block or the Teenmurti House, with forebodings of the Chinese threat. When asked to take the rap for the disaster, Gen. Thapar with the humility of a feudal servant, took off his Sam Browne belt and placed it on Nehru's table. This was the final humiliation that Nehru heaped upon the glorious track record of the Indian Army that had not only empowered the Allies to win two successive victories in both the world wars during the 20th century but also enabled the British Empire to sustain itself over its many, far-flung colonies.

Jammu and Kashmir now had two institutionalised interlopers in its territory. On its northern and western ends, Pakistan had established its powers and on its north-eastern ends, China established itself in strategic niches. The stage was now set to trap India into a pincer and make it bleed with a thousand cuts. This strategy was not the brainchild of either Zulfikar Ali Bhutto or Gen. Zia-ul-Haq but had its origins in the tenure of Lt. Gen. W. J. Cawthorn, who was the longest-serving ISI Chief from 1950–59. For the first six of these nine years, Pakistan was still a British dominion. So, it can be argued that despite Pakistan being a member of SEATO and CENTO, and despite being a part of the then British Empire, it had already begun to pursue a clandestine military and strategic alliance with China.

In 1954, Mao had discarded the ideological differences inherent in politically flirting with Pakistan. Often enough, Beijing expressed its views that it would not object to Pakistan joining CENTO and SEATO as long as the country stays away from any activity directed at China. At the Bandung Conference in April 1955, Pakistan Premier Mohammad Ali Bogra met Chinese Premier Chou En-lai.[10] It was in Bandung that these two leaders agreed that China and India were emerging as rivals fighting for leadership amongst Afro-Asian countries. They decided that China and Pakistan should cooperate to increase their leverage against Moscow and New Delhi and that the two countries could evolve a working relationship despite their ideological differences.

There is circumstantial evidence to suggest that as a consequence of these Chinese political overtures to the Pakistani leadership in the 1950s, there was a succession of meetings held between Cawthorn and the chief of China's Central Investigation Department, Kang Sheng. These meetings crystallised into a combined Sino-Pak approach to dealing with India and became a bedrock of the ISI's institutionalised strategic and tactical range of options against India. The creation of this Sino-Pak strategic and military calculus was the main reason for the extraordinarily long tenure of Cawthorn as the ISI Chief. The Bible of tradecraft that he conceived, probably still determines the actions of the ISI's dealings with India.

Pakistan's Second Bout of Adventurism

The years after Cawthorn's retirement were dominated by the strengthening of Sino-Pak relations and the Sino-Indian War of 1962. By 1965, the time was ripe to put into practice the elements of Cawthorn' s plan. In the same year, the Pakistani Army began continuous shelling of the Srinagar-Leh highway from vantage positions above Kargil.[11] After a tough battle, the Indian Army's 4th Rajput Regiment captured these positions on 17 May 1965 only to have them returned by the political leadership after a composite ceasefire was announced in June 1965. Undeterred and thankful for the return of these two positions, Ayub Khan launched Operation Gibraltar two months later, on 5 August 1965. This involved mixing so-called *Mujahideen* with regular Pakistan Army troops and infiltrating through seven thrust lines in Gurez, Kupwara, Uri, Poonch, Mendhar, Naushera and Akhnoor. By 12 August 1965, 1,200 infiltrators had been captured. India's western army Commander, Lt. Gen. Harbaksh Singh, retaliated and captured four significant heights on the Muzaffarabad-Kel Road and also captured the Haji Pir Pass. These very positions were captured in 1948 and returned to Pakistan after the 1949 ceasefire! Operation Gibraltar ended with a whimper.

The backup, face-saving plan to follow Operation Gibraltar was Operation Grand Slam. This was an artillery-led support operation in Chhamb, which commenced on 1 September 1965. The possibility of Pakistan capturing Akhnoor as a consequence of Operation Grand Slam was countered by Lt. Gen. Harbaksh Singh by brilliantly opening up two new fronts in Lahore and Sialkot in the plains of Punjab. On 16 September 1965, China served India with a dramatic ultimatum asking India to withdraw from 56 alleged incursions into Tibet within three days or 'face the consequences'. These incursions were, in some cases, crude shelters put up by the Indian Army for its observation posts to provide protection from the vagaries of weather. Because of the ambiguity of the watershed, in some places, they were in what the Chinese perceived to be their territory.

These could have been easily resolved by talks and did not merit an ultimatum. The ultimatum, however, provoked British Prime Minister Harold Wilson to promise to India the support of both the UK and the US, if China intervened. The threat of global war loomed. On 19 September 1965, Ayub Khan paid a visit to Beijing to confer with Premier Chou En-lai; this was the first manifestation of the Sino-Pak strategic and military calculus envisioned by Lt. Gen. Cawthorn. The Chinese extended the ultimatum by another three days, until 22 September 1965. By this time, they knew that contrary to their tacit exhortations to Pakistan to fight on, a ceasefire was already being negotiated. A ceasefire was declared after UN intervention on 23 September 1965. The formal ceasefire agreement known as the Tashkent Agreement was signed on 19 January 1966 and by 26 February 1966, both armies had pulled back to ground positions they previously held. Once again, India surrendered and allowed the recapture of her own territory in Jammu and Kashmir. History repeats itself.

The Master Cell Is Born

Like history, patterns repeat themselves as well. According to author Praveen Swami, as explained in his book, *India, Pakistan and the Secret Jihad: The Covert War in Kashmir, 1947–2004*, the ambiguity of the National Conference towards accession to India manifested itself in March 1964 in the form of certain fringe elements in the organisation establishing the Students' Federation (SF) and Young Men's League (YML) to push the case for separation from India more aggressively.[12] Three SF and

YML members, Ashraf Batku, Bashir Ahmed Kitchloo and Zafar-ul-Islam, along with another valley resident-turned-Pakistani spy, Ghulam Sarwar, set up what was called the Master Cell to supervise their covert campaign against Indian rule in Jammu and Kashmir.

Within two weeks of the launch of Operation Gibraltar on 5 August 1965, the Master Cell started printing and posting anti-India posters on the streets of Srinagar. On 29 August 1965, it organised a students' strike in Srinagar. They also set off a grenade, carrying the Pakistan Ordnance Factories' seal, on the same day in Srinagar's Regal Chowk. On 6 September 1965, they also convinced the students of the Government Medical College to go on a strike. On 11 September 1965, another grenade was let off in Lal Chowk. More grenade attacks followed and the campaign of terror unleashed by the Master Cell continued. These activities ran concurrently with the 1965 Indo-Pak War. However, Indian intelligence caught on to the tracks of the Master Cell and by early 1966, it was shut down.

Despite the clean-up, some remnants of the Master Cell remained. One of its sub-cells, Poster Cell-1, had a rather nondescript member called Ghulam Rasool Zahgir. In the book cited earlier, Swami has comprehensively catalogued and tracked the trajectory of the evolution of Zahgir as a master terrorist. In fact, it will not be out of place to credit Zahgir for being the father of Pakistani subversion in Jammu and Kashmir. In mafia parlance, he was the *capo di tutti capi* or the boss of all the bosses. Men like Masood Azhar, Hafiz Sayeed and Syed Salahuddin were worthy successors of this trailblazer. Zahgir showed the way to initiate and execute subversion in the valley with the support of the PIB and the ISI. The Jaish-e-Mohammed and Lashkar-e-Taiba had only to follow his trail.

Zahgir was detained on 21 October 1965. However, since he was then only on the fringes of the ring, he was released on parole in January 1966. Indian intelligence had unfortunately underestimated him. Upon his release, he established contact with intelligence operatives working out of the Pakistan

High Commission in New Delhi. They asked him to develop contacts with underground student groups like the Students' Revolutionary Council. Zahgir's arrival charged up this group and he took over their leadership. By December 1966, Zahgir and his group mailed posters bearing a map of India with Jammu and Kashmir coloured red and marked as a separate entity to a wide range of people in Jammu and Kashmir. This act caused his group to be named 'Red Kashmir'. However, his handlers at the Pakistan High Commission wanted him to do much more.

In Srinagar, on the night of 3 February 1967, a BSF constable was on duty at the Nawakadal Bridge. He was armed with a .303 army-issued rifle, loaded with five rounds in its chamber. Armed with daggers, Zahgir and Sarwar stabbed the BSF guard in the chest. Officials at the Maharaj Gunj Police Station registered a First Information Report recording the murder but had no information on who carried it out. The police investigation of the Nawakadal murder moved no further even after Red Kashmir claimed responsibility for the murder in the next issue of its newsletter. Soon after the murder, Zahgir was arrested under the Defence of India rules because of intelligence reports that said that he had resumed his anti-India activities. However, the Jammu and Kashmir Police had no idea that Zahgir was involved in either the Red Kashmir posters or the Nawakadal murder.

In April 1968, Zahgir was once again released from prison without the police linking him to the two crimes. In July 1968, Zahgir, along with Nazir Ahmed Wani, travelled across the Ramgarh-Sialkot border into Pakistan. The two met a Pakistani IB official, who identified himself as Zafar Iqbal Rathore; Rathore was to become their case officer. They also met a Maj. Tufail and Col. Bashir. Zahgir and Wani were instructed to send small groups of men for military training and were themselves to return again for a longer period of specialised training. Shortly after Zahgir's return from Pakistan, two new recruits joined him. They were Mohammad Aslam Wani and Zahoor Ahmad Shahdad. The two planned to rob rifles from an armoury used to store rifles for the National Cadet Corps, situated at the Islamia College. The robbery was a failure and one of the groups of robbers that was caught on the spot led the police to Wani and Shahdad. Once the dots had been joined, the trail revealed the role of Zahgir. He swiftly fled to Pakistan in November 1968. Over there, he was trained by the Pakistan Army field intelligence unit in all the skills he would require to wage a guerrilla war against the Indian state.

Master Cell's Transformation into Al-Fatah

As early as 1968, during the waning years of Ayub Khan's presidency, Pakistan's greater strategic imperatives were being integrated with the planning and execution of a widespread covert war with India. Zahgir became the nucleus of this effort. He had developed a map that would not just cause the defeat of the Indian security forces but would also bring down its entire apparatus of power and control. In this visionary plan, tax strikes, protests by the unemployed and demands by bureaucrats for higher pay—all had a role in the larger political struggle against India. Zahgir now chose the name Al-Fatah for his organisation. In Arabic as in Urdu, the name means liberation, salvation and conquest. The initiation of this major plan to subvert India through the starting point of Jammu and Kashmir predates the Bangladesh War and the new turn of militancy in the state beginning from 1987.[13]

In January 1969, Zahgir, Fazl-ul-Haq Qureshi and Musadaq Husain returned to India from Pakistan via Punjab. They then made their way back to Srinagar. Nazir Ahmad Wani was eagerly waiting for them. The old networks were reactivated and new members recruited. Having achieved this, in May 1969, Zahgir, Qureshi and Wani then travelled back to Pakistan where they received specific instructions from PIB's Zafar Iqbal Rathore, Brig. Asghar and Maj. Tufail. The latter two were, in all probability, ISI officers seconded to assist Rathore. Wani received military instruction and learnt how to operate machine guns, rifles, hand grenades and explosives. All of them were taught how to fabricate improvised explosive devices from easily available materials such as potassium chlorate and arsenic sulphide. In July 1969, they returned to India, again via Punjab and started teaching courses in guerilla combat tactics for eight recruits in the Hak-Khul forests above the village of Arizal, in Beerwah. Significantly, this was the same village where some years earlier, in May 1965, in the run-up to Operation Gibraltar, the subversive group of Hayat Mir, an affiliate of the Master Cell, had carried out a savage terrorist attack. It was also the place where an old prison mate of theirs, Salim Jehangir Khan, a former Pakistani covert operative, had opened a poultry farm. This poultry farm would serve as a cover for Al-Fatah's training activities. All of their time was spent in building up the organisation and fine-tuning their tradecraft. In January 1970, Zahgir again travelled to Pakistan, this time with two new members of Al-Fatah—Bashir Ahmed and Gulzar Ahmed 'Khaki'. Zahgir provided his case officer and the ISI support team with a detailed account of Al-Fatah's organisation-building activities as well as some intelligence of military value. The group was now told it was time to act. Rathore told Zahgir that he would shortly be posted to the Pakistan High Commission in New Delhi. A fortnight later, the group returned to Srinagar. Their first target would be the office of the education department at Pulwama.

Late on the night of 1 April 1970, Zahgir's group travelled in a stolen jeep to Pulwama. Outside the education department's office, they encountered three unarmed guards. Confronted with the heavily armed group, two of these guards promptly surrendered. One, who put up more of struggle, was injured in the process. The group then picked up the office safe and loaded it on to the back of the jeep and drove down the deserted Avantipora Koil road. The safe contained ₹71,847.60, an astronomical sum in those days. Not surprisingly, the Pulwama dacoity created a sensation and the police went into a tizzy trying to solve the case. They suspected the groups of Kashmir-based Naxalites. In the time the police spent in pursuit of the Naxalites, Zahgir was able to spend the cash without arousing suspicion. He found a piece of land in the village of Barsoo, in the district of Anantnag, which seemed an ideal location for Al-Fatah's new quarters. He spent ₹50,000 or so, to construct a building which was to serve as Al-Fatah's headquarters. Zahgir also rented a house in Srinagar's Buchwara, which served as the political headquarters for the activities of the YML and the SF. The rest of the funds were used to purchase equipment for Al-Fatah; notably, a camera, a tape recorder, a projector for viewing microfilm and a typewriter.

Interestingly, the National Conference had no qualms in permitting the YML and the SF from operating out of these premises. Does one wonder how many senior officials of the National Conference knew what these people were up to?

By May 1970, Zahgir was ready to report on his activities to intelligence officials at the Pakistan High Commission. Accompanying Abdul Hai to New Delhi, Zahgir carried an account of the Pulwama dacoity case as well as some military intelligence data that had been transferred to microfilm. It appears that the cash-strapped high commission had little to offer Zahgir for his efforts. His visit, however, compelled the PIB and the ISI to assess the credibility and efficacy of Al-Fatah.

While PIB's Rathore had not yet been posted to New Delhi, a suspected intelligence operative named Mufti Zia-ul-Haq, a resident of the village of Kreeri, who had left for Pakistan after Partition, visited the valley and held meetings with Zahgir, Nazir Ahmad and Fazl-ul-Haq Qureshi to discuss Al-Fatah's expansion plans. While Al-Fatah was focusing on recruiting new cadre in the valley, its unit in Doda was only involved in covert surveillance activities. Run by Ghulam Hasan Bhat, an ethnic Kashmiri who lived in the remote Kishtwar area, Al-Fatah's Doda unit generated much of the military intelligence the organisation gathered. It also engineered a dramatic robbery of potassium cyanide from the laboratory of a college in Bhadarwah. The members would use this as a means of suicide in the event that any of Al-Fatah's operatives were captured.

In April 1968, soon after Zahgir was released from jail, he had received a visit from the Plebiscite Front leader, Mirza

Afzal Beg. Beg was Abdullah's right-hand man and was the Founder-President of the Plebiscite Front in 1955, which would provide an attractive pool of recruits to promote Pakistan's subversion in the valley. He had also been jailed along with Abdullah in 1953 and was released in 1954. In a seminal treatise called *Report on Pakistani Organised Subversion, Sabotage and Infiltration in Jammu and Kashmir*, Surendra Nath, former Director General of Police, Jammu and Kashmir, bluntly stated that it was a political decision to release Beg from imprisonment to ensure that those close to Abdullah could at least, by proxy, participate in the deliberations of the constituent assembly. In later years, Beg became Abdullah's representative in talks with the Indian Government in 1974, clinching the 1975 accord between Abdullah and Indira Gandhi.

While Beg had expressed his support for Zahgir's activities, there is no available evidence to suggest that Beg knew precisely what these specifically were. However, both of them were united in their struggle to get Jammu and Kashmir to secede from the Indian Union. The relationship was to prove highly beneficial for both of them. Al-Fatah had a major concern—it needed a legitimate political front as a cover. It is surmised that, with a nod from Beg, two senior Al-Fatah members, Abdul Rashid Dar and Mohammad Yousaf Mir, were put in charge of building the YML and the SF. The political situation of the day required that Beg had access to Zahgir's network while Zahgir needed access to Beg's legitimacy. Moreover, after the arrests following the Islamia College robbery and the Nawakadal murder, a charge sheet was filed, and prosecution had been initiated. Zahgir had been named an offender in the murder, but he continued to evade arrest. A sympathetic lawyer was needed to defend Syed Sarwar, Mohammad Aslam Wani and Zahoor Shahdad, all of whom were behind bars. Afzal Beg was an excellent lawyer who had previously defended himself in the Kashmir Conspiracy Case. He had his own reasons to partner with Al-Fatah, despite the obvious risks of associating with Zahgir.

Praveen Swami has revealed that Abdul Rashid Dar was put in charge of maintaining contact with Beg, both to discuss the defence of the Al-Fatah members and to frame a common programme of political agitation. Soon after the Pulwama robbery, Zahgir, Dar and Beg held another meeting, this time in the Chashm-e-Shahi gardens on the banks of the Dal Lake in Srinagar. This time Afzal Beg had matters other than the law to discuss. General elections were due in 1971, and the Jammu and Kashmir Legislative Assembly elections were due in 1972. The 1967 elections had made it clear to Beg that the Plebiscite Front ran the risk of being marginalised.

What Beg and Zahgir never realised was that all their meetings were under surveillance of the security arms of the Indian state. Apparently, at another meeting on 14 November 1970, Afzal Beg finally told Zahgir that the Plebiscite Front was ready to contest the coming elections and that he was principally worried of the Congress party rigging the elections. One major concern was booth-capturing and its corollary of stuffing ballot boxes. Beg wanted the SF and YML to help the Plebiscite Front secure a respectable showing by being polling booth vigilantes. Beg, in parting, asked Zahgir if he had any message to pass on to the Pakistan High Commission, where he was scheduled for a visit the next month. Zahgir did not take up the offer because he did not want to expose his own links.

Praveen Swami goes on to relate a gripping account of how, in order to augment their supply of cash, Al-Fatah planned another robbery. Nazir Ahmad Wani identified Jammu and Kashmir Bank's Hazratbal branch as the target. The execution of the robbery was superlative—the payday for government employees fell on 2 January 1971 and it was on that day that Wani, dressed as the Deputy Superintendent of Police, confidently walked into the bank, claiming that he was investigating an embezzlement charge. He demanded that the manager and cashier hand over all funds and record books, and then accompany him to his vehicle. Thoroughly confused, both the manager and cashier complied. Just before they reached Lal Bazaar, Wani ordered the manager and cashier to get out of the car. Both of them, having realised that they had been taken for a ride, attempted to argue with the fake policemen. It was a futile effort, for the Al-Fatah operatives had guns. After scaring their hostages away, the bank robbers drove to meet Zahgir at a spot on the outskirts of Srinagar. There, they changed into civilian clothes, tossed their uniforms into a sack which was tossed into the Jhelum River.

In Srinagar, the police were about to make some headway in their hunt for Al-Fatah. The bank cashier told investigators that one of the robbers resembled a student he had known while he was a student at Srinagar's Sri Pratap College in 1967. When police officials presented the cashier with photographs of students who had been at the college around that time, he quickly identified the man he knew as Farooq Ahmad Bhat. Bhat, it turned out, was well-known as he was the son of a prominent politician who had served in the Jammu and Kashmir Legislative Assembly. Bhat's involvement in the Hazratbal robbery intrigued investigators; he had been an outstanding student who was elected to head the students' union. He was pro-India in his public pronouncements and decidedly secular in his personal life. Police officials promptly raided Bhat's home, but he had fled by the time they got there. They then searched the room he had occupied at the medical college hostel, even though he had vacated the room sometime earlier. The police were in luck. Among his books, they found a small diary with seven names scribbled on one page. One of these was of Bhat's cousin, Abdul Ghaffar. To the delight of police officials, Ghaffar was at home. During his interrogation, the scale and import of the Hazratbal robbery began to unveil itself for the first time. Abdul Ghaffar told the police that he had been recruited to Al-Fatah by a Kupwara resident named Ghulam Nabi Mir. Shortly afterwards, he said, Bhat had told him during a casual encounter that he knew of his decision to join the covert organisation. From this, Abdul Ghaffar had surmised that Bhat was a senior figure in Al-Fatah. During a subsequent meeting with Zahgir, Ghaffar said, his speculation was confirmed. But Ghaffar, however, knew the names of only a few low-level Al-Fatah operatives. What the police did learn, was that all of Al-Fatah's senior members were close to a Srinagar *paan* shop owner, Mohammad Yusuf Mir. For all of Al-Fatah's careful security measures, its top leadership had been careless enough to patronise this *paan* shop. Mir was arrested and interrogated for several days and finally, on 16 January 1971, he cracked and told police officials of the Al-Fatah safe-house at Barsoo. Deputy Inspector General of Police, Pir Ghulam Hassan Shah personally led the raid, along with another officer who acquired much prominence thereafter—Deputy Superintendent of Police, A. M. Watali.

Nazir Ahmad Wani and Farooq Bhat were both in the Barsoo safe-house when the police arrived and both opened fire with their revolvers but were arrested alive. Watali kept the premises under surveillance, which led to the arrest of Fazl-ul-Haq Qureshi and Abdul Hai. Fazl-ul-Haq Qureshi's interrogation was to finally lead the police to Zahgir. In the course of the day, he confessed further and revealed another safe-house that had been established in Srinagar's Shahidgunj area, just before the Hazratbal robbery. This is where Zahgir was living. Watali also placed these premises under surveillance and soon after, Zahgir was arrested by two police teams, who burst into his top-floor room and disarmed him. From Zahgir, police investigators learned, for the first time, the details of the Pulwama dacoity, the existence of the political wing of Al-Fatah and its links with Beg.

The police also found a treasure trove of documentation on the organisational structure of Al-Fatah in the safe-house, along with some classified Indian military papers. Soon afterwards, a large cache of Pakistan-supplied Sten guns was recovered at Charar-e-Sharief. During his interrogation, Zahgir told the police that he had planned to initiate a series of kidnappings and assassinations when campaign for the upcoming 1971 general elections began. Zahgir, the police recorded, said that the hostages would have been kept at the Barsoo safe-house.

According to Praveen Swami, Indian counter-intelligence had discovered that Al-Fatah's Abdul Rashid Dar had met Beg at

Jammu on 7 and 8 January 1971, days after the Hazratbal robbery. Beg, by this account, asked Dar for an escalation of the anti-India activities. Zahgir received Dar's message on 15 January 1971 and this was the same day when members of the YML and the SF attempted to hijack the stage during the Friday congregational prayers in Srinagar, Sopore and Anantnag to deliver anti-India speeches. Like the Master Cell, Al-Fatah had been shut down well before it could achieve its ends. The Pakistani IB and the ISI had hoped that Al-Fatah would serve as the nucleus for war, after the failure of Master Cell and the war of 1965.

As the year 1971 drew to a close with India's decisive victory against Pakistan, Prime Minister Indira Gandhi capitalised on this, and, in the next few years, used it to negotiate a political settlement with Sheikh Abdullah. Abdullah eventually agreed to some limited political autonomy for Jammu and Kashmir, renouncing his demand for a plebiscite once and for all. As part of the political settlement, Chief Minister G. M. Sadiq's successor in office, Syed Mir Qasim, launched a programme to win over the erstwhile members of Al-Fatah. Pir Ghulam Hassan Shah, the officer who finally broke the Al-Fatah network, was now charged with winning its cadre over. In 1975, having been unconditionally pardoned as a result of the accord between Abdullah and Indira Gandhi, the bulk of Al-Fatah's cadre went mainstream, forming the *Inquilabi Mahaz*, or Revolutionary Union, which supported the Indira Gandhi-Sheikh Abdullah agreement. The absolute collapse of this agreement and the grave error of entering into it is what still haunts the Indian state.

Chapter 9

Deeper Waters

The year 1975 brought some grim forebodings for Indira Gandhi, then in her ninth successive year as the Indian Prime Minister. Her great victory in the December 1971 war with Pakistan and her engineering the creation of the new nations of Bangladesh and a smaller Pakistan had long been forgotten. Despite signing the Shimla Agreement in July 1972 and the consequent return of over 90,000 Pakistani prisoners of war, coupled with the dropping of all charges of committing war crimes by Pakistan Army officers, the Pakistani Prime Minister, Zulfikar Ali Bhutto, had gone back on his word to transform the newly named and demarcated LoC in Jammu and Kashmir into an international border. Within India, Jayaprakash Narayan's movement demanding a 'total revolution' had gathered an ominous momentum and Indira Gandhi was facing a huge amount of political opposition. The Allahabad High Court was close to deciding on the election petition filed against Indira Gandhi's election from Rae Bareli in UP, and in the US, President Nixon had been forced to resign following the Watergate scandal.

After sacking Sheikh Abdullah in 1953, the government in New Delhi had ramped up financial assistance to Jammu and Kashmir to aid its economic development, with the planning commission committing to the state a sum that was then equivalent to US$15 million. But Abdullah's successor, Bakshi Ghulam Mohammed made no secret of his policy of buying out the support of Kashmiris; he came from a family of businessmen who had benefitted from military contracts and forest leases. Bakshi reached out to Abdullah's supporters and awarded

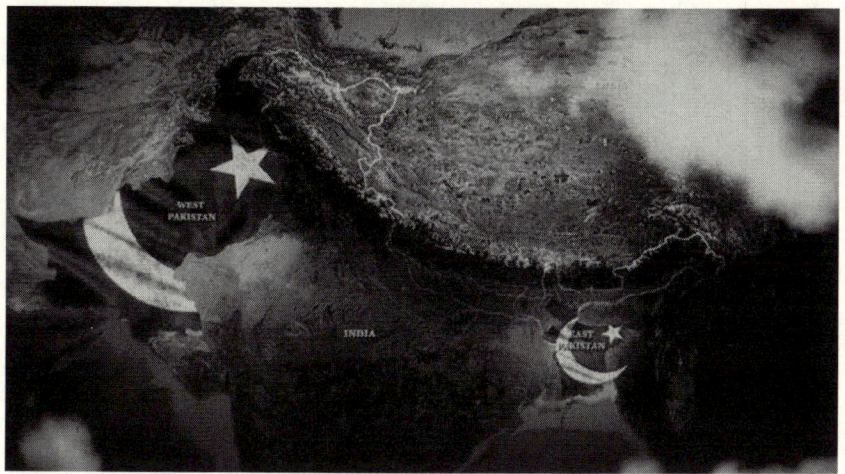

Image 9.1: West and East Pakistan, which later became the independent country of Bangladesh
Source: Archives of AIM Television Pvt. Ltd.

contracts and licences for forestland, transport and tourism, always asking for a price. Even though all this was quietly managed, unfortunately, all Kashmiris began to be viewed as people who would do anything for money. In reality, it was only the middle class that benefitted from these sops. Ironically though, this class had always been supportive of Pakistan, observes Wajahat Habibullah, an Indian civil servant who spent most of his career in the state, in his book, *My Kashmir: The Dying of the Light*.[1]

Across Jammu and Kashmir, communal polarisation between the Muslim-dominated valley and the Hindu-dominated Jammu had become a way of life. Before the 1975 accord, Abdullah had headed the Plebiscite Front that was known to receive funds from Pakistan and opposed the state's accession into the Indian Union. However, with the Al-Fatah gone, the anti-Congress opposition space in the valley was now occupied by the Jamaat-e-Islami and by the Jana Sangh in Jammu. When Abdullah was freed from prison following the 1975 accord, the state's Congress Chief Minister, Syed Mir Qasim, resigned on 23 February 1975.

He was soon replaced by Abdullah; he was now an almost one-man government supported by his long-time associate, Mirza Afzal Beg. Within months of becoming the Chief Minister, Abdullah, sensing the political winds blowing against Indira Gandhi, began to articulate his misgivings about the accord.

The 1975 Accord

Abdullah had killed two birds with this accord—he was back in power and the cadres of Al-Fatah had been pardoned. Zahgir, despite being tried for both murder and sedition, was released but certain key players like Fazl-ul-Haq Qureshi, Nazir Ahmad Wani, Hamidullah Bhat, Mohammad Shaban Vakil and Farooq Ahmad Bhat had rejected the deal.[2] Despite holding out, Qureshi struck his own deal with Abdullah's new government and was reinstated in his old government job, in 1980. This underscored the influence that both Abdullah and Beg exercised over Qureshi. Mirza Afzal Beg had faithfully protected his boys and delivered them their freedom.

With Abdullah in power, Al-Fatah lost its relevance but held on to the ethos and passion with which they functioned. Abdullah's return to mainstream politics had obviated, for some time, the necessity for organisations like the Master Cell and Al-Fatah. It is interesting that till 1975, the National Conference had used mainstream politics to attract agitated youth and then dispatched them into the twilight zone inhabited by the Master Cell and Al-Fatah. Pakistan, because of its own internal turmoil, was unsure of what position to take on Kashmir.

The accord of 1975 did not let Abdullah achieve his ambition of returning to the exact position of power that he enjoyed before his dismissal in August 1953. The accession of the state to India seemed final and Abdullah, in public statements, confirmed his acknowledgement of the current state of affairs. However, the accord did grant him the freedom to review all the laws of the state that had been enacted since 1953.

The 1977 elections in the state marked a turning point in its troubled history. The 1975 Kashmir accord, had now been shown to be an illusion. Abdullah was no longer the chosen instrument of the Indian Government. The rift in opinion between the people of the valley and Jammu residents was leading to communal tensions; the Hindus felt belittled because they thought the Muslims were ruling them and the Muslims believed that Jammu's Hindus were trying to break up the state. Abdullah had been endorsed by what can only be described as a Muslim voter base but in no way could he be seen to be the voice of Islam in Jammu and Kashmir. This space was now taken up by the Jamaat-e-Islami.

Abdullah's intent was made obvious not through a single manifesto but through isolated actions. In September 1977, for example, the state government took measures that indicated the beginnings of press censorship. In November, the state government assumed certain powers of detention, through ordinances like the Jammu and Kashmir Public Safety Ordinance 1977, that could last up to two years without the right of appeal. Abdullah explained that he needed a stronger hand in order to deal with undesirable 'infiltration' from Pakistan. By the beginning of 1978, these various draconian ordinances gave rise to demonstrations across the state. He also enacted the Agrarian Reforms (Amendment) Act of 1978 to garner support on the lines of the land reforms made in his first tenure, after his re-election in 1977.

In September 1978, suspecting that some of his colleagues were not wholeheartedly backing his decisions, Abdullah ordered all members of his cabinet to take a personal oath of loyalty to him. Mirza Afzal Beg, who had stood unflinchingly beside Abdullah for well over four decades, now broke up with his old friend. Beg, who was seen as a natural successor to Abdullah, was sidelined in what was to become a feudal order. Beg was expelled from the National Conference and his efforts to set up his own party, the *Inquilabi* (Revolutionary) National Conference, never really took off and his political career faded away. Thus, Beg, the godfather of the 'transients' within the 'twilight zone', was no longer there to shepherd his flock. He died in 1982, abandoned by his friends and beneficiaries.

In an address on 13 July 1980, Abdullah declared that 'no one would be allowed to enslave us again, whether it is India or Pakistan'. He had not, it seemed, abandoned his dream of an independent Jammu and Kashmir. Indira Gandhi was extremely annoyed at this and at a meeting with Abdullah in New Delhi, on 22 July 1980, she evidently made her feelings plain. Abdullah backed down a bit, as he had often done in the past. Gandhi, however, was not convinced. Through 1981, Abdullah resolved to loosen his grip on the reins of power and hand over the control of the state to his son Dr Farooq Abdullah, who, in 1981, became the President of the National Conference.

Dr Farooq Abdullah was now the heir apparent. Even though his political views were not clear at this juncture, it was evident that he wanted no less autonomy than his father. At the very least, he would fight for a return to the pre-1953 position. As support for the Abdullah's began to wane, the Jammu and Kashmir Resettlement Act of 1982—that took advantage of Article 7 of the Indian Constitution allowing migrants to enter Pakistan after Partition to resettle if any law permits them to do so—was initiated to allow Kashmiris, who had migrated to Pakistan, as state subjects. The fact that such an act would go against nationalist emotions across India was ignored. When Abdullah died in October 1982, Indira Gandhi had attended his funeral.

Enter Farooq Abdullah

A challenge to Farooq's succession was mounted by Ghulam Mohammed Shah, the husband of Khalida, Abdullah's favourite child. Farooq Abdullah eventually became Chief Minister after the elections of 1983, though not without the support of Indira Gandhi, who expected a political alliance between her Congress party and Farooq's National Conference. But being advised by his party to be independent, Farooq first vacillated and then confronted the Congress even though Indira Gandhi, in an unprecedented move, chose to campaign in the Jammu and Kashmir state elections. Relations between Farooq Abdullah and Indira Gandhi further strained after he chose to engage openly with some opposition leaders at a three-day National Opposition conclave that he had hosted in Srinagar in October 1983. It set the stage for the entry of a newly appointed Governor, Jagmohan, who was a trusted lieutenant of the Gandhi family. Farooq was replaced by his brother-in-law G. M. Shah as Indira Gandhi was reluctant to follow Jagmohan's advice of imposing Governor's rule by article 92 of the Jammu and Kashmir Constitution. Indira Gandhi's intention was apparently only to discipline the young Farooq Abdullah, but his removal only gave Farooq's popularity a boost, and it has been argued that Farooq's ouster had led to the insurgency that devastated the state since 1989.

Kashmir had also begun to see the revival of Islamist political parties in the 1980s. The MUF was established in August 1986 by a number of Muslim parties led by Jamaat-e-Islami (including the People's Conference), the Ummat-e-Islami and the Ittehad-ul-Muslimeen.[3] Simultaneously, Rajiv Gandhi worked towards the restoration of a constitutional government in Jammu and Kashmir. A dialogue with Farooq led to the Rajiv-Farooq accord in November 1986, but the Kashmiris viewed this initiative as a blow to their self-respect. Farooq lost much of the goodwill that had followed his ouster in 1983. By 1987, the stage was set for a political confrontation between the Jamaat and the National Conference; the Jamaat had, by then, emerged as the leader of the MUF under the leadership of Syed Ali Shah Geelani. He had steadily worked towards building its influence, since 1979, through *Madrasas* which were allowed to proliferate by Sheikh Abdullah. Apparently, his aim was to keep New Delhi on the edge by keeping alive the possibility of religious revival, in case it interfered with his government's freedom within Jammu and Kashmir. These developments hadn't gone unnoticed in Pakistan, where the military was back in power, after dismissing Bhutto in 1977.

Coinciding with the dismissal of Zulfikar Bhutto was the 1977 state assembly elections. It was regarded as a referendum of Abdullah's accord with Indira Gandhi in 1975. The 1987 elections turned out to be quite the opposite of that: allegations of mass malpractice against the Farooq Abdullah-led National Conference spread across the valley, even though an objective civil servant—the highly regarded Wajahat Habibullah—found them to be true in only 10 constituencies, mostly in Srinagar. Jagmohan later denounced the entire elections as rigged. There was open rigging in the Amira Kadal constituency, where Ghulam Moinuddin Shah, a close relative of Farooq, was pitted against Syed Mohammed Yusuf Shah of the MUF. They had allegedly replaced the ballot boxes and this, as Habibullah concedes, was a turning point after which the Kashmiri people had decided that they had had enough. When the Kashmiris, fed up with the manipulations of politicians in Srinagar and Delhi, raised a cry for independence following the rigged elections of 1987, it gave Pakistan the opportunity it was looking for. Many of those who were polling agents for Syed Mohammed Yusuf Shah were imprisoned without bail for months and subjected to harsh treatment. But when freed, these young men went on to become militant leaders of the insurgency that hit Kashmir in 1989. Shah went off to Pakistan to head the Hizb-ul-Mujahideen under the adopted name of Syed Salahuddin. In fact, Pakistan had begun to flood the valley with weapons, ammunition and trained militants just after the 1987 elections.

Even though New Delhi had continued to insist that the Shimla Agreement had resolved all areas of Indo-Pak disputes, including the Kashmir issue, the Pakistan Army, especially after the Soviet withdrawal from Afghanistan, became obsessed with 'doing a Bangladesh on India' in Kashmir. This coincided with a similar movement in eastern Europe as the Soviet Union broke up. And so, Pakistan initiated a well-planned operation to liberate the valley from India after a large number of Kashmiri youths, appalled with the 1987 elections, crossed the LoC, which was then an unfenced military boundary line with troops deployed on either side, into POK. They were welcomed, trained and armed by the Pakistan Army, and then pushed back into the valley to initiate an insurgency. A recent collection of interviews of these insurgents has been published on 10 March 2019 issue of *The Week*.

Zia's Operation Topac

On Gen. Zia-ul-Haq's orders, 'the ISI drew up a plan for Kashmir in 1984 that was to mature in 1991'[4] says Husain Haqqani in *Pakistan: Between Mosque and the Military*. The aim was to run this quasi-military operation in three phases: in phase one, Pakistan was to initiate a low-level insurgency in Kashmir, which it did from late 1989, while still allowing the local government to function so that central rule was not imposed by New Delhi. It would also have Pakistani sympathisers subvert the police forces, financial institutions and other government organisations along with their regular anti-India student and youth-led rioting to prepare Kashmir for secession and a Pakistani-led takeover of the valley. In phase two, as Kashmir remained on the boil, Pakistan would exert military pressure on the Indian Army on the LoC, forcing it to deploy the bulk of its troops along the LoC and in the Siachen region. This was to be followed by attacks on key military cantonments and posts along the LoC to divert the attention of the Indian Army from the turmoil in the valley. Pakistan would then cut off the Kashmir Valley and its airfields, tunnels and highways to prevent an Indian response to any subsequent Pakistani attack. And finally, in phase three, Pakistan would enable the liberation of the Kashmir Valley by creating a mini-Islamic state in the valley. The aim of this was to turn Kashmiris away from their centuries-old culture of Sufism by replacing it with Wahhabi Islam and cleanse the valley of non-Muslims.

Pakistan's generals had put together plans to first challenge the sanctity of the LoC and then to initiate the secession of the valley, in reverse order of their foiled plans of 1965. In the first part, their aim was to capture the Siachen Glacier. As the CFL/LoC ends abruptly at NJ 9842 near Leh, the Siachen Glacier—the source of about a 100 million cubic meters of water—lay in 'no man's land'.

Image 9.2: Line of Control/Ceasefire Line
Source: Archives of AIM Television Pvt. Ltd.

But, India's swift response of placing troops in the glaciated region stumped Zia's adventure, and since 1984, Siachen has remained the world's highest battlefield and an area of military dispute. Then, working to a plan, outlined in April 1988 by Gen. Zia-ul-Haq, Pakistan launched what is now their longest running quasi-military initiative against India—Operation Topac[5] (named so after a Latin American guerrilla movement).

Rajiv Gandhi, now India's Prime Minister following the assassination of Indira Gandhi, took to Jagmohan's advice to declare Governor's rule and dismissed the G. M. Shah government for communal rioting. New Delhi's biggest concern was that the communal tensions would end up posing as an additional security challenge, as Punjab was still unsettled. Kidnapping and grenade attacks on paramilitary posts became the norm in the valley, as the political leadership stood paralysed and confused. But the first to be at the receiving end of the steadily normalised violence were the Kashmiri Pandits, who were amongst the oldest inhabitants of the valley. Fifty Hindu homes were burned down in the Anantnag district of south Kashmir in February 1986, setting the stage for the mass exodus of Kashmiri Pandits, that began in February 1990. The Pandits had constituted 1,25,000 out of the 30,00,000 Kashmiris in the valley. Fearing further attacks, with threats being announced through Srinagar's Urdu daily *Al-Safa* and loudspeakers at mosques, and with official announcements that refugee camps were being set up in the valley, most Pandits chose to move to Jammu and other parts of India.[6] Slowly, the Pandit population was reduced from over 75,000 families in January 1990 to around 650 families in 2014. It was a blow to the philosophy of 'Kashmiriyat', from which the state has never quite recovered.

Even though much of the insurgency had thus unfolded according to Gen. Zia's plans, the Pakistan Army's hopes of liberating Kashmir were foiled. Zia had expected Indian troops to stay in Sri Lanka battling Tamil insurgents much longer, but they returned in March 1990 as India pulled out of Sri Lanka, just as the Pak-sponsored insurgency took off in the valley. Earlier, warnings by Indian Army commanders in Jammu and Kashmir were ignored by Rajiv Gandhi, who had just been bruised by a shoddily implemented intervention in Sri Lanka. But, once the contours of Pakistan's plan became more apparent, a panic-stricken New Delhi Government decided, for the first time, to launch the Indian Army in a counter-insurgency role (later for counter-terrorism operations) within the Kashmir Valley, in 1990. Soon, the AFSPA was implemented across the state of Jammu and Kashmir. It gave Indian troops legal cover to operate freely in the state, but the AFSPA soon came under a lot of criticism for the alleged human rights abuses by Indian troops. The central government remained in denial about the insurgency for quite some time, even though the police had arrested the first group of Pakistan-trained men in as early as September 1988. Their numbers kept increasing as they infiltrated across the LoC, guided by the local shepherds through craggy pathways. By mid-1989, Srinagar descended into violence and a 'Quit Kashmir' movement was launched; simultaneously the JKLF (a freedom-seeking secular group) was sidelined by the more radical pro-Pakistan Hizb-ul-Mujahideen. [7]

With Indian troops soon flooding the valley, many of whom had no idea of how to battle this new challenge, there were excesses committed that continue to plague the Kashmiris. One such case that still awaits closure is of the allegations of mass rape committed by Indian troops on the night of 23–24 February 1991 of at least 100 women of the twin villages of Kunan Poshpora. Several fact-finding missions—by civil servants, the army, and even NGOs—have led nowhere, as the statements of the victims (and their numbers) have been inconsistent. The only consistent fact is that none of those claiming to be rape survivors has accused an Indian Army officer of misconduct. Nevertheless, the considerable public outrage and condemnation of the Indian Army put enormous pressure on its soldiers, who were now battling militants and the public at large. But even then, as the militancy began to lose its momentum, Pakistan started pushing its veterans from its recent adventure in Afghanistan to lead the insurgency and scale up its military activities. By mid-1990s, the Hizb-ul-Mujahideen was sidelined by the Lashkar-e-Taiba, which still enjoys wide support amongst Pakistanis. Simultaneously, Pakistan also extended support for setting up All Parties Hurriyat Conference, a coalition of 26 anti-India political parties in March 1993 to keep raising the cause of Kashmiri separatism. But, they were a divided lot with Syed Ali Shah Geelani, a hardliner, and Mirwaiz Farooq, a moderate, leading the two groups. Over the years, Pakistani leaders visiting India insisted on engaging with them, promising them that 'freedom' was around the corner. Pakistani intelligence agencies funnelled money to the conference's leaders, as investigations have now revealed, to keep the fires burning.

Al-Fatah Rises from the Grave

Away from the spotlight of the insurgency, in the spring of 1988, eight years after his rehabilitation and while working in his government job, Fazl-ul-Haq Qureshi, the veteran of the struggles of the Master Cell and Al-Fatah, emerged from political hibernation to found the Armed Reserve Force, along with his close friend Abdul Majid Dar, who would go on to become Commander-in-Chief (Operations) in the Hizb-ul-Mujahideen. Qureshi was once again detained under the Terrorist and Disruptive Activities (Prevention) Act in February 1990 and released on 3 June 1992. Qureshi founded the PPF on 8 August 1993. Of those Al-Fatah members opposed to the Indira-Abdullah accord of 1975, the key ones—Nazir Ahmed Wani, Hamidullah Bhat and Mohammad Shaban Vakil—were party to the decision to revive Al-Fatah on 14 September 1991. Abu Khalid was made its new chief. Soon after its revival in the valley, the group claimed responsibility for the abduction of a French engineer, Silva Antonia, in the Doda district on 14 October 1991. Abu Khalid, talking of the need to revive the organisation, said that the old stalwarts had decided to make their contribution to the achievement of the right of self-determination. In October 1994, the SOG of the Jammu and Kashmir Police killed three Al-Fatah terrorists in a joint operation with the 26 Punjab Regiment at Koil Muqam and Malangam.[8]

The moot question is—was the split in Al-Fatah a genuine split or was it an engineered split to once again send agent provocateurs or 'transients' into the 'twilight zone'? The Al-Fatah story reveals the limitations of the process of political accommodation of violent secessionists and their induction into the mainstream. The unanswered question is—were there channels of communication and control between the National Conference and the breakaway group of Al-Fatah after 1975? Was Fazl-ul-Qureshi this link? Was his action of founding the Armed Reserve Force, along with Abdul Majid Dar, and its absorption into the Hizb-ul-Mujahideen, an act of extending the shadows of the 'twilight zone' into an overlap between Pakistan controlled non-state actors? And in this saga, the final question that emerges is—was the air crash that killed Surendra Nath, a former IPS officer, and in 1994 the Governor of Punjab, actually a political assassination executed by the ISI? Governor Nath was in the crosshairs of the ISI because he had exposed their duplicity in the valley and in Punjab. Perhaps it is time for the Government of India to revisit his seminal report and implement his conclusions, which could still be valid. All the militants of the Master Cell and Al-Fatah were beneficiaries of a political system that sought rapprochement, rather than the perpetual exile or neutralisation of those who transgressed its limits. It is obvious that rapprochement failed miserably in the valley and perhaps it failed because the doorkeepers to the 'twilight zone' wanted to keep the doors open for the continuing cross-fertilisation of newer 'transients' and never really wanted the rapprochement to succeed?

The Punjab Police had ruled out sabotage of Nath's aircraft, but civil aviation officials are still sceptical about the police's explanation.[9] Both the pilots of the Beechcraft were highly-trained and experienced, and the plane had so far logged zero-defect flights. The Punjab Government's inquiry to probe the cause of the crash was not conclusive nor was any forensic investigation undertaken. Nath became Punjab's Governor in August 1991 when it was the most sought-after seat in the country. The state was under President's rule and terrorism was at its worst. By putting to use his stints as a troubleshooter in Mizoram and Kashmir and as an advisor to Arjun Singh when he was Punjab Governor, Nath succeeded where his predecessors had failed.

Even though a unified command had been set up in 1993 by the Governor, General Krishna Rao, an ex-Indian Army Chief, there was little unity in the actions of several elements that were brought together to counter the Pakistan sponsored insurgency. The unified command included the state's chief secretary, the home secretary, the DG of police, the IGs of the BSF, CRPF and

Jammu and Kashmir Police, and representatives of the Indian Army's Srinagar-based XV Corps. But the conflicting approach of these elements became only too evident in the handling and the subsequent fallout of the siege, following the presence of armed militants, in two of Kashmir's important places of worship.

The Hazratbal crisis in late 1993, first put the administration in a spot. Hazratbal is a mosque on the outskirts of Srinagar, on the banks of the Dal Lake, in which the *Moi-e-Muqqadas*—a hair of the Holy Prophet—is preserved as a sacred relic. For most people in the valley, this was their primary symbol of Islam, even though the hardliners in the Jamaat considered the worship of the Prophet's relic, or even of Sufi shrines, unacceptable. This shrine had become the headquarters of JKLF, just like it had once been, before the insurgency, for Sheikh Abdullah. Reports that heavily armed militants had entered the shrine in October 1993 led to its siege. As negotiations followed to give the government and the militants a suitable closure, tension in the valley led to the imposition of a curfew. But even then, a protest march against the siege by about 400 people in Bijbehara led to, what many claim, unprovoked firing by the BSF. Reportedly, 28 people were killed and 60 or more injured. This was reported the world over and for years, photographs of this incident were used to highlight the Indian Army's 'excesses' in Kashmir. Despite that, negotiations finally brought the Hazratbal siege to an end, and a change in the attitude of at least some quarters (like the JKLF, which announced a ceasefire in 1994 following Yasin Malik's release) and a call for dialogue.

But India's good luck didn't last too long. On 8 March 1995, a siege was laid on Kashmir's most revered Sufi shrine, Charar-e-Sharief, near Shopian in south Kashmir, following information that terrorists had taken over its premises. The shrine is dedicated to the 14th-century saint Sheikh Nur-ud-Din Wali, who along with his mentor Lal Ded, merged Kashmir's Shaivite mystical tradition with Sufism. From then on, Sufi shrines have been revered places of worship. As word spread about the shrine being taken over by militants who showed scant regard for its sanctity, a siege was laid by the army and the police to protect the shrine. But the negotiations with those holed up in the shrine left to junior police officers, led nowhere. Eventually, on 10 May (the day of Eid), a big fire in the area led to burning down of the exquisite walnut carvings in the shrine. The confusion following the fire let the leader of the militants, Mast Gul—from Peshawar and an Afghan war veteran—escape with his band of fanatics to Pakistan, where they were greeted with processions in many cities. It was a botched-up operation, and once again Pakistan used the burning down of the shrine by a fire—that was most likely started by the cornered militants—to claim that India was now targeting the Islamic traditions of the Kashmiris, when it was Pakistan's new generation of hardliners who wanted to undo Kashmir's Sufi traditions in the first place. Thus, the start of the phase of Operation Topac was now in place, that is, to turn Kashmiris away from their centuries-old culture of Sufism by replacing it with hard-line Wahhabi Islam and cleansing the valley of non-Muslims like the Pandits.

Wahhabi Islam Shapes the Insurgency

With the growing influence of Wahhabi Islam, a more fundamental Islam has grown in Kashmir, especially since 2000, following the setting up of thousands of Wahhabi *Mullah*-led mosques that many say were funded by Saudi Arabia and their representatives in Pakistan. Though their growth—in thousands—had been noticeable for years, as their architecture differed from the earlier types of mosques, these were passively allowed to grow by political parties in Kashmir. These mosques not only served as gathering places for locals, but they soon began to be used by politicians for their speeches and by hard-line *mullahs* for their (often anti-India) sermons. Today, large sections of the Kashmiris in the valley appear to be sympathetic—either by choice or coercion—to the more fundamental ways of Islam. The fear of Pakistan's intelligence agencies (such as the ISI) and the targeted assassinations of those who dared to challenge their narrative have left the moderates with no choice but to silently abide by such norms being enforced.

A large number of youth, who are victims of disruptions to their education and social life due to the battles against militancy and with few opportunities to earn a living, have been recruited into stone-pelting mobs, often getting paid as little as 100 rupees a day. They are egged on by local politicians and the Hurriyat leaders to attack police and paramilitary men on patrols or to disrupt counter-insurgency operations by giving cornered militants an exit route. Drawing upon an old and local tradition of stone pelting and the model of the Palestinian Intifada, they have challenged the patience of Indian troops. Many policemen were injured by these stone-pelting mobs which forced them to use pellet guns in response, in order to deter the stone-throwing mobs. When in 2017, the Indian Army warned that it wouldn't spare those disrupting their operations, the anti-India cries of the secessionists further garnered popular support. However, Islamabad's 'secret war' aimed at 'bleeding India by a thousand cuts' has been repeatedly exposed by several militants who have been captured or surrendered in the valley. And despite the insurgency having gone through many violent cycles and violent uprisings, politicians in New Delhi and Srinagar have failed to address the core issues of the Kashmiri people's grievances, while Pakistan's military intelligence agencies have continued to exploit this indecisiveness.

Peace and dialogue to restore their autonomy, perhaps even more than the freedom to lead a life of their choice, seems to be what most Kashmiris want. And recognising this, India's two former prime ministers, Atal Bihari Vajpayee and Dr Manmohan Singh, had both announced their intentions to offer that,[10] at the Sher-e-Kashmir stadium in Srinagar, during their respective tenures. Even Pakistan's military ruler, Gen. Musharraf, was willing to offer his '7 regions' proposal, a sort of halfway mark to the traditional Indo-Pak stand on Kashmir, as India ruled out a redrawing of the boundaries on the map. But whether it was a result of India's steady efforts at coercive diplomacy or the new fencing along the entire 740-kilometre LoC, India did see a drop-in infiltration from POK. Musharraf's promise of 'turning off' the tap of militants also worked for a while, with the announcement of a 'ceasefire' on the LoC and as Musharraf saw that his offer made little headway, a fractured ceasefire took its place.[11] Once he abdicated power, Pakistan's terror minders were back to their tried and trusted methods to keep Kashmir on the boil.

Since then, Pakistan's Army has reverted to providing artillery fire to those it trains and pushes across the LoC to keep the Kashmir boiling. This has resulted in fiery duels between the two armies on the LoC and a short but sharp conflict, known as the Kargil War that erupted in the summer of 1999, just after both the countries had become nuclear weapon states. Though the aim of Gen. Musharraf—then Pakistan's Army Chief—was to contest the sanctity of the LoC by putting regular and irregular soldiers on the mountainous heights around the northern Kashmiri town of Kargil, India's firm but measured military response pushed back Pakistani troops. More importantly, it led the US and the world at large to accept that the LoC was now the *de facto* border in Jammu and Kashmir. More importantly, it showed that these two nuclear-armed neighbours could fight a conflict for several weeks, without showing signs of using their nuclear arsenals.

Thereafter, attacks by Pakistani trained and armed militants—including a few suicide attacks—have largely been focused on Indian troops and military installations. However, sometimes, a terror attack on a military installation becomes too serious for the New Delhi Government to ignore; like the one in September 2016 on the rear echelons of an Indian Army base in Uri—on the LoC, along the Srinagar-Muzaffarabad Road—that killed 19 Indian soldiers and left even more wounded. The public outcry—with the media leading the charge—left Prime Minister Modi with little choice. What followed were simultaneous commando raids, popularly referred to as 'surgical strikes', on seven targets, several kilometres across the LoC on terrorist-training camps and their launch pads in POK. It left scores of militants dead with Indian special forces having suffered no casualties. But the Pakistan Army, which zealously guards its image as the guardian of the state, threatened the Indian Government with serious escalation if the details and photographic evidence of these 'strikes' were made public. The Modi government thus chose not to display film footage and other evidence of the strike, even though they briefed diplomats and sections of the media about the remarkable operation. The government's decision to not display evidence allowed his political opponents and all those sympathetic to Pakistan—especially amongst India's liberal intellectuals—to say that it was all a charade. The evidence was eventually made public much later, but by then Pakistan had dismissed it as a doctored publicity stunt!

But almost 30 months later, an explosive-laden vehicle driven by a Kashmiri youth, rammed into a CRPF convoy in Pulwama, on the Jammu-Srinagar highway in February 2019. It left over 40 soldiers dead, and even as the blame game continued within the Indian establishment on why and how this had happened, Prime Minister Modi and his advisors chose to do something even more daring than the surgical strikes across the LoC. India's armed forces had orders to hit back 'at a place and time of their choice', and they did precisely that. In the most audacious air strikes since the 1971 Indo-Pak War, the Indian Air Force bombed a major terrorist camp in Balakot, in Pakistan's Khyber Pakhtunkhwa province. During the Kargil conflict in 1999, Prime Minister Vajpayee had insisted that India's military responses should be limited to the Indian side of the LoC. Most importantly, it showed that India wasn't going to be held hostage to Pakistan's decades-old strategy to keep using terrorism to push its anti-India foreign policy, under the umbrella of its nuclear weapons, assuming that India would bear the repeated attacks in silence.[12] Once again, Pakistan's establishment was first shocked, until it carried out, a day later, an air intrusion across the LoC, dropping bombs at Indian military installations that fortunately missed their targets. India's swift response to the Pakistani air intrusion led to a dog fight between a vintage MiG-21 and Pakistan's F-16s, in which a

MiG-21 took down the F-16. Later, the MiG was shot down by a Pakistani air-to-air missile. But Pakistan's Inter-Services Public Relations, and its state-controlled media, continues to deny that one of their F-16s was shot down.

Even though China wants Pakistan's military to keep India on the back foot, is a party to the Kashmir dispute and has strategic interests in the region with projects in POK, it is also now giving Pakistan all the support that it desperately needs to extricate itself from the corner it has dug itself into, as the epicentre of terrorism in the region. India's responses have pushed Pakistan's deep state into an abyss. Clearly, Pakistan's three-decade-long *jihad* may now have run its course. But without India willing to confront China on its support for Pakistan, New Delhi's efforts to get the world to isolate Pakistan further would bear little fruit.

The realisation should dawn on India's strategists that Pakistan and China are very close, like the lips and teeth epithet originally coined by Mao in relation to North Korea. Today, Pakistan has replaced North Korea in terms of its importance to the Middle Kingdom.[13] The last chapter will show how inextricably China and Pakistan are entwined and how this clasp is not going to slacken any time in the future.

Chapter 10

Rising Tsunami

Amidst the borders of the vast Taklamakan Desert in Sinkiang, north of the Siachen Glacier, lies an unlikely green oasis, and nestled within this oasis is a newly built manufacturing facility that is going to alter the dimensions of the geostrategic equations between the US, China and India. This factory is soon going to become one of the world's largest plants to manufacture polysilicon, a substance that is an intermediate product in the manufacturing process of silicon wafers that are then transformed into an innumerable range of microchips for multiple applications.

The world is powered by microchips that run everything from pacemakers to mobile phones to geostationary satellites. There is an emerging cold war between the US and China which is going to rapidly divide the world between those that have access to advanced microchip technology and those that do not. The US is positioning itself to weaponise the innovation, technology and intellectual property ecosystem in microchips, just as the Chinese have leveraged their size and economic assistance for the Belt and Road Initiative. The US is now telling its friends to stop using Chinese giant Huawei's telecom products that use microchips made by its subsidiaries.

China's Card Is Revealed

On 21 November 2016, the US Navy's US$ 4.4 billion guided missile destroyer USS Zumwalt, while traversing the Panama Canal, suffered a catastrophic propulsion failure;[1] just two days later, on 23 November, the British Royal Navy's US$ 1.2 billion hi-tech destroyer HMS Duncan suffered a catastrophic propulsion failure, while on NATO manoeuvres.[2] The reasons identified for this failure have been identified as what is called Chinese 'chip destroyers'—which are a type of microchip manufactured by the Chinese PLA, that the US Navy was forced to buy by the tens-of-thousands as a cost-cutting exercise.

The US Department of Defence's most critical electronics components are built to MilSpecs and are sourced from Taiwan, Japan and the US.[3] These microchips are supposedly built under rigorous military specifications to handle a nuclear environment. However, since the US lost its superconductor supremacy earlier in this century, globalisation has thoroughly muddied the marketplace. US and Japanese corporations like ADM, Motorola, Intel, NEC and Qualcomm have been outsourcing from their corporate subsidiaries and third-parties that supply low-cost chips from mainland China, with the parent company's brand on them.

When forensic technicians were deployed to back-engineer the faults on the USS *Zumwalt*, they found that all of the microchips received from a particular manufacturer had the same flaw.[4] Instead of being laser-etched with the MilSpec equivalent of an electromagnetic pulse (EMP), these had civilian wiring equivalent to a 3-amp fuse. In general, electronic components are connected together like a daisy-chain. Even if 10 hardened microchips soldered in a series survive a short burst of electromagnetic energy called an EMP—and this never happens—that component will fail. And if this happens during a war or conflict, there will be no replacements easily available. All the spares warehoused on a ship or ashore will also get roasted by the same invisible pulse or EMP. There are so many embedded semiconductors wired on a nanoscale that to rectify them, each one would have to be inspected and re-certified at test centres equipped with specialised equipment, which is an impossibility.[5]

In fact, it has been proven as a consequence of the mishaps in these two ships that the Chinese microchips reportedly also have backdoors installed for easy hacking. To compound issues, even the drydock used to build the *Zumwalt* at the Bath Iron Works in Maine is a Chinese-made drydock. A cooperation agreement signed in 2014 between the US Navy and Royal Navy may have further allowed these dangerous devices to be placed in Britain's other warships, weapons and communication systems.

These mishaps were followed by a trail of forensic investigations that led to the blacklisting of Chinese tech company Huawei by the US Department of Defence. In August 2018, President Trump signed the National Defence Authorisation Act for fiscal year 2019,[6] which bars all US Federal Agencies from, among other things, purchasing equipment or services from Chinese companies like Huawei, ZTE and others, and from contracting with any entity that uses equipment or services provided by these companies as a substantial or essential component of any system.

Further, China imported over US$230 billion worth of microchips in 2018 from the US, Japan and Taiwan.[7] In order to not lose its overwhelming position as the world's factory for a vast majority of products, the Chinese Government embarked upon an urgent plan to step up the domestic production of microchips. China's National Integrated Circuits Industry Investment Fund, a central government subsidy programme aimed at reducing the country's reliance on foreign microchips, has raised around 200 billion yuan (US$32 billion) in 2018 for this purpose.[8] The first round of about 140 billion yuan (US$ 22.4 billion) was allocated to more than 20 companies, including ZTE.[9]

But money isn't the only factor in this ensuing cold war. Microchips require two critical raw materials, sand and freshwater. A 30 cm silicon wafer requires almost 10,000 litres of freshwater for its manufacture. All of China's major rivers like the Yangtze, the Yellow River and the Mekong are already choked with effluents. The Taklamakan Desert provides sand in abundance and there is a huge reserve of water stored in the lakes, rivers and glaciers in the Himalayan and Karakoram mountain ranges. Leading Chinese polysilicon and silicon wafer producer, GCL-Poly Energy Holdings, is completing a 130,000 MT polysilicon plant outside Kashgar in Sinkiang.[10] When completed, it could become the world's leading low-cost, high-quality polysilicon production base for modified Siemens method polysilicon manufacturing.

Chinese Hunt for Water

Is this quest for water one of the driving forces behind China's Belt and Road Initiative in Pakistan? As has been shown in Chapter 7, way back in 1954, China encroached into Indian territory in Aksai Chin, which is an extension of the Taklamakan Desert and occupied the whole of Aksai Chin[11] ostensibly to build a road linking Sinkiang and Tibet, both of which the country had recently annexed. But even then, the farsighted Chinese strategists were interested in the Shaksgam Valley, which is home to over 242 glaciers and considered to be the most heavily glaciated region in the world outside of the two poles.[12] Aksai Chin provides alternate access to the Shaksgam Valley.[13] The Shaksgam Valley fell into Pakistan's lap in 1947 as a consequence of British perfidy in orchestrating the Gilgit rebellion during Partition. The Chinese and Pakistanis were in secret negotiations in 1962 when China invaded India. Their border deal and the transfer of the Shaksgam Valley to China took place in early 1963.

But even before the Sino-Pak deal on the Shaksgam Valley was signed, China had surveyed plans for a transportation corridor stretching from the Chinese border to Pakistan's deep-water ports on the Arabian Sea. It was in this connection that Pakistan purchased Gwadar from Oman in 1958. In fact, Oman had first offered this to India and Nehru turned it down. After the purchase of Gwadar, the Chinese started construction of the Karakoram Highway in 1959. Warning bells should have been sounded in India,[14] but nobody seemed to be worried. In fact, in 1960, India signed the Indus Waters Treaty thereby gifting Pakistan a lion's share of the waters from the six major rivers of north India.

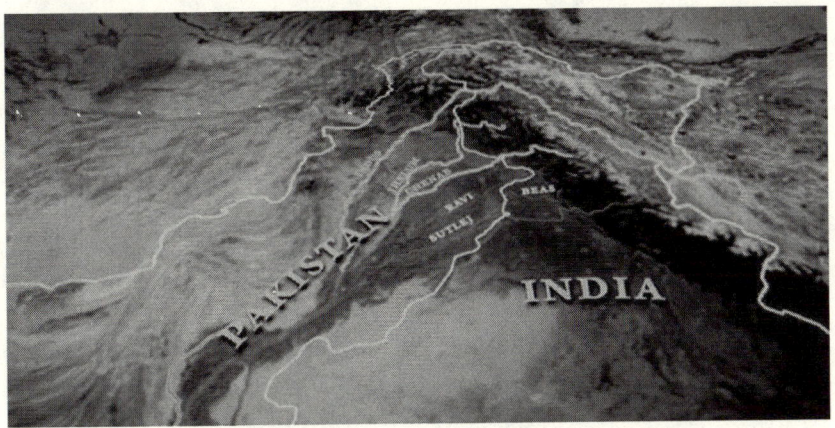

Image 10.1: Map of all the rivers of Indus Basin
Source: Archives of AIM Television Pvt. Ltd.

The treaty signed between India and Pakistan in 1960 divided the Indus and the five rivers of Punjab between the upper riparian state India and the lower riparian state Pakistan. While the waters of the Sutlej, Beas and Ravi went exclusively to India, India is allowed to tap into 19.48 per cent of the run-of-the-river water of the Indus, Chenab and Jhelum that flow through. In fact, when India and Pakistan had six rounds of talks in 1963 to settle the issue of Kashmir, Pakistan demanded 90 per cent of the Buddhist majority Ladakh because the Indus flowed through it. Was the Chinese incursion into Aksai Chin in 1954, Pakistani purchase of Gwadar in 1958, the commencement of the construction of the Karakoram Highway in 1959, the Indus Waters Treaty of 1960, the 1962 war and the Sino-Pak border deal on Shaksgam Valley in 1963, all interconnected milestones in a far-reaching conspiracy to steal India's waters?

The 1,300 km long Karakoram Highway, whose survey work was started in 1959, took 20 years to complete.[15] In between this period, in China, the failure of the Great Leap Forward in 1960 and the effect of the Cultural Revolution from 1966 to 1971 delayed the completion of this project. Added to this was the sheer engineering challenge of building such a highway. In 1966, when the Karakoram Highway was being constructed, Pakistan initially favoured routing it through the Mintaka Pass. However, China, citing that Mintaka Pass would be more susceptible to air strikes, recommended the steeper and more secure Khunjerab Pass instead.[16] Ultimately, the new Karakoram Highway was built further south and west, passing over the Khunjerab Pass. The highway started from Kashgar in Sinkiang, ending at Hasan Abdal in Punjab, Pakistan.[17] This highway now provided the Chinese instant road access into the Indian subcontinent.

Was India's consolidation of its ground presence on the Siachen Glacier in 1984 really the pre-emption of Sino-Pak moves to grab hold of the glacier? After all, the Siachen Glacier rubs shoulders with the Ghent and peak 30 glaciers in the Shaksgam Valley.[18] By physically taking possession of the Siachen Glacier, India has negated the terms of the China and Pakistan border agreement of 1963. As quoted in the agreement, the boundary in the area near the Siachen Glacier runs along 'the top of the Broad Peak, the top of the Gasherbrum Mountain, Indira Col Pass and the top of the Teram Kangri Peak, and reaches its south-eastern extremity at the Karakoram Pass'.[19] Importantly, China signed this agreement with Pakistan as the party in control of the area, and Article VI of the agreement states that following a settlement of the Kashmir dispute, negotiations will be reopened if the sovereignty of the area is with India.

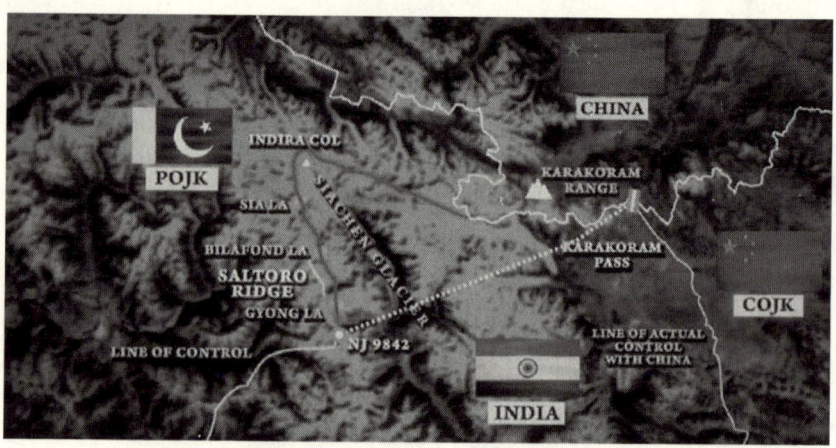

Image 10.2: Location of Siachen Glacier
Source: Archives of AIM Television Pvt. Ltd.

The physical control of the Siachen area by India places the status of Pakistan as the party in control of the area in question by shifting the presumed India and Pakistan and China tri-junction from the Karakoram Pass, almost 100 km to the west, near Indira Col. If a settlement of the India and Pakistan boundary is reached by extending the LoC up to Indira Col, it would require China to renegotiate this section of the boundary with India.[20]

The Sino-Pak Boundary Agreement of 1963 was clearly a case of collusive cartographic aggression by both China and Pakistan against a weakened India.[21] The Kargil War was an example of Pakistan trying to emulate India but failing miserably in securing control of the heights in the Kargil area and thus endangering the Srinagar-Leh highway. If the Kargil War had ended in Pakistan's favour, notwithstanding India's nuclear status, the Chinese would have come down from the Shaksgam Valley to the Urdok Glacier and then onto the Indira Col. Coupled with a thrust from the east, from Daulat Beg Oldie, Chinese forces would have captured the Indian Army in a pincer movement.

The waters from Indira Col drain in the south to the Siachen Glacier and to the Nubra and Shyok rivers, to finally merge with the Indus.[22] If Indian control was eliminated from this region, modern hydro-engineering could increase the flow of the Indus right up to and beyond Turtuk, the last village on the Indian side of the LoC. This would lead to a much more intense flow of the river and consequently make the generation of electricity much easier in the future.[23] Waters to the north of Indira Col would drain into the Urdok Glacier, Shaksgam River, Yarkand River, Tarim and Qyurug rivers to merge with the Lop Nor Lake in Sinkiang, close to China's nuclear testing site.[24]

It is clear that China's interest in the Shaksgam Valley was largely because of the waters of the four rivers that flow through it.[25] The country was setting up Lop Nor in Sinkiang as a nuclear testing site and in the event that the Lop Nor Lake was contaminated or it dried up, it wanted to ensure an available supply of water to the region. In 1962, China was still a non-nuclear nation and was yet to invade Ladakh and Arunachal Pradesh, then known as NEFA. For China to enter secret negotiations with Pakistan during those days, required a lot of courage because Pakistan, through its membership of SEATO and CENTO, was a frontline state against communism. What did China and Pakistan discuss during those talks? Did the Government of India have any intelligence inputs on them or did the agreement in 1963 come as a big shock to Nehru?[26]

Further, after the Sino-Indian War of 1962, China established *de jure* control over Aksai Chin in India. After encroaching into Aksai Chin in 1954 to build a road linking Sinkiang and Tibet, China was able to take over the Aksai Chin Lake, which is fed by Aksai River and many other streams. Its closed catchment occupies an area of about 8,000 sq km.[27]

As a result, the Chinese quest for water originating in the Karakoram-Himalaya region[28] has resulted in the Chinese acquiring Aksai Chin in Ladakh by force and the Shaksgam Valley in Gilgit-Hunza by an illegal treaty with Pakistan.[29] This farsighted Chinese planning has resulted in a windfall gain for them today. The only joker in the pack is India's right to exploit 19.48 per cent of river water of the three rivers flowing through the state of Jammu and Kashmir. India has not exploited any of the waters of the Indus cascade and has only partially exploited the waters of the Chenab and Jhelum. It is because of the ineptitude and the lack of will on the part of the Government of India that it has never realised the fact that it is sitting on a very potent weapon whose deterrent capacity is enormous. It could curtail the enormous consumer surplus being enjoyed by Pakistan in terms of the excess water that it has been using for the last 59 years. Here the argument is not even referring to the encroachment of water from Pakistan's share but only the full legal utilisation of India's share.

After the US invasion of Afghanistan following the 9/11 attacks, the US put collateral pressure on Pakistan to cease cross-border terrorist raids into Jammu and Kashmir by terror groups like the Jaish-e-Mohammed and the Lashkar-e-Taiba.[30] November 2003 saw a surprise offer of ceasefire across the LoC by the then Pakistan President Musharraf. Vajpayee travelled to

Islamabad in January 2004 and the ceasefire was implemented and terrorism took a back seat. The borders became quiet and illegal traffic across them ceased. During the next four years, Musharraf and Manmohan Singh, who succeeded Vajpayee as the Prime Minister of India in May 2004, tried to thrash out a deal on the state without changing the borders. Before the deal could be struck after four long years of complex negotiations, Musharraf abruptly resigned in August 2008 as the President of Pakistan. Before this, he resigned as the Army Chief in November 2007 and was succeeded by Gen. Ashfaq Parvez Kayani.

The Truth Behind Kishenganga

Taking advantage of the peace on the borders, in 2007, India's National Hydroelectric Power Corporation (NHPC) and its sub-contractor, Hindustan Construction Company started construction of the US$864 million run of the river hydroelectric project on the Kishenganga River near the Gurez Valley in Bandipore district of the state, located within line of sight of the LoC. The Kishenganga River is as the Neelum River in POK. Although construction of this project started in 2007, it halted in 2011 as Pakistan took India to the World Court in the Hague over this project.[31] Pakistan was rattled that India was now exploiting its legal right to tap into the water of the Jhelum and it decided to prepare a similar project on the Pakistani side of the river. This gave rise to the Neelum hydropower project. Reading between the lines, the Pakistanis consulted with the Chinese and, as a result, awarded the contract to a Chinese company in 2008. While India claimed that the Kishenganga Dam was only going to tap into 10 per cent of the river's waters, Pakistan claimed that it would affect 33 per cent of the flow of the river. The Neelum hydropower project, in fact, is in many ways a mirrored replica of the Kishenganga hydropower project. Both these projects tap into the waters of the same river on opposite sides of the LoC and then drain the waters back into the Jhelum River.

The year 2008 saw pro-*azaadi* or freedom demonstrations erupt in the valley. On 26 May 2008, the Government of India and the state government reached an agreement to transfer 99 acres of forest land to the Shri Amarnath Shrine Board in the valley to set up temporary shelters and facilities for Hindu pilgrims. This caused a controversy, with demonstrations from the Kashmir Valley against the land transfer. The largest demonstration saw more than 500,000 protestors at a single rally, among the largest in Kashmir's history. Six people were killed and 100 injured when police fired into a crowd of protestors in Srinagar. The separatist JKLF (R) organised a march to the site of the controversial land in Baltal. Senior separatist leaders Shabir Ahmed Shah, Syed Ali Shah Geelani and Mirwaiz Umar Farooq, leaders of the Hurriyat, which planned the protests, were placed under house arrest. Throughout the Srinagar area, most public buildings and many businesses remained closed. This was no coincidence. These protests caused the Kishenganga project to be substantially delayed as work slowed down and completion milestones began to get delayed. Were these protests engineered by the ISI after almost five years of peace in the valley so as to delay commencement of work on the project?

On 11 June 2010, violent protests erupted in Srinagar on account of a case of a fake encounter by the Indian Army, killing three locals in the Machil sector of the Kupwara district.[32] Between 1 May 2010 and 21 September 2010, around 110 people were killed and 537 civilians were injured as a result of being caught in the cross responses to stone pelting. Further, 1,274 CRPF men and 2,747 police personnel were injured during the same period across the valley. Adding to the eruption of violence in the valley was the constant shelling across the LoC by the Pakistani Army. This shelling provided cover for waves of militants to cross the LoC. Thus, a vicious circle of violence was initiated which started scaring away migrant labour employed on the project.

The IB and Army Intelligence claimed that these protests and demonstrations were part of the covert operations of the ISI. Media reports earlier in March had suggested that with ISI direction, Pakistan had once again revived a vicious return of militancy in the state. It was reported that in a meeting held in Muzaffarabad in mid-January 2010, which was chaired by former ISI Chief Lt. Gen. Hamid Gul, the Pakistani Army-created United Jihad Council had called for a reinvigorated *jihad* until Kashmir was free of Indian occupation. Interestingly, in May 2010, increased activities of militants were reported from across the border in the Neelum Valley in Pakistan-administered Gilgit-Baltistan. The locals reported that large numbers of militants had set up camps in the area with plans of crossing into the Kashmir Valley. This entire cycle of violence saw migrant labour fleeing the Kishenganga project in droves. Further, design changes had to shift key aspects of the project underground to insulate them from attacks by militants. Were these acts of violence in 2010 actually the second step in a smokescreen to provide a host of collateral reasons to make India completely scrap the Kishenganga project?

That Pakistan's orchestration of this violence was primarily geared towards sabotaging the Kishenganga project became clear when it went to the World Court, praying for work to be halted. It achieved momentary success when the court temporarily halted work on the project in October 2011. This was the third step in Pakistan's attempt to sabotage the project. After the World Court ruled in favour of India in 2013 and permitted the construction to restart, Pakistani proxies in the valley engineered a wave of local protests in Bandipore, thereby halting construction once again.[33] This time the protestors had targeted the project contractor, alleging that the project had violated environmental laws. This attempt at delay did not last long and the fourth step in sabotaging the project also failed.

The year 2013 was a significant year for the evergreen China-Pakistan relationship. The CPEC was announced and, in many ways, was the fulfilment of the full vision behind the commencement of the Karakoram Highway way back in 1959.[34] The full extent of this vision was later expanded in 2017 to include the construction of five dams forming the North Indus River Cascade that China had promised to finance and build in Pakistan and in POK.³⁵ The first dam would be built at Bunji near Skardu, and would have a 22 km long reservoir along the Indus. The second dam, the Diamer Bhasha Dam would have a live storage of 6.4 million-acre feet of water. The third dam in the cascade would be the Dasu Dam with a 74 km long reservoir along the Indus which will stretch all the way to the Diamer Basha Dam. The fourth dam would be a little distance downstream at Patan with a 35 km long reservoir that goes up to the Dasu Dam. The fifth dam would be a little downstream—the 4,000 MW Thakot Hydropower Project which would divert the Indus waters through four headrace tunnels to generate electricity.³⁶ By the time the Indus emerges from the tunnels, it will be close to the existing dam at Tarbela, which had been in operation since 1976.³⁷

Clearly the question is, once electricity has been generated from water, would the water then be released for irrigation or would it be used to make microchips? If the latter is the case, then it explains Pakistan's reaction to the Kishenganga project. Take the Indus out of the picture and you have to rely only on the waters of the Jhelum and the Chenab, both flowing through Jammu and Kashmir into Pakistan. Therefore, India's resolve to complete the Kishenganga project had to be broken.

Aggressive action from Pakistan started in January 2016, when for the first time ever, terrorists from Pakistan crossed the border and attacked a military asset in India. This was the frontline Pathankot Air Force Station, which is part of the western air command of the Indian Air Force. The ISI-backed and Pakistan-based United Jihad Council was quick to claim responsibility. The attackers, who were wearing Indian Army combat fatigues, were subsequently suspected to belong to Jaish-e-Mohammed which is led by Masood Azhar. Telephone calls made by the attackers were tracked down to two Pakistani numbers, one of which belonged to the terrorists' handler, a Jaish-e-Mohammed operative. This attack was meant to test the resolve of the Government of India and assess how it reacts.

The next attempt came in July 2016 and started with the killing of Burhan Wani, a commander of the POK-based Islamic militant organisation, Hizb-ul-Mujahideen, by Indian security forces.[38] After his killing, anti-Indian protests started in all 10 districts of the Kashmir Valley. Protestors defied curfews with attacks on security forces and public properties. The valley remained under 53 days of consecutive curfew, with the government having to rush in additional forces to contain the agitation.[39] The unrest, which went on for months till February 2017, resulted in the deaths of more than 90 civilians and left over 15,000 injured. This 2016–17 unrest in Kashmir is also known as the 'Burhan aftermath'.[40]

While the state was still reeling from this unrest, Pakistan struck once again. On 18 September 2016, four heavily armed militants, later identified to be members of Jaish-e-Mohammed attacked brigade headquarters of the Indian Army outside Uri. It was reported as 'the deadliest attack on security forces in Kashmir in two decades'.[41] This time India struck back. On 29 September 2016, 11 days after the dreadful Uri attack, the Indian Army announced that it had successfully conducted surgical strikes against suspected militants in POK.

Two months later, shelling intensified in and around the Kishenganga Dam and the intensity and regularity of shelling continued till the end of the year.[42]

Many of the temporary workers at the dam left only to return when the Burhan aftermath ended in 2017. The Pakistani Army intensified shelling in the Gurez sector causing the workers to periodically take shelter in tunnels as the Pakistanis were clearly targeting the dam. It was only when the Indian Army brought in its heavy artillery and gave the Pakistanis a taste of their own medicine did the intensive shelling subside. Today, the Indian Army has permanently stationed artillery near the Kishenganga Dam to provide deterrence against any new Pakistani misadventure in this sector. Eventually, all the three units of the dam were commissioned and synchronised with the electricity grid by 30 March 2018. On 19 May 2018, Indian Prime Minister Narendra Modi inaugurated the Kishenganga hydropower project. The project is a symbol of the tenacity and resilience of the Government of India, which stood steadfast with true grit, without yielding to the extreme provocation it was subjected to. The amount of electricity generated by the NHPC from Kishenganga is only 1,713 million units. This may be insignificant in relation to the scale of the national grid, but the project has allowed India to assert its control over Kashmir's natural resources. Across the LoC, frantic activity on the Neelum project enabled it to be connected to Pakistan's national grid on 13 August 2018.

Interestingly, it is useful to analyse Chinese moves in Ladakh during the period of construction of the Kishenganga project. Is there any pattern that is evident? Looking at 2008, when the work on the Kishenganga project was commencing and pro-*azaadi* demonstrations had restarted in the valley in June 2008, we saw Chinese incursions into Indian territory across the LoC suddenly increased during that summer. There were 2,285 instances of border violations in Ladakh in 2008, particularly in Demchok, Koyul and Chushul. Further near Chumar and Skagjung, in the Chang Tang National Nature Reserve, China forced Tibetan shepherds from its side of the border to send in cattle near the village of Dungti to establish a claim to 'traditional grazing' grounds. As the government wasn't able to join the dots,[43] India's reaction was tepid to say the least.

In 2013, when the CPEC was announced and construction restarted at Kishenganga and there were demonstrations against the project at Bandipore along with intensive Pakistani shelling in the Gurez sector, the Chinese PLA intruded 19 km deep into Indian territory at Burthe in the Daulat Beg Oldie sector in Ladakh. This was a serious incident intended to put pressure on a domestically weakened UPA-2 government in New Delhi. India's resolve was once again put to test in a Sino-Pak pincer move.

Image 10.3: Location of Daulat Beg Oldie
Source: Archives of AIM Television Pvt. Ltd.

Further, when Modi invited Xi Jinping to India in September 2014, the PLA in a brazen act of intimidation intruded into the Chumar and Demchok sectors in Ladakh. Once again, India's resolve was being tested. With every incursion into Indian territory, the Chinese extend their claim line further into India. They have steadfastly refused to resolve the border issue and demarcate the Line of Actual Control, because their intention is to keep testing India's resolve until it cracks significantly. In 2016, the Chinese made 260 incursions into Indian territory. In fact, in October 2016, extensive police raids in the Baramulla area of the valley lead to the seizure of Chinese flags and other incriminating documents from terrorist safehouses.[44]

The Wahhabi-Salafi Nexus

Apart from this coordinated approach of overt and covert pressure by China and Pakistan in the state, there is another dimension to this problem that has altered the perception of a majority of the inhabitants of the valley. This has been the Wahhabisation of Islam in the valley since the insurgency started in 1989. This is an austere, puritanical interpretation of Islam promoted by Saudi Arabia that is making deep inroads into the valley due to the efforts of the Jamaat Ahl-e-Hadith, which calls itself a religious and welfare organisation.

Across the border in Pakistan, Markaz-e-Jamiat Ahl-e-Hadith of Allama Sajid Mir is the best-known political organisation promoting the Wahhabi line, apart from Hafiz Jama'at-ud-Dawa which was formerly known as Dawatul Irshad with its *jihadi* wing, Lashkar-e-Taiba. The greatest asset of Jamaat Ahl-e-Hadith is its central Wifaq al-Madaris which looks after the Wahhabi seminaries all over Pakistan. It has eight subsidiary organisations, among which the Ahl-e-Hadith Youth Force is quite important. Because of its ability to mobilise and act, it is often called the 'spine' of the Jamiat. The next important subsidiary is Tehreek al-Mujahideen which is a fighting outfit headed by Sheikh Jameelur Rehman who also heads the ISI-controlled United Jihad Council, the apex body of all militias fighting in the Kashmir *jihad*. It trains near Muzaffarabad in Azad Kashmir and has resisted efforts for a merger with Lashkar-e-Taiba. Tehreek al-Mujahideen is funded by Al-Haramain Islamic Foundation which funnels money from Saudi Arabia into South Asia. The contact with Saudi Arabia was established after the Ahl-e-Hadith of Pakistan started a movement of protection of Mecca and Medina after the Shia tried to hold meetings at Kaaba. In 1985, Imam Kaaba and a representative professor of Medina University became members of this foundation. Mansur bin Abdul Rehman al-Qazi of Al-Haramain Islamic Foundation declared in the Tehreek journal *Shahadat* in July 2000 that he was satisfied by the Tehreek's spreading of the Salafi faith in India-held Kashmir.[45] Tehreek al-Mujahideen claims that 500 of its warriors died in *jihad* in Kashmir after killing 3,000 Indian soldiers and officers. Among the Pakistanis killed, 215 were from Punjab, 49 from Sindh, 45 from Azad Kashmir and 19 from the NWFP. In all, 70 Muslims of Indian-held Kashmir were killed. The Tehreek received a setback when in 1999 its commander Abu Waseem Salafi was killed by Indian security forces. In February 2001, it received another blow when its leader Maulana Abdullah Ghazali was captured by Indian security forces. The Wahhabi Salafi warriors of Tehreek al-Mujahideen have made efforts to spread their faith in the valley by converting many Barelvi mosques in Poonch and Kupwara into Ahl-e-Hadith mosques.[46]

Because local belief in Sufism was so strong, the puritans represented by the Wahhabi Salafi followers took a back seat in the valley.[47] However, once Operation Topac was launched by the ISI in 1989, the puritans forced their way to prominence and pre-eminence.[48] The descent of a plethora of ISI-trained *jihadi* groups, flush from their victory over the Red Army in Afghanistan, hijacked the local sentiment for *azadi* and steered the struggle and manipulated it to fit into their rhetoric of a holy war demanding an Islamic caliphate and secession from India. The sinister process of 'fundamentalist indoctrination' is alive and underway in Wahhabi madrasas and schools in the valley today.[49] According to JKPF's Chairman Fayyaz Ahmad Bhatt, based on a district-wise count, there are nearly 7,000 Wahhabi mosques in the state.[50] Of these, 911 alone function in Srinagar and preach the orthodox Wahhabi brand of Islam. Nearly all funding for them come in through unofficial *'hawala* channels'.[51] Admitting massive cash inflows to the valley, senior state intelligence officers reveal that the bulk of the illegal funds meant for Wahhabi groups[52] and other hardline factions are physically transferred across the LoC and at the border trading station in Uri, in the form of real and fake Indian currency notes, taking advantage of the barter trade being permitted between Jammu and Kashmir and POK. Checks by customs officers are at best cursory; there are no X-ray machines and other standard international border control equipment. The army merely observes the goings-on and does not interfere. The officers add that it is impossible to quantify the smuggled funds and that no government agency has made any effort to do so. What concerns police and intelligence officials more is the possibility of Lashkar-e-Taiba and Tehreek-ul-Mujahideen militants relying on Ahl-e-Hadith members to provide them safehouses.[53] Indoctrinated Wahhabis, funded from across the border, are unlikely to bite the hand that feeds them. In fact, in south Kashmir, local Wahhabi mosques are recruiting grounds for stone pelters and militants.[54]

So far, under the principle of freedom and equality of religious beliefs, the Government of India has not interfered in the rapid Wahhabisation of the state.[55] The fig leaf of religious freedom enshrined in the Constitution of India has enabled the ISI to exploit it to the hilt and set in place a process that not only challenges the syncretic nature of India but also ruptures the ties that bind the state to the larger country of India. Simultaneously, in collaboration with China, the ISI has tested India's resolve to an extreme in its quest to sequester from and deny India its legal right to exploit 19.48 per cent of the water from the Jhelum, Chenab and Indus rivers.[56]

The problem in Kashmir is not one of granting more or less autonomy to the political leadership of the state; the problem is to protect the encroachment of the state's natural resources, its territory and, by extension, the sovereignty of the Indian nation. The British, when they ruled India, realised this and for the first time in 1889 took charge of the state directly by dispossessing the then ruler. In the succeeding years and centuries, the Government of India has followed the pattern of the intervention of central rule in the state, just as the British did. However, the British never faced the onslaught of Wahhabisation and their resolve was steadfast. The Government of India has so far shown its resolve by combating the combined sabotage of the Kishenganga project by the

ISI-China syndicate. However, its responses to the combined Sino-Pak pincer have been diffident.

India has a nuclear triad in place and if it decides to dig into its heels, there is only so much that Sino-Pak forces can pressure it to do. India has allowed China to lock her into a continuously unfavourable balance of trade. India has not exercised its might yet, but it is now time to do so. It is also time to use Japanese and South Korean money and expertise to rapidly set up hydropower projects on the Jhelum and Indus to fully exploit our legal share of these waters.

India's Options

In the ultimate analysis, India has to choose sides in the coming microchip technology cold war. It has to cut itself loose from the age-old policy of appeasing China and boldly join the US-led alliance in this war. Choosing to sit on the fence will cut India off from technological power and deny it a place at the high table in the comity of nations like Japan, South Korea and the EU that are on US's side in the coming cold war. It is inevitable that the Chinese are going to construct a series of microchip manufacturing hubs in Gilgit-Baltistan. They will be fed with intermediate raw materials from the GCL-Poly Energy Holdings Kashgar plant. GCL-Poly is controlled by the Zhu Gongshan family and the Poly Group of China.[57] The Poly Group is a state-owned Chinese business group, one among the 102 central state-owned Enterprises under the Supervision of State-owned Assets Supervision and Administration Commission of the State Council. In other words, it is a Chinese Government corporation. Zhu Gongshan is an elusive Chinese billionaire extremely close to Xi Jinping.[58] The Zhu Gongshan family is also married into the Deng Xiaoping family.[59] If the Government of India is unaware of these facts, then it has only itself to blame. The Indian partners of GCL-Poly are the Adani Group and the Essel Group.

Image 10.4: Map showing connectivity from Gwadar Port to Kashgar
Source: Archives of AIM Television Pvt. Ltd.

As the forthcoming cold war intensifies, the militancy in Jammu and Kashmir is going to intensify. This is best illustrated by the Pulwama attack on 24 February 2019 and India's retaliatory air strike at the Jaish-e-Mohammed camp at Balakot in Khyber-Pakhtunkhwa on 26 February 2019. That Pakistan carried out a retaliatory but unsuccessful air intrusion the next day, underscores the Pakistani resolve to climb the escalation matrix. It is not rocket science to conclude that this resolve is buttressed by China's presence in the game. Funding the militancy costs the Sino-Pak syndicate a fraction of what it costs India to fight it. It has become a zero-sum game. The Government of India can only continue to ignore the big picture in the background at its peril.

Postscript

The first indications that fresh winds of change were going to blow away the existing structures of governance in the state of Jammu and Kashmir were noticed on Monday, 22 July 2019, when the Pakistani Prime Minister Imran Khan, the Pakistan Army Chief Gen. Jawed Bajwa and the ISI Chief Lt Gen. Faiz Hameed met the US President Trump at the Oval Office in the White House. The Pakistani ruling troika desperately needed to regain their clout with the US in order to balance their current vassal like the relationship with China.

With the US Congressional elections due in November 2019 and the start of campaigning in January 2020 for the US Presidential elections, Trump is desperate for the plan of an honourable American exit from Afghanistan to be in place by 1 September 2019, after an 18-year deployment in that country. Pakistan has promised to deliver this as it controls the Taliban opposition in Afghanistan. In return, Pakistan desires a resumption of military aid from the US to help push India to the talks' table on Kashmir, and to have a decisive say in the future of Afghanistan with the elimination of India's role in that war-torn country.

Trump immediately delivered all of Pakistan's demands by not only announcing a US$125 million preliminary military-aid package but also by declaring that he had spoken to Prime Minister Modi and offered US mediation to resolve the long-standing Kashmir dispute.

Even though the US and India are strategic partners, their interests in Afghanistan have often clashed. India wants the US to remain in Afghanistan as its presence over there prevents the Pakistani army from using Afghanistan both as a 'strategic depth' to fall back into in the event of a major Indian invasion following the continuous Pakistani use of terror as an extension of their anti-India foreign policy, and as a base for building their terror machinery against India, as they did during 1995–2001. The US wants to exit Afghanistan, as the American public is unwilling to both bear, by now, the astronomical costs of this never-ending war and also continue to receive body bags of dead US soldiers killed in combats.

India realises that once the US pulls out of Afghanistan, Pakistan is going to invite China to send its troops into Afghanistan, as they themselves cannot bear the costs of using Afghanistan for their tactical and strategic moves against India. And China needs to regulate a post-US Afghanistan because it not only needs to deny the use of that country as a launching pad for Uighur freedom fighters into neighbouring Chinese-occupied Xinjiang, but also to further pressurise and bleed India in Kashmir.

For India, an imperative was to pre-emptively act in moving its own dominoes on this dynamic chessboard and not react to the changes that would be put into place within the next few months when the US withdrawal from Afghanistan would be over. An indication was provided by the sudden spike in cross-border shelling across the LoC that intensified in Jammu & Kashmir, and the return of the *jihadi* fighters back to the LoC, as soon as Pakistani Prime Minister Imran Khan and his generals returned home from the US. Attacks by Pakistan's Border Action Team (BAT) on India's forward posts were intercepted by the Indian Army, and also successfully fought off BAT incursions at locations in the Keran, Gurez, Machil and Tangdhar sectors along the LOC by even killing some Pakistan-based intruders.

On Friday, 2 August 2019, the Government of India asked all pilgrims undertaking the pilgrimage to the Amarnath shrine and all tourists and outsiders in the Kashmir Valley to immediately leave the state as soon as possible citing a security threat based on intelligence inputs. And in an unusually rare move, the Jammu & Kashmir Government also officially cancelled the pilgrimage for this year. Thereafter, Section 144 of the Indian Penal Code was put in place in the entire state banning an assembly of more than four persons. Late at night, on Sunday, 4 August 2019, all important politicians in the state were put under house arrest.

The final coup de grâce to the debate on the special status of the state of Jammu & Kashmir that had been continuing since 1953, when Jana Sangh leader, Shyama Prasad Mookerjee, first raised it, was delivered in the morning of Monday, 5 August 2019, in the Parliament by Union Home Minister Amit Shah. He announced that the government has decided to repeal both Article 370 and Article 35A of the Constitution which grants special status to the state. The government may have moved the Parliament to remove Article 370 but before doing so, it first rendered the provision toothless by revoking the 1954 Presidential proclamation through a gazette notification that very morning. With that revocation order, Article 35A, which granted special privileges about property ownership in Jammu & Kashmir to Kashmiri residents (or state subjects) now ceases to exist. reason being that this was inserted through a presidential proclamation of 1954, drawing powers from Article 370 itself. The Government of India has also decided to bifurcate the state into two Union territories—Jammu and Kashmir, which will have a legislature, and Ladakh, which will be without a legislature. The order passed on 5 August 2019, thus, made it possible for the government to introduce legislation to separate Ladakh from Jammu & Kashmir and make the remainder of the state a Union Territory with an assembly.

There are reasons to argue that as a collateral outcome, these changes have resulted in the people of Jammu and Ladakh to appear to have finally been freed from the tyranny of majoritarianism that the politicians in the Valley had subjected them to for the last 72 years. It can also be argued that for the common people of the Valley, the Maharaja's feudal rule had been replaced by the feudal rule of a minuscule minority that had boxed them into a vicious circle of economic deprivation. This had been complemented over the past decade or more, by the steady implementation of an austere brand of Wahhabism. Both these shibboleths now seem suddenly shaky.

Once again, as it had done so for the first time in 1889, the Government of India has pre-empted international changes from wantonly impacting the fortunes of this state. In 1947, two parts of the entire state of Jammu & Kashmir that had acceded to India, namely Gilgit and it's vassal states and the Muzaffarabad belt, were swallowed up by Pakistan. In the 1950s, China swallowed up a large part of Ladakh. So, the Government of India can hardly be blamed for this internal reorganisation as it prepares to meet the newly emerging Sino-Pak threat to the state, as also to finally put an end to the dominance of a handful of families in the sociopolitical equations in Kashmir, who had stalled every attempt of New Delhi to extend the rights that citizens of India enjoy outside Jammu & Kashmir, by holding the people of the state hostage to the fear that 'Kashmiriyat' would be soiled when they engage with the rest of India. The story of Kashmir is now clearly headed for a new chapter.

Endnotes

Chapter 1: Unfathomable Depths

1. Plutarch, Arrian and Q.C. Rufus. *Alexander the Great: The Brief Life and Towering Exploits of History's Greatest Conqueror—As Told by His Original Biographers*, ed. T. Gergel (UK: Penguin Books, 2004).
2. P. H. L. Eggermont. *Alexander's Campaign in Southern Punjab* (Belgium: Peeters Publishers, 1993).
3. H. Kersten. *Jesus Lived in India: His Unknown Life Before and After the Crucifixion* (India: Penguin Books).
4. M. K. Kaw. *Kashmir and Its People: Studies in the Evolution of Kashmiri Society* (India: A. P. H. Publishing, 2004).
5. P. N. Razdan (Mahanori). *Gems of Kashmiri Literature and Kashmiriyat: The Trio of Saint Poets-I* (Delhi: Samkaleen Prakashan, 1999).
6. C. Snedden. *Understanding Kashmir and Kashmiris* (London: Hurst Publishers, 2015).
7. K. M. Panikkar. *Gulab Singh (1792–1858): Founder of Kashmir* (London: Martin Hopkinson Ltd., 1930).
8. G. D. Bakshi. *Footprints in the Snow: On the Trail of Zorawar Singh* (India: Lancer Publishers, 2002).
9. M. Alex. *History of Tibet* (London: Routledge, 2003).
10. S. R. Robert. *The Life and Campaigns of Hugh, First Viscount Gough, Field-Marshal. Vol. 1* (Westminster: Archibald Constable, 1903).
11. India Army. *Frontier and Overseas Expeditions from India, Volume 6* (Simla: Govt. Monotype Press, 1907–11).
12. A. Lamb. *The China India Border: The Origins of the Disputed Boundaries* (London: Oxford University Press, 1964).
13. A. Lamb. *Kashmir: A Disputed Legacy, 1864–90* (London: Roxford Books, 1964).
14. S. Michael. Executive Summary from *British Military Involvement in Transcaspia: 1918–19* (Camberley: The Defence Academy of the United Kingdom, 2004).
15. NAI/ Foreign Sec. No. 353 (K.W) Prog. 1884.
16. C. H. Ellis. *The British Intervention in Transcaspia 1918–19* (Berkeley and Los Angeles: University of California Press, 1963).
17. Foreign., Sec. E, No. 354, Prog. May 1894.
18. Resident to Government of India, 3 August 1920, File No. 19-P/1924.
19. Ibid., 16 August 1920, File No. 19-P/1924.
20. Resident to Maharaja, 26 August 1920; Maharaja to Resident, 28 August 1920, File No. 19-P/1924.
21. Note by J. B. Wood, 21 August 1920, File No. P-19/1924.
22. Note by H. R. Lynch Blose, 23 September 1925, File No. 19-P/1925.-P/1925.

Chapter 2: Cloudy Waters

1. Telegram, First Assistant to Resident, 23 September 1925, File No. 19 (10)-P/1925.
2. Note by H.R. Lynch Blose, 24 September 1925, File No. 19-P/1925.
3. Ibid.
4. Ibid.
5. Telegram, Secretary of State, 5 October 1925, File No. P-19(10)/1925.
6. Telegram, Secretary of State, 7 October 1925, File No. P-19(10)/1925.
7. Memorandum of an interview between Political Secretary Major Neal and B. J. Glancy, 4 October 1925, File No. 19-P/1925.
8. That this term was then not used 'with reference to the particular circumstances of the present case' was made clear by the Resident to Hari Singh in a private meeting—From John Wood, 18 October 1925, File No. 19-P/1925.
9. Hari Singh's Kharita, 14 October 1925, File No. P-19(10)/1925.
10. Telegram, First Assistant to Resident, 28 September 1925, File No. P-19(10)/1925.
11. Telegram, Resident, 18 October 1925, File No. P-19/1925.
12. Telegram, To Resident, 7 October 1925, File No. 19(10)-P/1925.
13. Note by J. P. Thompson, 5 October 1925, File No. 19-P/1925; see also Telegram to Secretary of State, 5 October 1925, File No. 19(10)-P/1925.
14. A. Lamb. *Kashmir: A Disputed Legacy, 1864–90* (London: Roxford Books, 1964).
15. Foreign. Sec. Nos. 1–17, Mar. 1921; Note by J. P. Thompson, 26 September 1925, File No. 19-P/1925.
16. S. M. Abdullah. *The Blazing Chinar* (Kashmir: Gulshan Books, 2016).
17. Bruno De Cordier. 'International Aid, Frontier Securitization and Social Engineering: Soviet-Xinjiang Development Cooperation During the Governorate of Sheng Shicai (1933–44)'. *Central Asian Affairs*, 3 (2016) pp. 49–76.
18. K. P. S. Menon. *Delhi-Chungking: A Travel Diary* (India: Oxford University Press, 1947).
19. W. Brown. *Gilgit Rebellion* (UK: Pen & Sword Military, 2014).
20. 'Maharaja Hari Singh'. *Daily Excelsior*. 24 August 2014. http://www.dailyexcelsior.com/maharaja-hari-singh/
21. D. Hiro. *The Longest August: The Unflinching Rivalry Between India and Pakistan* (USA: Nation Books, 2015).
22. A. Lamb. *Kashmir: A Disputed Legacy, 1864–90* (London: Roxford Books, 1964).
23. W. Brown. *Gilgit Rebellion* (UK: Pen & Sword Military, 2014).

Chapter 3: Emerging Ripples

1. J. Korbel. *Danger in Kashmir* (Princeton: Princeton University Press, 1966).
2. A. Lamb. *Kashmir: A Disputed Legacy, 1864–90* (London: Roxford Books, 1991).

3. *Tibet, Government of India Policy; Military Aid to Tibet, September 1945–May 1946.* Original File No.: L/WS/1/1042 File WS.17058.
4. A. Lamb. *The China India Border: The Origins of the Disputed Boundaries* (London: Oxford University Press, 1964).
5. P. Brobst. *The Future of the Great Game: Sir Olaf Caroe, India's Independence and the Defense of Asia* (Ohio: Akron University Press, 2005).
6. Z. Chaudhary. 'A tribute to Heritage of Poonch.' *Counter Currents.* 26 October 2006. https://www.countercurrents.org/kashmir-choudhary261006.htm
7. W. Brown. *Gilgit Rebellion* (UK: Pen & Sword Military, 2014).
8. R. Ankit. 'By George: The Cunningham Contribution'. *Epilogue.* 4 (3) 2010) pp. 33–35.
9. W. Brown. *Gilgit Rebellion* (UK: Pen & Sword Military, 2014).
10. The two-nation theory is the basis of creation of Pakistan. It argues that Muslims and Hindus belong to two separate nations. Therefore, Muslims should be able to have their own separate land in the Muslim majority areas of India. The two-nation theory gained currency after the Pakistan Resolution of March 1941 passed in Lahore at the All India Muslim League meeting.

Chapter 4: Swelling Crests

1. D. Duncan. *Mutiny in the RAF: The Air Force Strikes of 1946* (Socialist History Society Occasional Papers, Series No. 8, 1998).
2. R. Specter. 'The Royal Indian Navy Strike of 1946.' *Armed Forces and Society.* 7#2, pp. 271–84.
3. G. D. Bakshi. *Bose, An Indian Samurai : Netaji and the INA, A Military Assessment.* (New Delhi: K. W. Publishers Pvt. Ltd., 2016).
4. R. J. Moore. *Making the New Commonwealth* (UK: Clarendon Press, 2016).
5. C. Bell and B. Ellemen, eds. *Naval Mutinies of the Twentieth Century: An International Perspective* (London: Routledge, 2003).
6. L. Zuckerman. *Earl Mountbatten of Burma, KG, OM 25 June 1900–27 August 1979* (Biographical Memoirs of Fellows of the Royal Society, 1981).
7. J. Colville. *Winston Churchill and His Inner Circle* (New York: Wyndham Books, 1981).
8. A. Lamb. *Kashmir: A Disputed Legacy, 1864–90* (London: Roxford Books, 1991).
9. H. T. Lin. *Tibet and Nationalist China's Frontier: Intrigues and Ethnopolitics, 1928–49* (British Columbia: Contemporary Chinese Studies Series, UBC, 2011).
10. D. Marston. *The Indian Army and the End of the Raj* (New York: Cambridge University Press, 2014).
11. A. Whitehead. *A Mission to Kashmir* (New Delhi: Penguin Global, 2008).
12. W. Brown. *Gilgit Rebellion* (UK: Pen & Sword Military, 2014).
13. Ibid.
14. R. Ankit. 'By George: The Cunningham Contribution'. *Epilogue.* 4 (3), 2010.
15. W. Brown. *Gilgit Rebellion* (UK: Pen & Sword Military, 2014).
16. John W. Cell. 'Review: White Mutiny: British Military Culture in India by Peter Stanley.' *The American Historical Review.* Vol. 104, No. 3. (June 1999) pp. 888–89.

17. O. P. Sharma. 'Gandhi's Only Kashmir Visit'. *Kashmir Life*. 2 October 2017. https://kashmirlife.net/gandhis-only-kashmir-visit-152254/
18. Z. Hasan. *The Times And Trial of the Rawalpindi Conspiracy, 1951: The First Coup Attempt in Pakistan* (Karachi: Oxford University Press, 1998).
19. C. Bell and B. Ellemen, eds. *Naval Mutinies of the Twentieth Century: An International Perspective* (London: Routledge, 2003).
20. A. Ishtiyaq. *The Garisson State: Origins, Evolution, Consequences (1947–2011)* (Pakistan: Oxford University Press, 2013).
21. C. C. Trench. *The Frontier Scouts* (New Delhi: Rupa Publications, 1985).
22. N. Hajari. *Midnight's Furies: The Deadly Legacy of India's Partition.* (USA: Houghton Mifflin Harcourt, 2015).
23. V. Schofield. *Kashmir in Conflict: India, Pakistan and the Unending War* (London: I. B. Tauris, 2003).

Chapter 5: Lashing Waves

1. A. Lamb. *Kashmir: A Disputed Legacy, 1864–90* (London: Roxford Books, 1991).
2. K. Singh. *Heir Apparent: An Autobiography* (London: Oxford University Press, 1983).
3. A. Lamb. *Kashmir: A Disputed Legacy, 1864–90* (London: Roxford Books, 1991).
4. Ibid., pp. 121.
5. H. Husain. 'Pak Tribal Areas...' *Improveacrati*. 26 February 2018. https://improveacrati.wordpress.com/2018/02/26/prelude-to-indo-pak-war-1947-48/
6. O. Ali. '16th Light Cavalry. A Historic Picture and an Anecdote from Kashmir'. *Brown Pundits*. 30 May 2017. https://www.brownpundits.com/2017/05/30/16th-light-cavalry-a-historic-picture-and-an-anecdote-from-kashmir/
7. Brig. S. Bhattacharya. *Nothing But!* (India: Partridge, 2013).
8. S. N. Prasad and P. Dharm. *Operations in Jammu and Kashmir 1947–48* (New Delhi: Thomas Press, 1987).
9. S. M. Abdullah. *The Blazing Chinar* (Kashmir: Gulshan Books, 2016).
10. S. N. Prasad and P. Dharm. *Operations in Jammu and Kashmir 1947–48* (New Delhi: Thomas Press, 1987).
11. K. S. Bajwa. *Jammu and Kashmir War (1947–48) Political and Military Perspective, Military Affairs Series* (New Delhi: Har-Anand Publications Pvt. Ltd., 2003).
12. M. Y. Effendi. *Punjab Cavalry: Evolution, Role, Organisation and Tactical Doctrine 11 Cavalry, Frontier Force, 1849–1971* (Karachi: Oxford University Press, 2007).
13. M. I. Khan. *The Kashmir Saga.* (Mirpur: Vering, 1965).
14. J. Bhagyalakshmi ed. *Capital Witness: Selected Writings of G. K. Reddy* (New Delhi: Allied Publishers, 1991).
15. S. M. Abdullah. *The Blazing Chinar* (Kashmir: Gulshan Books, 2016).
16. K. Singh. *Heir Apparent: An Autobiography* (London: Oxford University Press, 1983).
17. W. Brown. *Gilgit Rebellion* (UK: Pen & Sword Military, 2014).

18. Ibid.
19. R. Singh. *Major Defence Operations Since 1947* (India: Prabhat Books, 2010).
20. W. Brown. *Gilgit Rebellion* (UK: Pen & Sword Military, 2014).

Chapter 6: Temperamental Tides

1. S. M. Abdullah. *The Blazing Chinar* (Kashmir: Gulshan Books, 2016).
2. R. Ankit. *Kashmir, 1945–66: From Empire to the Cold War*. Unpublished PhD thesis: University of Southampton, 2014.
3. S. M. Abdullah. *The Blazing Chinar* (Kashmir: Gulshan Books, 2016).
4. A. Lamb. *Kashmir: A Disputed Legacy, 1864–90* (London: Roxford Books, 1991).
5. P. N. Bazaz. *The History of Struggle for Freedom in Kashmir* (New Delhi: Kashmir Publishing Company, 1954) pp. 120–22.
6. A. Lamb. *Kashmir: A Disputed Legacy, 1864–90* (London: Roxford Books, 1991).
7. Memoirs of Sir Olaf Caroe, MSS Eur C273, Caroe Papers, IOR, p. 106; also see, P. Brobst. *The Future of the Great Game: Sir Olaf Caroe, India's Independence and the Defense of Asia* (Ohio: Akron University Press, 2005).
8. Speech by Cunningham (8/1244) 3 June 1946, Speech by Caroe (8/1498) 4 February 1948, RIIA.
9. 15th Meeting of the Defence Committee, MD1/D43, Mountbatten Papers, 20 November 1947, CB 6(15)/47.
10. Lockhart to ACB Symon, File No. 8310-154-77 to 105, 18 December 1947, Lockhart Papers, NAM.
11. Bucher to Baldev Singh, File No. 19 – Part I, BN Rau Papers (I Instalment), 17 November 1947, NMML and Bucher to Elizabeth Bucher, File No. 7901-87-6-1, 24 September 1948, Bucher Papers, NAM.
12. See Cunningham's diary, MSS Eur D670/6 and Cunningham to Caroe, MSS Eur F 164/19, 2 April 1948, IOR; also see R. Ankit, 'The Cunningham Contribution', *Epilogue* (Volume 4, Issue 3), March 2010; also see DO 142/494, TNA and (No. KR-456), First Series, Volume IX, 8 December 1947, Jinnah Papers.
13. Short to States Ministry, MB1/D240 (Folder 1), 17 October 1947; for Nehru's complaint against Mudie, see letter to Mountbatten dated 7 October 1947, MB1/D241, Mountbatten Papers.
14. Mountbatten-Elmhirst meeting, MB1/D80 (Folder 1), 28 May 1948, Mountbatten Papers.
15. Bucher-Mountbatten meeting, MB1/D78 (Folder 1), also see MB1/D216, 10 April 1948, Mountbatten Papers.
16. CRO to New York, T. No. 2569, L/WS/1/1152; G 2275/30, L/WS/1/1142, 8 and 18 June 1948, IOR.
17. Shone to CRO, T. No. 1804, L/WS/1/1142, 9 June 1948, IOR.
18. 11 June 1948, Shone to CRO, T. No. 1844, L/WS/1/1142, 9 June 1948, IOR; also see MB1/D272, Mountbatten Papers and Dasgupta, War and Diplomacy, pp. 151–54.
19. Pol Ext 16232/48, FO 371/69719, 14–16 June 1948, TNA.
20. Elmhirst to Bucher, 23 June 1948, Bucher to Patel, Subject File 19-Pt I (1947–48), 24 June 1948, Rau Papers.
21. Grafftey-Smith to Carter (CRO), S/41, DO 133/80, 23 June 1948, TNA.

22. Gracey to Elmhirst, ELMT 3/1, Elmhirst Papers, 21 June 1948, CAC.
23. Grafftey-Smith to CRO, T. No. 161, PREM 8/801, 15 July 1948, TN.
24. Speech by Messervy at the RIIA (Ref. 8/1558), 25 June 1948, Chatham House.
25. Bucher to H.M. Patel and T.W. Elmhirst, File No. 19 – Part I, BN, 24 June 1948, Rau Papers (I Instalment), NMML and 13 December 1948, Bucher to Elizabeth Bucher, File No. 7901-87-6-1, Bucher Papers, NAM.
26. Shone to CRO, T. No. 2247, L/WS/1/1142, 12 July 1948, IOR.
27. CRO to Grafftey-Smith, 17132/111, PREM 8/801, 6 July 1948, TNA.
28. CRO to Shone, T. No. 1186, PREM 8/801, 16 July 1948, TNA.
29. PIN/21/48, 28 June 1948; Grafftey-Smith sent this to Carter (CRO) on 9 July 1948, S/24, DO 142/429, TNA.
30. Gracey to Bucher, File No. 7901-87-6-2, 30 October 1948, NAM; also see R. Ankit, 'The Defiant Douglas', *Epilogue* (Volume 4, Issue 1), January 2010.
31. Mudie to Maurice Hallett, MSS Eur D 714/84, Mudie Papers, 11 November 1948, IOR.
32. MSS Eur F 164/12, MSS Eur F 164/48, IOR; also see, R. Ankit. 'Whose was Kashmir to be?', *Epilogue* (Volume 4, Issue 10), 2010.
33. Mudie to Hallett, MSS Eur D 714/84, Mudie Papers, 22 February 1950, IOR 61 Speech by W. J. Cawthorn at the RIIA (8/1575), 28 September 1948, Chatham House.
34. File No. 7901-87-6-3, Bucher Papers, January 1951, NAM; also see R. Ankit, 'Right Man in the Wrong Place', *Epilogue* (Volume 4, Issue 7), July 2010.

Chapter 7: Stormy Seas

1. A. Lamb. *Kashmir: A Disputed Legacy, 1864–90* (London: Roxford Books, 1991)
2. Ibid.
3. R. Ankit. *Kashmir, 1945–66: From Empire to the Cold War.* Unpublished PhD thesis: University of Southampton, 2014.
4. K. Singh. *Heir Apparent: An Autobiography* (London: Oxford University Press, 1983).
5. Ibid.
6. 6 July 1949, TASS report on India, Fond 82, Opis 2, No. 1208, Molotov Papers, RGASPI.
7. DO 133/138 and DO 133/185; Iyengar to William Strang, January 1949, STRN 2/5, Strang Papers, CAC.
8. 5 March 1949, PIN/8/49 and 14 June 1949, PIN/20/49, Reed to Oliver, DO 142/528, TNA.
9. Noel-Baker to Attlee, 12 July 1949, 76/49, DO 142/536.
10. 28 June, 5 and 12 July 1949, PIN/22/49 and S/24, Reed to Oliver, DO 142/528.
11. 6 December 1950, CIA-CREST Records NARA-II
12. 24 January 1951 (Box 63, Folder Kashmir), Office Files of Harry Howard, 1945–60 (Entry A1 1291) (Lot 61D214) RG 59, NARA-II.
13. 10 January 1951, FO 371/92863, TNA.
14. 22 January 1951, Memo on "problems of military assistance" submitted by Military Attaché of American Embassy, New Delhi (Box 4, Folder New Delhi Documents, 1951), (Entry A1 1534; Regional Conferences and

Country Files, Bureau of Near-Eastern and South-Asian Affairs, 1951–55 (RG 59), NARA-II.
15. 13 March 1951, Combined letter from C-in-C NELM and C-in-C, ME to the UK CoS and the US JCS, MIL/3039/ME and 6 April 1951, Shinwell to Gordon-Walker, DO 35/3008, TNA .
16. 9 July 1951, State Department Memo, CDF (1950–54) Box 2998 (690 D.91) RG 59, NARA-II.
17. 14 July 1951, Acheson to Karachi/Delhi, CDF (1950–54) Box 2998 (690 D.91), 19 July 1951 (Box 14, Folder 1, 1950–51), Office of UN Political and Security Affairs, 1945–57 Subject Files (Lot 58D742 and 59D237).
18. 31 July 1951, Norman Cousins to B.N. Rau, Subject File Serial No. 27, Rau Papers (I and II Instalments).
19. 14 February 1949, 'Communism in Kashmir', SDR (India: Internal Affairs, 1945–49, Part I – reel 14).
20. 4 February 1952, Paris to FO, No. 78, FO 371/101203, TNA.
21. 22 January 1952, FO's note, FO 371/10121, TNA.
22. 17 January 1952, Selwyn Lloyd to FO, No. 32, FO 371/10121, TNA.
23. 31 January 1952, No. 5781, P. Chaudhry and Vanduzer-Snow, eds. *The United States and India: A History Through Archives – The Formative Years* (New Delhi: Sage and ORF, 2008), p. 468.
24. A. Lamb. *Kashmir: A Disputed Legacy, 1864–90* (London: Roxford Books, 1991).
25. R. Rohmetra. 'A Tribute to Mukherjee'. *Daily Excelsior*. 23 June 2013. http://www.dailyexcelsior.com/a-tribute-to-mookerjee/
26. 24 November 1952, Abdullah to Singh, 3395/PRS, Subject File 114, JJ Singh Papers (I and II Instalments).
27. 10 September 1952, OCI No. 8871, CIA-CREST Records (accessed on 26 August 2013), NARA-II.
28. 3 July 1952, CRO's Memorandum on 'position of Sheikh Abdullah', DO 35/6650, TNA.
29. 7 November 1952, Information Report, CIA-CREST Records (accessed on 26 August 2013), NARA-II.
30. K. Singh. *Heir Apparent: An Autobiography* (London: Oxford University Press, 1983).
31. Ibid.
32. Ibid.
33. S. Raghavan. *War and Peace in Modern India* (UK: Palgrave Macmillan, 2010).
34. 2–4 May 1953, Box 441, Folder 5 (Walter Johnson Tape Transcripts), Stevenson Papers.
35. 25 April 1961, Pandit to Kaul, Correspondence File, Pandit Papers .
36. 26 May 1953, Stevenson to George Allen, Box 2, Folder 13, Stevenson Papers .
37. 4 and 21 August 1953, Allen to Adlai, Box 2, Folder 13, Stevenson Papers.
38. 23 August 1953, Stevenson to Allen, Box 2, Folder 13, Stevenson Papers .
39. 28 June 1954, Mehta to Nehru, No. 93-A/54, Subject File Serial No. 1, Mehta Papers (III and IV Instalments).
40. 6 March 1953, IB report D1507-K/53, File No. 8/15-K/51 (MOS, Kashmir), NAI .
41. File Nos. F 8 (9)-K/54 and 18 (7)-K/54 (GOI, MOS, Kashmir), NAI .

42. 25 February 1953, B. P. L. Bedi's talk with N. Pastukhov, report of the talk was sent to Moscow on 16 March and was forwarded to Molotov and Grigoriyan on 7 April, Fond 5, Opis 28, No. 94 (Reel 22, 5094), RGANI.

Chapter 8: Emerging Abyss

1. R. Ankit. *Kashmir, 1945–66: From Empire to the Cold War*. Unpublished PhD thesis: University of Southampton, 2014.
2. S. M. Bajwa. 'Gen. Nath's Recee in Aksai Chin'. *Hindustan Times*. 22 January 2013. https://www.hindustantimes.com/chandigarh/gen-nath-s-recce-in-aksai-chin/story-Uhf9oNAzdHjgN9K0J2JCTK.html
3. A. Parthasarthi. 'Chinese Perfidy'. *Mainstream Weekly*. 5 May 2018. http://www.mainstreamweekly.net/article7931.html
4. The Baghdad Pact was a defensive organisation for promoting shared political, military and economic goals, founded in 1955, by Turkey, Iraq, Great Britain, Pakistan and Iran. The main purpose of the Baghdad Pact was to prevent communist incursions and foster peace in the Middle East. It was renamed the Central Treaty Organization, or CENTO, in 1959 after Iraq pulled out of the Pact.
5. SEATO was an international organisation for collective defence in Southeast Asia created by the Southeast Asia Collective Defense Treaty, or Manila Pact, signed in September 1954 in Manila, Philippines.
6. M. Afridi. 'Searching Friends and Strengthening Security: Pak-China Relations in 1950s'. *International Journal of Social Science Studies*. 3. 10.11114/ijsss.v3i2.699. 2015.
7. B. Riedel. *JFK's Forgotten Crisis: Tibet, the CIA, and the Sino-Indian War* (New York: Harper Collins, 2015).
8. K. Singh. *Heir Apparent: An Autobiography* (London: Oxford University Press, 1983).
9. V. Ahuja. *Military Perspective: Genesis of the Sino-Indian Border Dispute—The Konkgka La incident*. PhD Thesis: Auburn University, 2011. https://www.slideshare.net/VivekAhuja1/kongka-la-incident-7421863
10. A. Shahi. 'A Historical Watershed'. *Dawn*. 14 May 2005. https://www.dawn.com/news/1067837
11. A. Lamb. *Kashmir: A Disputed Legacy, 1864–90* (London: Roxford Books, 1991).
12. P. Swami. *India, Pakistan and the Secret Jihad: The Covert War in Kashmir, 1947–2004* (London: Routledge, 2006).
13. F. A. Rao. Making of Al'Fatah Kashmir Armed Resistance. 10.13140/2.1.4459.2968. (2012).

Chapter 9: Deep Waters

1. W. Habibullah. *My Kashmir: The Dying of the Light* (London: Penguin Books Limited, 2014).
2. P. Swami. 'India- Summertime? Reflections on the Peace Process in J&K'. *South Asian Intelligence Review*. Volume 3, 2004.
3. K. Santhanam et al. *Jihadis in Jammu and Kashmir: A Portrait Gallery* (New Delhi: Sage, 2003) pp. 87–89.

4. H. Haqqani ed. *Pakistan: Between Mosque and Military* (London: Penguin Books Limited, 2016).
5. R. Wirsing. *Pakistan's Security Under Zia* (London: Macmillan, 1991).
6. W. Habibullah. *My Kashmir: The Dying of the Light* (London: Penguin Books Limited, 2014).
7. A. Bhattacharjea. *Kashmir: The Wounded Valley* (New Delhi: UBSPD, 1994).
8. P. Swami. 'Tackling Terror'. *Frontline*. 9 May 1998. https://frontline.thehindu.com/static/html/fl1510/15100650.htm
9. R. Vinayak. 'Governor of Punjab Surendra Nath dies in plane crash'. *India Today*. 31 July 1994. https://www.indiatoday.in/magazine/indiascope/story/19940731-governor-of-punjab-surendra-nath-dies-in-plane-crash-809425-1994-07-31
10. A. S. Dulat. 'The Problem'. *Seminar Magazine*, #709, 2018.
11. A. G. Noorani. 'Questions about the Kashmir Ceasefire'. *Economic and Political Weekly*. Vol. 35, No. 45, 2000.
12. C. C. Fair. *Fighting to the End: The Pakistan Army's Way of War*. (London: Oxford University Press, 2014).
13. Zhongguo or the Middle Kingdom or Middle Country is the Mandarin name for China. It dates back to 1000 BC when land was designated to the Chou Empire, on the North China Plain. The Chou people, unaware of high civilisations in the West, believed their empire occupied the middle of the earth, surrounded by barbarians.

Chapter 10: Rising Tsunami

1. 'China Turns Most Powerful US and UK Destroyers into Tin Cans'. YouTube, uploaded by Report Pravada, 28 November 2016, https://www.youtube.com/watch?v=wq7KVvzLXic
2. S. Faal. 'Most Expensive US-UK Warships Ever Built Lay "Dead In Water" Due To China Chip Destroyer'. *The Unhived Mind News*. 26 November 2016. https://theunhivedmind.com/news/2016/11/25/most-expensive-us-uk-warships-ever-built-lay-dead-in-water-due-to-china-chip-destroyer/
3. W. Thomas. 'Faulty Chips Could Cripple U.S. Attack On Iran-FLASHBACK TO 2007'. *The Unhived Mind News*. 25 November 2016. http://theunhivedmind.com/news/2016/11/25/faulty-chips-could-cripple-u-s-attack-on-iran/
4. D. Nidess. 'Don't Trust the Chinese to Make Microchips for the Military'. *Wall Street Journal*. 26 October 2017. https://www.wsj.com/articles/dont-trust-the-chinese-to-make-microchips-for-the-military-1509059023
5. P. W. Singer and C. August. *Ghost Fleet: A Novel of the Next World War* (Boston: Houghton Mifflin Harcourt, 2015).
6. B. Krebs. 'Supply Chain Security is the Whole Enchilada, But Who's Willing to pay for it?' *Krebs on Security*. 5 October 2018. https://krebsonsecurity.com/2018/10/supply-chain-security-is-the-whole-enchilada-but-whos-willing-to-pay-for-it/
7. R. Jordan and R. Michael. 'The Big Hack: How China Used a Tiny Chip to infiltrate U.S. Companies'. *Bloomberg*. 4 October 2018. https://www.bloomberg.com/news/features/2018-10-04/the-big-hack-how-china-used-a-tiny-chip-to-infiltrate-america-s-top-companies

8. '8 Things You Should Know About Water and Semiconductors'. *China Water Risk*. 11 July 2013. http://www.chinawaterrisk.org/resources/analysis-reviews/8-things-you-should-know-about-water-and-semiconductors/
9. J. Horwitz. 'Why the Semiconductor Is Suddenly at the Heart of US-China Tech Tensions'. *Quartz*. 24 July 2018. https://qz.com/1335801/us-china-tech-why-the-semiconductor-is-suddenly-at-the-heart-of-us-china-tensions/
10. M. Osborn. 'GCL-Poly to Expand new Xinjiang Polysilicon Production Plant to 60,000MT'. *PVTech*. 29 October 2018. https://www.pv-tech.org/news/gcl-poly-to-expand-new-xinjiang-polysilicon-production-plant-to-60000mt
11. S. Shiv. 'Chinese Roads and Infrastructure in Aksai Chin—A Google Earth Study'. *Defence Forum India*. https://defenceforumindia.com/chinese-roads-infrastructure-aksai-chin-1978
12. V. Phan, R. Lindenbergh and M. Menenti. 'Geometric Dependency of Tibetan Lakes on Glacial Runoff. Hydrology and Earth System Sciences'. 10. 729–68. 10.5194/hessd-10-729-2013.
13. R. Vats. 'Is China's Road in Kashmir's Shaksgam Valley a Threat to India?' *Swarajya*. 5 May 2018. https://swarajyamag.com/defence/is-chinas-road-in-kashmirs-shaksgam-valley-a-threat-to-india2?utm_content=buffercac5eandutm_medium=socialandutm_source=twitter.comandutm_campaign=buffer.
14. 'Detailed Satellite Map of Karakoram Pass'. 2019. http://www.maphill.com/search/karakoram-pass/detailed-satellite-map/
15. M. Rankl, S. Vijay, C. Kienholz and M. Braun. 'Glacier Changes in the Karakoram Region Mapped by Multi-mission Satellite Imagery'. *The Cryosphere Discussions*. 7. 4065-4099. 10.5194/tcd-7-4065-2013. https://www.researchgate.net/figure/Overview-map-of-the-Karakoram-Range-The-orange-line-indicates-the-delineation-of-the_fig8_260965568
16. M. Z. Ispahani. *Roads and Rivals: The Political Uses of Access in the Borderlands of Asia* (USA: Cornell University Press, 2015).
17. J. Summers. 'Traveling China's Karakoram Highway—Traveler's Guide'. *Farwest China*. 16 July 2017. https://www.farwestchina.com/travel/karakoram-highway-china-guide/
18. H. Alifu, Y. Hirabayashi, B. A. Johnson, J. Vuillaume, A. Kondoh and M. Urai. 'Inventory of Glaciers in the Shaksgam Valley of the Chinese Karakoram Mountains, 1970–2014'. *Remote Sensing*. 10(8), 1166; doi:10.3390/rs10081166
19. C. Arpi. 'The Aksai Chin Blunder'. *Claude Arpi*. 1 February 2017. http://claudearpi.blogspot.com/2017/02/the-aksai-chin-blunder.html
20. M. S. Sondhi. 'The India-China-Tibet Triangle'. *Mainstream Weekly*. 23 December 2018. http://www.mainstreamweekly.net/article8449.html
21. Brig. V. Anand. 'Nehru Era's Defence and Security Policies and Their Legacy'. 2014. https://www.vifindia.org/sites/default/files/nehru-era-s-defence-and-security-policies-and-their-legacy.pdf
22. J. D. Ives, R. B. Shrestha and P. K. Mool. 'Formation of Glacial Lakes in the Hindu Kush-Himalayas and GLOF Risk Assessment'. Report submitted to International Centre for Integrated Mountain Development, Kathmandu, 2010.

23. The Water Centre. 'The Impact of Ice: Glacial Studies in the Karakoram'. *The University of Utah*. 2 August 2018. https://water.utah.edu/2018/08/02/the-impact-of-ice-glacial-studies-in-the-karakoram/
24. G. Rahul, Q. Chaudhry and A. Mahmood. 'Glaciers and Glacial Lakes under Changing Climate in Pakistan'. 2019.
25. S. N. A. Gilany and Dr J. Iqbal. 'Geospatial Analysis of Glacial Dynamics in Shigar and Shyok Basins'. Unpublished research paper: Institute of Geographical Information System, National University of Science and Technology, Islamabad, Pakistan, 2016.
26. C. Arpi. 'The Aksai Chin Blunder'. *Claude Arpi*. 1 February 2017. http://claudearpi.blogspot.com/2017/02/the-aksai-chin-blunder.html
27. R. Kattelman and T. Watanabe. 'Draining Himalayan Glacial Lakes Before They Burst'. Presented at Destructive Water: Water-caused Natural Disasters, Their Abatement And Control Conference held at Anaheim, California, June 1996.
28. M. Yahuda. 'China and the Kashmir crisis'. *BBC*. 2 June 2002. http://news.bbc.co.uk/2/hi/south_asia/2020788.stm
29. S. Goldenberg. 'Glacier Lakes: Growing Danger Zones in the Himalayas'. *The Guardian*. 10 October 2011. https://www.theguardian.com/environment/2011/oct/10/glacier-lakes-melt-himalayas
30. International Crisis Group. *Kashmir: Confrontation and Miscalculation*. (Belgium: International Crisis Group, 2002).
31. C.A. Brebbia. *Water and Society II* (Boston: WIT Press, 2013).
32. M. Jaleel. 'Fake Encounter at LoC: 3 Arrested, Probe Ordered'. *Indian Express*, 24 November 2011. http://archive.indianexpress.com/news/fake-encounter-at-loc-3-arrested-probe-ordered/626105
33. T. Bhat. 'Braving Harsh Weather, Pakistani Shelling: How India built Kishenganga Project'. *The Week*, 19 June 2018. https://www.theweek.in/news/india/2018/05/19/how-india-built-kishenganga-power-project-near-loc.html
34. A. Tarapore. 'Along the Karakoram Highway: A Photo Essay (Part 1)'. *Lowy Institute*. 2 August 2016. https://www.lowyinstitute.org/the-interpreter/along-karakoram-highway-photo-essay-part-1
35. S. Dharmadhikary. 'Mountains of Concrete—Dam Building in the Himalayas'. Report submitted to International Rivers, California, 2008.
36. J. Gupta. 'Indus Cascade: A Himalayan Blunder'. *Eco-Business*. 25 May 2017. https://www.eco-business.com/opinion/indus-cascade-a-himalayan-blunder/
37. J. Gupta. 'Going Ahead with the Indus Cascade Will Be a Himalayan Blunder'. *The Wire*. 24 May 2017. https://thewire.in/environment/indus-cascade-himalayan-blunder
38. 'Hizbul Mujahideen "Poster Boy" Burhan Wani Killed in Joint Encounter'. *Indian Express*. 28 July 2016. https://indianexpress.com/article/india/india-news-india/burhan-muzaffar-wani-hizbul-mujahideen-dead-killed-death-jk-2902044/
39. PTI. 'Curfew Lifted from Valley, One Killed in Clash in Sopore'. *Deccan Herald*. 31 August 2016. https://www.deccanherald.com/content/567874/curfew-lifted-valley-one-killed.html/

40. S. Yasir. 'Kashmir Unrest: What Was the Real Death Toll in the State in 2016?' *FirstPost*. 22 April 2016. https://www.firstpost.com/india/kashmir-unrest-what-was-the-real-death-toll-in-the-state-in-2016-3183290.html
41. BBC News. 'Militants Attack Indian Army Base in Kashmir "Killing 17"'. *BBC*. 18 September 2016. https://www.bbc.com/news/world-asia-india-37399969
42. P. Sawhney. 'China Lists the Kashmir Conflict as its Top Priority'. *Force India*. 23 October 2017. http://forceindia.net/china-lists-kashmir-conflict-top-priority/
43. C. Arpi. 'China-Pakistan's Dam Projects in Gilgit-Baltistan Should Worry India'. *DailyO*. 11 June 2017. https://www.dailyo.in/politics/china-obor-cpec-gilgit-baltistan-indus-water-treaty-pakistan/story/1/17750.html
44. R. Kumar. 'What are Chinese flags Doing in Kashmir?' *Financial Express*. 19 October 2016. https://www.financialexpress.com/india-news/what-are-chinese-flags-doing-in-kashmir/423657/
45. M. S. Siyech. 'Salafism in India: Diversity and Challenges'. *Counter Terrorist Trends and Analysis*. Vol. 9, Issue 4. 2017.
46. K. Ahmed. 'The Power of the Ahle-Hadith'. *Hindu Vivek Kendra*. 12 July 2002. http://www.hvk.org/2002/0702/106.html
47. T. Mir. 'Kashmir: From Sufi to Salafi'. *Pulitzer Center*. 5 November 2012. https://pulitzercenter.org/reporting/kashmir-sufi-salafi
48. A. Karim. 'Wahhabism in South Asia'. *Indian Defence Review*. 13 September 2014. http://www.indiandefencereview.com/news/wahhabism-in-south-asia/
49. A. T. Singh. 'Here's How School of Faith, Mobiles Are Radicalising Kashmir'. *Times of India*. 18 July 2017. https://timesofindia.indiatimes.com/india/how-mosques-and-mobiles-are-radicalising-kashmir/articleshow/59507200.cms
50. A. K. Dubey. 'Jammu and Kashmir: Wahabi-controlled Mosques on the Rise, Security Forces Tightening Vigil'. *India Today*. 2 June 2017. https://www.indiatoday.in/mail-today/story/jammu-and-kashmir-wahabi-controlled-mosques-ahle-hadith-sufi-shrines-militancy-madarsas-980513-2017-06-02
51. A. Olly. 'Saudi Charities Pump in Huge Funds Through Hawala Channels to Radicalise the Valley'. *India Today*. 23 December 2011. https://www.indiatoday.in/magazine/special-report/story/20120102-saudi-charities-pump-in-funds-through-hawala-channels-to-radicalise-kashmir-valley-750136-2011-12-23
52. S. Jain. 'Controversial Texts, Mystery Funds: On The Trail of Saudi-Style Islam in India'. *NDTV*. 25 September 2016. https://www.ndtv.com/india-news/controversial-texts-mystery-funds-on-the-trail-of-saudi-style-islam-in-india-1466303
53. Y. Sikand. 'Islamist Militancy in Kashmir: The Case of the Lashkar-e-Taiba'. *The Practise of War: Production, Reproduction and Communication of Armed Violence* (New York: Berghahn Books, 2008).
54. H. Mir. 'Why Does India Consistently Push the (False) Narrative Of Radicalisation in Kashmir?' *Scroll*. 6 May 2017. https://scroll.in/article/836632/why-does-india-consistently-push-the-false-narrative-of-radicalisation-in-kashmir

55. A. Gupta. 'Countering Radicalization in Kashmir Valley'. *Indian Defence Review*. 3 December 2015. http://www.indiandefencereview.com/news/countering-radicalization-in-kashmir-valley/
56. M. Katju. 'I Suspect the Chinese Hand Behind Kashmiri Separatist Militancy'. *Huffington Post*. 11 December 2018. https://www.huffingtonpost.in/markandey-katju/the-chinese-hand-in-kashmiri-separatist-militancy_a_21431905/
57. I. Clover. 'GCL Partners with Adani for Solar PV Operations in India'. *PV Magazine*. 28 September 2015. https://www.pv-magazine.com/2015/09/28/gcl-partners-with-adani-for-solar-pv-operations-in-india_100021259/
58. Press Trust of India/UNI. 'Soft Bank Arm, Essel Group to Jointly Develop 500 MW Solar Park'. *Economic Times*. 31 October 2018. https://economictimes.indiatimes.com/industry/energy/power/softbank-arm-essel-group-to-jointly-develop-500-mw-solar-park/articleshow/66451918.cms
59. P. Tisheva. 'Essel, GCL Plan 5 GW Solar Manufacturing Hub in India's Andhra Pradesh'. *Renewables Now*. 15 January 2008. https://renewablesnow.com/news/essel-gcl-plan-5-gw-solar-manufacturing-hub-in-indias-andhra-pradesh-509278/

Index

A

Abbas, Chaudhry Ghulam, 35, 50
Abdullah, Farooq, 136–37
Abdullah, Sheikh, 21–23, 34–36, 42, 46, 50, 54, 56, 69, 75, 77–81, 89–93, 98–100, 102–8, 111, 131–32, 137, 145
   acclaimed secularism, 92
   accord with Indira Gandhi, 127, 131, 137
   agenda, 42
   ambition, 134
   emergency government, 90
   first taste of power, 80–81
   founder of National Conference, 23
   imprisonment, 22
   'leading light' of communism in administration, 97
   Naya Kashmir manifesto, 95
   political craftiness, 27
   political lineage of the Congress, 23
   release of, 77
   rise of, 21–23, 78
   single-point agenda, 95
   written vision for Kashmir, 92
Abdullah-Stevenson summit, 109
Accession, 69–70
Acheson, Dean, 100, 112
Afghan-Russia threat, 84
Afridi Battalion, 62
AFSPA, 141
Agrarian Reforms (Amendment) Act of 1978, 135
Ahl-e-Hadith, 166–68
Aksai Chin, 5, 9, 26, 111–13, 116–18, 154, 158
Alexander, 1–4, 8, 10
Al-Fatah, 124–31, 133–34, 143–44
   credibility and efficacy of, 126
   expansion plans, 126
   ideal location for new quarters, 126
   organisational structure of, 130
   political wing of, 130
   relevancy, 134
   training activities, 125

Al-Haramain Islamic Foundation, 166
All India Muslim League, 27
All Parties Hurriyat Conference, 142
Al-Qazi, Abdul Rehman, 166
Al-Safa, 141
Amarnath shrine, 172
Ambedkar, B. R., 98
Anglo-Afghan War, Second, 10
Anglo-American aggression against USSR, 96
Anglo-Russian Convention (1907), 13, 15
Anglo-Sikh War, 6–7
Anglo-Soviet Pact, 27
Anjuman-e-Nusrat-ul-Islam, 21
Ankit, Rakesh, 94, 96
Anti-India cries, 147
'Armed coexistence' policy of PLA, 117
Arpi, Claude, 111
Associated Press, 76
Attlee, Clement, 43, 45, 47, 49, 66, 82–83, 87–88, 96
Auchinleck, Field Marshal, 62
Ayyangar, Gopalaswami, 79, 98
Azad Kashmir, 38, 76, 78, 89, 166–67
  formation of, 39
Azhar, Masood, 122, 162

B

Bacon, Lt. Col. Roger, 40–42, 49–53, 55–56, 70–73
Bajwa, B. S., 67, 108
Bajwa, Jawed, 171
Baku, 16
Balakot, surgical air strike, 149, 170
Bandung Conference, 119
Bangladesh War, 124
Bannihal Pass tunnel, 93
Barelvi mosques, 167
Batku, Ashraf, 122
Batra, R. L., 59, 77
Battle of To-Yo, 5
Bedi, B. P. L., 97, 109
Beg, Mirza Afzal, 21, 27, 90, 97, 102, 134–35
Bevan, Aneurin, 86
Bhartiya Jana Sangh. *See* Jana Sangh
Bhat, Farooq, 130
Bhatt, Fayyaz Ahmad, 167
Bhutto, Zulfikar Ali, 114, 119, 132, 137
  dismissal of, 137
Big Landed Estates Abolition Act, 93
Blitz, 109
Bogra, Mohammad Ali, 119
Booth-capturing, 128
Border Action Team (BAT), 172

Bose, Rash Behari, 16
Bose, Subhash Chandra, 44–46
Breakdown in the public transport system, 43
Brigade, Tal, 61–62
British Cabinet Mission, 27
British East India Company, 3
British Joint Commission, 20
British policy, major objective of the, 46
British-Russian enmity, 16
Brown, Capt. William, 31–32, 34, 40
Brown, Maj., 51, 53, 56, 67, 70–72, 74
BSF, 123, 144–45
Buddhist Association of Ladakh, 103

C

Caroe, Sir Olaf, 37, 61, 82
Caucasus Indicus, 1
Cawthorn, Gen. W. J., 85, 119
Ceasefire, 88–89, 118, 120–21, 145, 148, 158–59
CENTO, 114, 116, 119, 158
Central Rule in Kashmir, 11–13
Charar-e-Sharief, 130, 145
Chashm-e-Shahi, 128
Chenab, control over the water of, 85
Chetty, R. K. S., 79
China
    Belt and Road Initiative, 154

card, 151–54
'chip destroyers', 152
cultural revolution, 155
encroachment in Ladakh, 112–17
friendship with Pakistan, 113
hunt for water, 154–59
incursion into Aksai Chin, 113, 155
interest in the Shaksgam Valley, 154–57
microchips, 152
National Integrated Circuits Industry Investment Fund, 153
relations with Pakistan, 161
Xinjiang, 172
Christ in Kashmir, 1–4
Churchill, Winston, 41, 45–46, 56, 63
Civil and Military Gazette, 76
Civil War, 15
Cobb, Lt. Col. E. H., 40
Cold war, 45–46
Communal tensions, 135, 140
Communism, 15, 44, 84–85, 95, 98, 101–2, 109, 158
Constitution of India, 91–92, 98–99, 103, 105, 136, 168
Article 6, 136
Article 35A, 173
Article 370, 98–99, 105; repeal of 173
Article 371, 91

Council of Regency, 11, 16
Council of State, 16, 18–19
Counter-insurgency, 141, 147
Counter-terrorism operations, 141
Crimean War of 1853–54, 15
Cunningham, George, 37, 40–41, 45, 47, 49, 52, 56, 61–62, 72–74, 84
Currie, Frederick, 28

D

Dar, Abdul Majid, 143
Dar, Abdul Rashid, 127–28, 130
Dehra Compass, 117
Delhi Accord, 102, 104, 106
Dhar, D. P., 102, 106, 108
Dhar, Shyam Sunder Lal, 77
Divide and rule, 37–39
Divided Muslim Opposition, 23–24
Dixon, Owen, 100, 105, 107
Dogra dynasty, 27, 94, 99, 105
Dogra logistics, 5
Dogra, G. L., 108
Dogra, Prem Nath, 38, 104, 106

E

East India Company, 6–7
Emergency evacuation orders, 66

F

Fake encounter by Indian Army, 160
The Far-flung Frontiers, 67
Farooq, Mirwaiz Umar, 160
First Kashmir War 1947–48, 67
First War of Independence in 1857, 8
Folklore, 2
Forward Policy, 117–20
Frontier Constabulary, 61, 68, 73
'Fundamentalist indoctrination', 167

G

Gandhi, Mahatma, 53–55
Gandhi, Indira, 127, 131, 132, 134, 136–37, 140
Gandhi, Rajiv, 137, 140–41
Ganga Ram, Wazir, 27
Gas scarcity, 43
Geelani, Syed Ali Shah, 137, 142, 160
Ghazali, Maulana Abdullah, 167
Gilgit Agency, 31–34, 40–42, 48, 50–52, 54, 56, 67, 70–72, 78, 80, 82–83, 88–89, 103, 113
    accession of, 32
Gilgit Scouts, 25, 32, 40, 51–52, 67, 71
Gilgit
    British consolidation, 31–34
    British preparation to snatch, 24–26
    control of, 39–42
    Pakistan's interest, 72–74
    Kashgar boundary, 37

Glancy Commission, 25
Glancy, B. J., 22, 26
Global depression, 25
Gracey, Lt. Gen. Douglas, 85
Great Trigonometrical
　Survey of India, 9
Guerrilla war, 70, 124–25
Gul, Gen. Hamid, 161

H

Habibullah, Wajahat, 133, 138
Haqqani, Husain, 139
Hasan, Shaikh Sadiq, 75
Hassnain, Fida, 2
Hawala, 167
Hazratbal crisis, 145
Hazratbal robbery, 129–31
Hebrew tradition, 2
Hindu-dominated
　government, 107
Hindu-German conspiracy
　of 1914–17, 16
Hindu Mahasabha, religious
　chauvinism of, 109
Hindustan Construction
　Company, 159
Hizb-ul-Mujahideen, 138,
　142–44, 163
Huawei, 153
Huq, A. K. Fazlul, 27
Husain, Musadaq, 124

I

Iftikharuddin, Mian, 67, 75
Ili rebels, 48

Imperialism, 16, 110
INA, 44, 67
*India, Pakistan and the Secret
　Jihad*, 121
Indian National Congress,
　85
Indian Penal Code, Section
　144, 172
Indira-Abdullah accord of
　1975, 131, 143
Indo-Pak talks on Kashmir,
　116
Indo-Pakistan war (1965),
　122
Indo-Pakistan war (1971),
　132
Indo-Pakistani military
　rapprochement, 113
Indus Waters Treaty, 154–55
Indus, control over the
　water of, 85
Infiltration, 39, 66, 135, 148
Inquilabi Mahaz,
　(Revolutionary Union),
　131
Instrument of Accession,
　60–61, 69, 77, 81, 83, 98,
　102
Inter-generational
　bitterness, 29
Invasion plan of Valley, 66
Irshad, Dawatul, 166
ISI, 85, 96, 119–20, 122,
　124–26, 131, 139, 144, 146,
　160–62, 166–69, 171

Islamia College robbery, 127
Ismay, Hastings, 41, 45–52, 55–56, 60, 63, 70, 72, 74, 83, 87
    treachery, 50–53
Ittehad-ul-Muslimeen, 137

J

Jagirdari, abolition of, 99
Jagmohan, 137, 140
    advice of imposing Governor's rule, 137
Jaish-e-Mohammed, 122, 158, 162–63, 170
Jama'at-ud-Dawa, 166
Jamaat Ahl-e-Hadith, 166
Jamaat-e-Islami, 135, 137
Jammu and Kashmir Public Safety Ordinance, 135
Jammu and Kashmir Resettlement Act of 1982, 136
Jana Sangh, 104, 133, 173
    religious chauvinism of, 109
Jhelum, control over the water of, 85
Jihad, 150, 161, 166
Jinnah, Mohammed Ali, 23, 27, 36, 47, 49–50, 52, 59, 66, 68, 75, 83, 90
    demand for Pakistan, 27
    visit to Srinagar, 36
JKLF, 142, 145, 160
Johnson, W. H., 9

K

Kabailis, invasion force of, 68
Kak, Ram Chandra, 35–39, 42, 46, 50, 52, 54–55, 58–59
Kalkat, Onkar Singh, 63–70
Karakoram Pass, 9, 26, 48, 156–57
Karanjia, Rusi, 109
Kargil War, 148, 157
Kashmir accord (1975), 134–36
Kashmir Conspiracy Case, 127
Kashmir Plan, 93
Kashmir Times, 75–76
Kashmiri Pandits, mass exodus of, 141
'Kashmiriyat', 3, 141
Katoch, Nishchant Chand, 55, 77
Kaul, B. M., 108
Kaul, Sir Hari Kishan, 21
Kayani, Gen. Ashfaq Parvez, 159
Kersten, Holger, 2
Khan, Abdul Ghaffar, 84, 129
Khan, Akbar, 68
Khan, Ayub, 113, 115–16, 120–21, 124
Khan, Imran, 171–72
Khan, Khan Abdul Qayyum, 52, 56–57, 61, 71, 75

Khan, Liaquat Ali, 66, 83, 96
Khan, Muhammad Ibrahim, 30, 34, 39, 42, 56, 67–68, 75–76, 78
Khan, Salim Jehangir, 125
Khan, Sher Ali, 10
Khan, Yulbar, 101
Khurshid, K. H., 75
Khyber Rifles, 62
Kiani, Maj. Zaman, 67
King George VI, 45
Kirkbride, Maj. G., 26
Kishenganga Dam, 159, 163
Kishenganga river, 159–65
Kitchloo, Bashir Ahmed, 122
Koh-e-Khizr, 31, 39, 52

L

Ladakh-Tibet trade mission, 106
Lahore Resolution, 23, 26–27
Lal Ded, 145
Lashkar-e-Taiba, 122, 142, 158, 166, 168
Lawrence, Henry, 6–7
Legislation to separate Ladakh from J&K, 173
'Light of the Faith', 3
Limbuwala (radio operator), 56
Listowel, Lord, 47
Lockhart, Rob, 84
Logistical tactics, 13

M

MacDonald, Sir Claude, 115
Madhok, Balraj, 104
Madrasas, 137
Mahajan, Mehr Chand, 65, 77
Majoritarianism, tyranny of, 173
Malakand Battalion, 62
Malik, Jacob, 101
Malik, Yasin, 145. *See also* JKLF
Malleson, Sir Wilfrid, 15
Manekshaw, Field Marshal, 67
Markaz-e-Jamiat Ahle-Hadith, 166
Masoodi, Maulana, 102
Master Cell, 121–22, 124–25, 131, 134, 143–44
transformation into Al-Fatah, 124–31
Mathieson, Jock, 40, 51–52, 72
Mayne, J. D., 14
Mazar-i-Sharif, 10
McCartney-MacDonald Line, 115
McMahon Line, 117
Mehta, G. L., 109
Menon, Krishna, 118
Menon, V. P., 69
Mersh, Allen, 101
Messervy, Lt. Gen. Sir Frank, 62

Militancy, 57, 124, 142, 147, 161, 170
Military intervention, 82
Mini-Pakistan, 104
Mir, Allama Sajid, 166
Mir, Ghulam Nabi, 129
Mir, Mohammad Yusuf, 130
Mirali, Mir Ali, 63
Mirza, Lt. Col. Iskander, 73
Mittha, Abdul Rahman, 75
Modi, Narendra, 148–49, 164–65, 171
Mohammad, Mirwaiz, 21–22, 35
  imprisonment, 22
  ultra-conservative religious mindset of, 23
  rise of, 21–23
Mohammed, Bakshi Ghulam, 90, 102, 106, 108, 132
Moi-e-Muqqadas (hair of Holy Prophet), 145. *See also* Hazratbal
Moinuddin, Ghulam, 138
Mookerjee, Shyama Prasad, 104, 108, 173
Mountbatten, Lord 45–54, 59–60, 69–71, 79–81, 83, 86
Mountbatten, Edwina, 50
Mudie, Sir Robert Francis, 84
Mujahideen, 120, 142, 166
Mukherjee, Abani, 16
Mullick, B. N., 106–7, 112

Murray, C. P., 63
Musharraf, 147–148, 158–59
Muslim Conference, 22–23, 35–36, 38–39, 58, 77, 90
  rising powers of the, 29
Muslim League, 23, 38, 56, 67
Muslim subjects, mobilisation and militarisation of, 29
My Kashmir: The Dying of the Light, 133
Mysore model, 91, 99

N

Narayan, Jayaprakash, 132
Nath, Surendra, 127, 144
National Cadet Corps, 123
National Conference, 23, 27, 35–38, 77, 90, 93–95, 100, 102, 105, 107, 109, 121, 126, 134–37, 143
National Defence Authorisation Act (US), 153
National Health Service, 44
National Herald, 109
National Hydroelectric Power Corporation (NHPC), 159
National Opposition conclave, 137
Naxalites, 125
Naya, or New, Kashmir proposals, 92

Nedou, Willi, 102
Neelum hydropower project, 159
Neelum project, 164
NEFA, 157
Nehru, Jawaharlal, 23, 35–36, 38, 46–47, 50, 53–54, 58–59, 66–67, 69–70, 75, 78–81, 83, 86–91, 94, 96, 102–4, 106–7, 109–10, 118, 154, 158
  disillusionment with Abdullah, 102–7
  friendship with Edwina Mountbatten, 50
  'Tryst with Destiny' speech, 58
Nisbet, Parry, 11
Noel-Baker, 87, 95
Noor, Uplift and Burj, 97
North Indus River Cascade, 162
Nund Rishi, 3
NWFP, 37, 40–41, 49, 52, 56, 61–62, 65, 68, 73, 75, 84, 167

O

Olson, Suzanne, 2
Operation Datta Khel, 68, 71, 81, 83
Operation Gibraltar, 120, 122, 125
Operation Grand Slam, 120

Operation Gulmarg, 56, 60, 63, 65, 68–69, 72–74, 78, 81
Operation Topac, 139–42, 140, 146, 167. *See also* Zia-ul-Haq
Opium War, First, 5

P

Pakistan: Between Mosque and the Military, 139
Palestinian Intifada, model of the, 147
Pamir Boundary Commission, 11
Panchsheel Agreement, 112–13
Partition, 3, 49, 52, 61–62, 82, 84, 126, 136, 154
Pastukhov, N., 109
Patel, Sardar Vallabhbhai, 53, 69, 79, 81–83, 90–91, 95
  outmanoeuvred, 82–83
Pathankot Air Force Station terror attack, 162
Pax Britannica, 41, 51, 70
'Peculiar diarchy', 90
Pir of Manki Sharif, 56–57, 61, 68, 75
Pishin Scouts, 62
Plebiscite, 69, 80–81, 83, 89, 99, 131
  principle of, 81
Plebiscite Front, 126–28, 133

Political mobilisation of Muslim, 22
Political polarisation, 38
Poonch
  confiscated by Sikh Empire, 39
  imbroglio, 28–31
  loss of autonomy, 39
Poonch-Muzaffarabad belt, 89
Powel, Richard, 55, 58
Praja Parishad, 100, 104, 106, 108
  agitation, 106, 108
  religious chauvinism of, 109
Presidential Proclamation, 173
Primogeniture, principle of, 14
Pro-*azaadi* demonstrations, 160, 164
Provincial Azad Jammu and Kashmir government, 68
Pulwama dacoity case, 125–26, 130
Pulwama terror attack, 149
Punjab Boundary Commission, 54–55

Q

Qadeer, Abdul, 21
Qadir, Manzur, 114
Qasim, Syed Mir, 102, 131, 133
Queen's Proclamation of 1858, 11
Quit Kashmir movement, 27, 35, 94, 142
Qureshi, Fazl-ul-Haq, 124, 126, 130, 134, 143

R

RAF mutiny (1946), 44, 51
Rai, Lt. Col. V. R., 79
Rajatarangini, 3
Rajendra Nath, 112
Rajiv-Farooq accord, 137
Rajya Hindu Sabha, 38
Rao, General Krishna, 144
Rathore, Zafar Iqbal, 123–24
Red Army, 167
Red Kashmir, 123
Red line of Partition, 41
Reddy, G. K., 76
Right-wing elements, 110
Ringzin, Chhewang, 103
Round Table Conference, London (1930), 21, 24
Roy, M. N., 16
Rozabal shrine, 2
RSS, 39, 104
Russian Civil War, 15
Russian Revolution of 1917, 15

S

Sadr-e-Riyasat, 103, 105, 107–8

Sadiq, G. M., 21, 90, 97, 102, 105, 110, 131
Said, Capt. M., 53
Salahuddin, Syed, 122, 138
Sanjeevi, T. G., 94
Sant Dev, Swami, 59
Saraf, Pandit Ram Lal, 107–8
Sarwar, Ghulam, 122. *See also* Master Cell
Sathe, R. D., 101
Sayeed, Hafiz, 122
Scott, Maj. Gen., 50–55, 58
SEATO, 114, 116, 119, 158
Security Council, 101
Shah, Amit, 173
Shah, G. M., 130–31, 136–37, 140
Shah, Shabir Ahmed, 160
Shah, Syed Mohammed Yusuf, 138
Shahadat, 166
Shahdad, Zahoor Ahmad, 123
Shimla Agreement, 132, 138
Shri Amarnath Shrine Board, 160
Siachen Glacier, 139, 151, 156–57
Sikh Empire, confiscation of Poonch, 28
Sikh governors, 5
Silk Route, 2
Singh, Amar, 14, 16, 19
  death, 16
  political ambitions, 14
Singh, Baldev, 29, 65–67, 79, 83
Singh, Dhyan, 4, 28, 30
Singh, Duleep, 6–7, 10
Singh, Ghansara, 53–54, 67, 71–72
Singh, Gulab, 4–8, 12, 14–15, 17, 27–29, 78–79, 82, 89, 103, 105
  complete autonomy over his own army, 4
  emergence of, 4–8
  independent sovereignty, 7
  role in the death of his brother Dhyan Singh, 28
  rule of, 9
  secret alliance with the British, 6
  tactical and strategic boost for the East India Company, 6
Singh, Harbaksh, 120
Singh, Hari, 14–22, 25, 27, 29–31, 33, 35, 38–39, 46, 48, 50, 53–58, 67, 76–78, 116
  accession to the throne, 21
  attitude towards the British, 31
  bitterness towards the British, 19
  create a constitution for the state, 22
  dilemma, 58
  endgame for, 76–80
  growing political ambitions, 25

imposition of constitution, 22
intent and actions of, 25
marginalisation policy, 29
Round Table Conference (1930), 25
under Pressure, 67–69
Singh, Hira, 6
Singh, Jagat Dev, 15, 18–19, 29–30, 34, 39, 78
death of, 38
Singh, Janak, 56, 58–59
Singh, Jawahar, 'treacherous conspiracy', 28
Singh, Karam, 116
Singh, Karan, 95–96, 99, 104–8
Singh, Kulwant, 65, 67
Singh, Manmohan, 147, 159
Singh, Pratap, 10–11, 13–15, 18–20, 29, 34, 78
Singh, Ranjit, 3–6, 22, 28
Singh, Moti, 28–29
Singh, Pratap, 10–11, 14–15, 17, 22, 25, 29, 34
erosion of powers, 13–17
loyalty of, 17
political freedoms, 22
Singh, Raja Amar, 11, 14–15, 29, 34
Singh, Raja Dhyan, 15, 28–29, 78
Singh, Ranbir, 8–11, 14, 28
Singh, Ratan Dev, 30
Singh, Sardar Baldev, 65–66, 79

Singh, Sher, 28
Singh, Shiv Ratandev, 38
Singh, Zorawar, 5
Sino-Indian relations, 114
Sino-Indian War of 1962, 120, 158
Sino-Pak alliance, 118
Sino-Pak Boundary Agreement (1963), 115, 157
Sino-Pak deal, 116, 154
Sino-Pak strategic and military calculus, 120–21
Sino-Pak syndicate, 170
Sino-Pak threat, 174
Sloan, Maj. R. E., 87
Socio-religious equations, 27
Standstill agreement, 49, 56, 59–61, 66, 70
Stevenson, Adlai, 109
Stone pelting, 147, 160
Struggle for the Throne, 18–23
Hari Singh's claim, 19
Raja Jagat Dev Singh's claim, 18
rules of succession of a natural heir, 18
Students' Federation (SF), 121
Students' Revolutionary Council, 123
Sufi traditions, 146
Sufism, 139, 145–46, 167
Suicide attacks, 148
Sultan dynasty, 3

Sunni Muslim, 2
Surgical strikes, 148–49, 163
Swami, Praveen, 121, 128, 130

T

Tajuddin, Malik, 76
Taliban, 171
Taseer, Muhammad Din, 75
Tashkent Agreement, 121
Tehreek al-Mujahideen, 166–67
Tehreek-ul-Mujahideen, 168
Templer Report, 88–89
Terrorist and Disruptive Activities (Prevention) Act, 143
Thapar, Gen. P. N., 65, 118
Transfer of power, 41, 44, 46–49, 51, 54, 56, 59, 61
  mechanics for, 27
Treachery in NWFP, 61–63
Treaty of Amritsar (1846), 7, 10–12, 28, 60, 78, 104
Treaty of Chushul, 5–6, 113
Treaty of Lahore, 7
Treaty of Nanjing, 5
Tribal Afghans or *Kabailis*, 65
Trump, Donald, 153, 171
Tucker, Lt. Gen. Sir Francis, 61
Turmoil in Valley, 26–28
Two-nation theory, 42, 81

U

Ummat-e-Islami, 137
UN resolution, 89

UN's Kashmir Observers, 97
UN-sponsored plebiscite proposals, 95
United Jihad Council, 161–62, 166
Uri terror attack, 148, 163
US mediation on Kashmir, 171
US Presidential elections, 171
US's withdrawal from Afghanistan, 171–172

V

Vajpayee, Atal Bihari, 147, 149, 158–59

W

Wahhabi Islam, 139, 146–50
Wahhabi madrasas, 167
Wahhabi-Salafi Nexus, 165–69
Wahhabisation of Islam, 166
Wahhabisation of state, 168
Wakefield, G. E. C., 21
Wakhan Corridor, 11
Wali, Sheikh Nur-ud-Din, 3, 145
Wani, Burhan, killing of, 163
Wani, Mohammad Aslam, 123, 127
Wani, Nazir Ahmad, 124, 126, 128, 130, 134
Watali, A. M., 53, 130
Watergate scandal, 132
Wavell, Lord, 36, 44
Welfare state, 43

Wifaq al-Madaris, 166
Wilson, Harold, 121
Wood, Sir John, 18–19
World Court, 159, 161

Y

Young Afghan Party, 85
Young Men's League (YML), 121

'Yuz Asaf', 2

Z

Zafar-ul-Islam, 122
Zahgir, Ghulam Rasool, 122–31, 134
Zhob Brigade, 62
Zia-ul-Haq, 119, 126, 139–40